PSYCHOLOGY

MARK BILLINGHAM
HELEN J. KITCHING

This resource is endorsed by OCR for use with OCR Level 1/2 GCSE (9–1) in Psychology specification J203.

In order to gain OCR endorsement, this resource has undergone an independent quality check. Any references to assessment and/or assessment preparation are the publisher's interpretation of the specification requirements and are not endorsed by OCR. OCR recommends that a range of teaching and learning resources are used in preparing learners for assessment. OCR has not paid for the production of this resource, nor does OCR receive any royalties from its sale. For more information about the endorsement process, please visit the OCR website, www.ocr.org.uk.

Photo acknowledgements

p.4 © mrkornflakes/Shutterstock; **p.7** © Andrey_Popov/Shutterstock; **p.10** © Andrey_Popov/Shutterstock; **p.19** © michaeljung/Shutterstock; **p.21** © ZUMA Press, Inc./Alamy Stock Photo; **p.34** © chrisbrignell/Shutterstock; **p.39** b © Chase Sutton/Alamy Stock Photo, t © REUTERS/Alamy Stock Photo; **p.42** © Monkey Business Images/Shutterstock; **p.49** © Graeme Black/Shutterstock; **p.57** © blvdone/Shutterstock; **p.60** © Jasmin Awad/Shutterstock; **p.66** © SpeedKingz/Shutterstock; **p.73** © James Boardman/Alamy Stock Photo; **p.77** ©oliveromg/Shutterstock; **p.81** © nelen/Shutterstock; **p.85** © Dima Sidelnikov/Shutterstock; **p.93** b © Marcos Mesa Sam Wordley/Shutterstock, t © Diego Cervo/Shutterstock; **p.94** © Helen J. Kitching; **p.98** t © Rafael Ben-Ari/Alamy Stock Photo, b © Universal History Archive/REX; **p.102** © CLICKMANIS/Shutterstock; **p.108** © earl young/art directors/Alamy Stock Photo; **p.110** © Pete Maclaine/Alamy Stock Photo; **p.114** © Paul Davey/Alamy Stock Photo; **p.130** © JOHN DEE/REX/Shutterstock; **p.135** © Eric Isselee/Shutterstock; **p.139** © Doug Lemke/Shutterstock; **p.147** © dolgachov/123RF; **p.151** © PR Image Factory/Shutterstock; **p.164** © Robert Kneschke/Shutterstock; **p.170** © Sam Toren/Alamy Stock Photo; **p.179** © Monkey Business Images/Shutterstock; **p.182** © Marina Pousheva/Shutterstock

Practice questions

Questions in the *Practice questions* pages of this textbook have been written by the authors, Mark Billingham and Helen J. Kitching. They have not been produced by OCR.

Acknowledgements

To Sarah for all of her patience and support. To Caitlin, Violet and Tess for making psychology real! And to Ben – never to be forgotten. MB

To mum, my inspiration and my constant support and champion. To Emmie and Christopher for their love and hugs and not minding when mummy had to take her laptop camping. And to Tom for listening. HK

Every effort has been made to trace all copyright holders, but if any have been inadvertently overlooked, the Publishers will be pleased to make the necessary arrangements at the first opportunity.

Although every effort has been made to ensure that website addresses are correct at time of going to press, Hodder Education cannot be held responsible for the content of any website mentioned in this book. It is sometimes possible to find a relocated web page by typing in the address of the home page for a website in the URL window of your browser.

Hachette UK's policy is to use papers that are natural, renewable and recyclable products and made from wood grown in sustainable forests. The logging and manufacturing processes are expected to conform to the environmental regulations of the country of origin.

Orders: please contact Bookpoint Ltd, 130 Park Drive, Milton Park, Abingdon, Oxon OX14 4SE. Telephone: (44) 01235 827720. Fax: (44) 01235 400454. Email education@bookpoint.com Lines are open from 9 a.m. to 5 p.m., Monday to Saturday, with a 24-hour message answering service. You can also order through our website: www.hoddereducation.co.uk

ISBN: 9781471899577

© Mark Billingham, Helen J. Kitching 2017

First published in 2017 by
Hodder Education,
An Hachette UK Company
Carmelite House
50 Victoria Embankment
London EC4Y 0DZ

www.hoddereducation.co.uk

Impression number   10 9 8 7 6 5 4 3 2
Year   2020   2019   2018   2017

All rights reserved. Apart from any use permitted under UK copyright law, no part of this publication may be reproduced or transmitted in any form or by any means, electronic or mechanical, including photocopying and recording, or held within any information storage and retrieval system, without permission in writing from the publisher or under licence from the Copyright Licensing Agency Limited. Further details of such licences (for reprographic reproduction) may be obtained from the Copyright Licensing Agency Limited, Saffron House, 6–10 Kirby Street, London EC1N 8TS.

Cover photo © iStock/Getty Images/Thinkstock

Illustrations by Peter Lubach & Elektra Media Ltd

Typeset by Elektra Media Ltd

Printed in Slovenia

A catalogue record for this title is available from the British Library.

Contents

Introduction ... iv
1 Criminal Psychology ... **3**
2 Development ... **27**
3 Psychological problems ... **54**
4 Social influence ... **92**
5 Memory ... **121**
6 Sleep and dreaming ... **147**
7 Research methods ... **170**
Glossary ... 210
Index ... 217

Introduction

Psychology is a great subject to study because it offers such a varied set of skills, from considering different theories to looking at evidence from research to carrying out investigations to in-depth evaluation of controversial debates. You will learn about a variety of really interesting topics, such as what happens to our memory if we have a brain injury, why certain people become criminals, what is meant by schizophrenia, how we develop mentally, what makes us obey others and why we dream. You'll also learn about how to conduct research and analyse the results, as well as how to think critically.

This textbook is endorsed by OCR and is designed to cover the specification content for OCR GCSE (9–1) Psychology. Each chapter focuses on a different topic including a clear focus on mental health, a theme developed in conjunction with the Time to Change organisation. Each chapter covers the six key areas:

- biological
- cognitive
- developmental
- social
- individual differences
- research methods.

Apart from research methods, each chapter introduces you to key concepts within the topic, considers two competing theories, details two key studies and looks at how research can be applied to real-life environments. Within the chapters, there are a number of different activities to reinforce your knowledge and understanding of the content. There are also extension tasks to take each topic a bit further.

Features

Learning objectives
Found at the beginning of each chapter, learning objectives outline the key objectives for the chapter and how these relate to the specification.

DIY
Mini investigations to try out yourself

STUDY HINT
Handy tips for studying psychology

Time for some maths
Maths questions and activities to help you brush up on your maths skills

Key terms
A short definition of key vocabulary. Key terms are highlighted in the text at their first mention in each chapter. They are defined in the main text and in the glossary.

Neuropsychology now
You will find sections relating to neuropsychology throughout the book. Where these sections occur, they will be called 'Neuropsychology now'.

Check your understanding
Short, knowledge-based questions to help you check you've understood different topics

Extension
Extension activities to take what you've learnt further

Challenge
Short tasks and activities that help to reinforce learning

SUMMARY
Each chapter finishes with a summary of key points covered in the chapter

Practice questions
Questions designed to offer study practice

Something to think about
Questions or issues for you to consider

Cross references to required research methods skills

1 Criminal Psychology

There are many different professionals who work in the area of crime, such as police officers, social workers, lawyers and forensic scientists. A psychologist's interest in criminal psychology can be quite varied, from looking at how decisions are made in a courtroom to how an eyewitness' memory can be improved. Psychologists are also interested in the reasons behind why people commit crimes, and how this mentality and behaviour can be changed to prevent repeated offences or a crime being committed in the first place.

> This chapter should enable you to:
> - develop awareness of different types of crime
> - develop understanding of crime as a social construct, including deviation from norms and the role of culture in defining criminal and anti-social behaviour
> - develop understanding of how crime is measured: official statistics and self-report
> - explain and evaluate the Social Learning Theory of criminal behaviour, with specific reference to identification with role models, the role of observation and imitation, the process of vicarious reinforcement, the role of direct reinforcement and internalisation, and criticisms of the theory including the nature/nurture debate
> - describe and evaluate Cooper & Mackie's (1986) study into video games and aggression in children
> - explain and evaluate Eysenck's Criminal Personality theory with specific reference to the central nervous system, extraversion, neuroticism, psychoticism, synapses and dopaminergic neurons, dopamine reward systems, the reticular activation system, the cerebral cortex, the autonomic nervous system, the limbic system, early socialisation and difficulties in conditioning, and the issue of individual differences
> - describe and evaluate Heaven's (1996) study into delinquency, extraversion, psychoticism and self-esteem
> - understand the role of rehabilitation in reducing criminal/anti-social behaviour in increasing pro-social behaviour, including restorative justice and the use of positive role models
> - understand the effects of punishment and deterrents in reducing criminal/anti-social behaviour, including the use of prisons, community sentences and fines.

Defining criminal behaviour

In simple terms, criminal behaviour is an act that is against the law. However, there are many laws, and so there are many different types of crime.

Criminal behaviour ranges from minor crimes, such as motoring offences, to much more serious crimes, such as murder. Psychologists are generally more interested in more serious crimes, as the offenders tend to be 'different' to law-abiding people. It is also important to find out what causes people to commit serious crimes, such as **violent**, **drug related**, **acquisitive**, **sexual** and **anti-social offences**, as these can impact negatively on individuals and society.

Violent offences
Aggressive crimes resulting in physical harm or death to the victim.

Drug related offences
Crimes involving trading in or using illegal substances.

Acquisitive offences
Crimes where capital or belongings are acquired through illegal means, e.g. theft.

Sexual offences
Crimes where a victim is forced to commit or submit to a sexual act against their will.

Anti-social offences
Criminal acts that cause harassment, alarm or distress to people who do not share a home with the perpetrator.

OCR GCSE Psychology

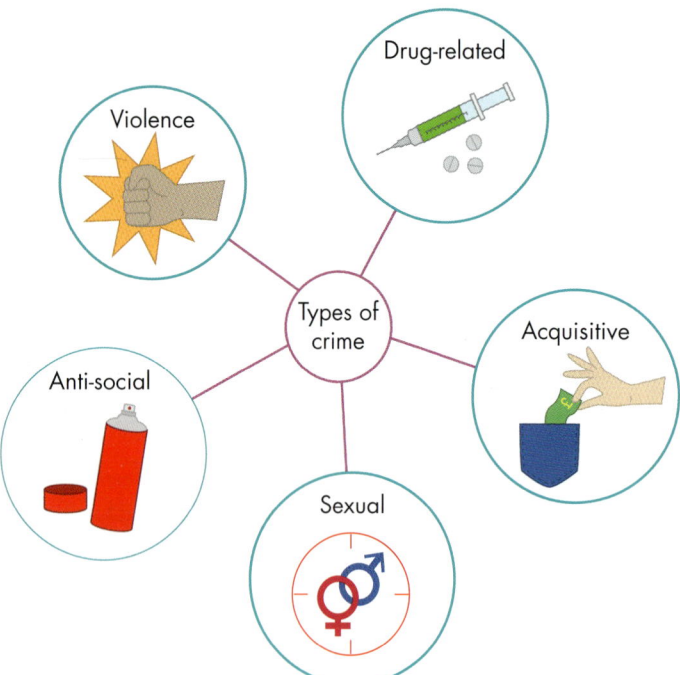

▲ Crime covers a range of offences, but all of them cause damage in some form or another. This is why we want to stop or reduce them.

We often talk or write about different types of crime as though we are dealing with facts. For example, a report may state that acquisitive crimes are more common than violent crimes, or politicians may discuss the best way to tackle drug related crime. When some psychologists investigate the causes of crime, they assume that criminal behaviour is a product of human nature and is therefore inevitable. Some psychologists are looking for a gene that causes criminal behaviour. However, some people believe that criminal behaviour is **subjective** rather than objective. This is the idea that criminal behaviour is a **social construct**, meaning that societies determine what is considered criminal, often based on what is considered acceptable at that particular point in time. For example, in some societies assisting a terminally ill person to die (euthanasia) is considered acceptable and is not against the law. In contrast, in the UK euthanasia is legally wrong, although it may not always be considered to be morally wrong. As a result, if someone in the UK helps a terminally ill patient to die they would be considered a criminal.

Challenge

Look at the following offences. What type of crime would each of the offences be categorised as?
- Rape
- Murder
- Supplying cocaine
- Use of child pornography
- Burglary
- Fraud
- Possession of cannabis
- Graffiti
- Drunk and disorderly
- Physical assault
- Theft
- Urinating in public

STUDY HINT

Make sure you can do more than just define the different types of crime. It would be useful to know how they are different from each other. For example: their frequency, their likely perpetrators, or how they are punished.

Subjectivity
Based on personal opinion rather than fact.

Social construct
A concept that exists as the result of interactions between people who make up a society.

▲ The crime of 'stalking' did not exist before this century. Does this mean it did not happen before then? Did society create a crime for people to commit?

> **Extension**
> Draw up a table, listing each of the types of crime listed on page 1. For each one, decide how far you agree that the crime is a social construct, as opposed to something which is objectively unacceptable.

Deviation from norms
When an act or behaviour goes against the accepted standards of a society.

Culture
A collective set of norms and values that determine the way of life of a group of people.

> **Challenge**
> Working in groups, see who can come up with the most examples for each of the following:
> 1 Acts that deviate from norms but are not criminal.
> 2 Acts that are 'normal' (most people do them) but are criminal.
> 3 Acts that used to be illegal in the UK but are not any more.

Anti-social behaviour
'Behaviour by a person which causes or is likely to cause harassment, alarm or distress to one or more persons not of the same household as the person' (Antisocial Behaviour Act 2003 & Police Reform and Social Responsibility Act 2011).

> **Challenge**
> In groups, see who can come up with the longest list of why people may not report crimes.

> **Extension**
> Carry out research on the types of crimes which are most likely to go undetected including reasons why.

This discrepancy between what different societies consider to be a crime makes it difficult to investigate the causes of criminal behaviour. For example, an eighteen year-old who has sex with a fifteen year-old can be branded a paedophile, and therefore a criminal in the UK, because a child under the age of sixteen does not have the legal capacity to consent to sex. As psychologists, we may then begin to investigate this person's biology or family background to see what made them this way. However, if the offender moved to a country where the age of consent is younger, he would no longer be classed as a criminal, despite his biology and background being unchanged.

So, how does society decide which activities are criminal, and which are not? The distinction is often based on norms, or acceptable standards of behaviour. If behaviour is different from what society expects, then this is an example of a **deviation from norms**, which can be labelled as a crime. For example, walking around naked in public breaks norms and is therefore considered a criminal offence, called 'indecent exposure'.

Norms are often based on what the majority do or expect others to do. For example, most people do not deal drugs and therefore this activity breaks norms and is seen as criminal. However, there are exceptions. For example, having an abortion was illegal in the UK until the late 1960s. This may be partly due to the fact that it was not something practised by the majority. Nowadays, most women still do not go through the experience of having an abortion, yet society is more tolerant and understanding of the procedure. Most people in the UK would see it as unreasonable to treat someone as a criminal because they had had an abortion.

The above examples show the importance of the role of **culture** in defining criminal and **anti-social behaviour**. As cultures change, so do their norms, and this leads to changes in the law if there is a strong shift in opinion. For example, the UK has many more anti-smoking laws now compared to in the past. Additionally, big changes in the use of technology has meant many societies need new laws to deal with this, and has resulted in offences relating to online fraud, illegal downloading, abuse on social media and use of internet pornography. Cultures are also deeply embedded in their history, and some societal differences may always be visible in the law. For example, in certain countries (e.g. Saudi Arabia, Egypt) it is normal for a man to have more than one wife, but in the UK this is a criminal act known as bigamy. In short, cultures define our way of life and determine which behaviours we will tolerate and which need to be punished.

> **Something to think about**
> There are many examples of cross-cultural differences in criminal behaviour. But what acts are considered criminal wherever you go? Why do you think this is the case with these particular acts?

How crime is measured

Although it is difficult for researchers to agree on a definition of crime, the law obviously identifies what counts as a crime, and then society also tries to measure the extent of different types of crimes. Official statistics give a measure of crime – for example, telling us which crimes are more common, or which ones are on the increase or decrease. Official statistics are collected and published by the government, and are based on crimes that have been reported to and recorded by police forces. There is a clear problem here. Not all crimes are reported – indeed, some crimes may take place without even being detected. This is why researchers also rely on **self-report** surveys to begin to uncover the 'dark figure' of crime. Self-report surveys are sometimes confidential surveys which ask convicted criminals about other crimes they have committed, besides the ones they have been charged for, or sometimes ask the general public about their offences. Another alternative is to use victim surveys, where people can report crimes they have experienced even if they had decided not to report them to the police.

Check your understanding

1. What type of crime involves taking property without consent?
2. What is meant by the phrase 'deviation from norms' and how does it relate to criminal behaviour?
3. What is the link between crime as a social construct and culture?
4. What is the difference between official statistics and self-reports as measures of crime?

Explanations of why criminal and anti-social behaviour occurs

Psychologists offer many explanations for why people turn to criminal behaviour or behave anti-socially. We will look at two theories that attempt to explain crime in general: **Social Learning Theory** and Eysenck's Criminal Personality Theory.

Social Learning Theory

Social Learning Theory proposes that we learn all of our behaviour from others. This theory can be used to explain all kinds of behaviour, including criminal behaviour.

Social Learning Theory starts with **role models**. These are people that we look up to and respect, such as parents, older siblings, peers, and people and characters we see in the media. We go through a process of **identification**, where we decide we want to be like these people; we watch what they do and try to copy them. These are the processes of **observation** and **imitation**.

In relation to criminal or anti-social behaviour, think carefully about the following examples:

Firstly, a young girl might identify with her older sister, who is in a group of friends who get into trouble, and secondly, a teenage boy may identify with a gangster character from his favourite film. The older sister and the gangster become role models and their behaviour is carefully observed. Over time, the children may believe that they are in a position to try to imitate behaviours they have seen. For example, the girl may form her own gang and go out on the streets and intimidate others. The boy may start dealing in drugs and using knives because that is what he has observed his hero doing.

But what is it that motivates us to imitate people in the first place? Social Learning Theory states that **vicarious reinforcement** is important here. This describes a situation where we observe others being rewarded for their

Self-report
A method that involves participants reporting on themselves through answering questions.

STUDY HINT
It is really important that you know how to apply Social Learning Theory to criminal behaviour to earn the highest marks for a description of the theory. For example, don't just write about learning from others – be clear who those 'others' would be in the context of criminal behaviour.

Social Learning Theory
A theory that explains behaviour in terms of observation and imitation.

Role model
A person held in esteem by another.

Identification
The process where a person aligns themselves with another.

Observation
The process where people pay attention to behaviours and retain them in memory.

Imitation
A process where people recall behaviours and reproduce them in their own actions.

Vicarious reinforcement
When a behaviour is strengthened by an individual observing this same behaviour being rewarded in another.

Extension
Whether or not we imitate a certain behaviour is also affected by something called self-efficacy. Do some research on what this term means in the context of Social Learning Theory. How might self-efficacy be used in an explanation of criminal behaviour?

Chapter 1 Criminal Psychology

STUDY HINT
When you have a long list of terms to learn and remember – like those in Social Learning Theory – it can be helpful to use a mnemonic to aid recall. Does the phrase '**R**ude **M**onarchs **I**nvite **O**ld **I**nvestors **V**ery **R**arely to **D**ine on **R**oyal **I**slands' mean anything to you? If not, perhaps you could come up with a better one of your own for the key words on pages 6 and 7!

▲ The police and other agencies are concerned about how many criminal acts we get to see and hear about in this day and age. Media output is massive and difficult to control. The problem is that this increases the chance of 'copycat' crimes, which are explained through Social Learning Theory.

Direct reinforcement
When a behaviour is strengthened and likely to be repeated due to positive outcomes for the individual.

behaviour; we then decide that we want the same rewards, and believe that by imitating this behaviour we will receive the same outcomes. For example, the young girl may see her older sister treated with respect because others fear her. This is vicariously reinforcing for the young girl, who views respect as rewarding. The teenage boy may see the gangster making money through his criminal activity. The money is vicariously reinforcing; the boy thinks he will make money too, if he copies what he has seen in the film.

Of course, in these examples, the young girl and the teenage boy may *not* be rewarded when they imitate the behaviour. For example, the young girl's gang may not be as respected as her sister's, or the teenage boy may be caught and punished for his crime. However, if they experience **direct reinforcement** for their behaviours by receiving the same or similar rewards, they have an incentive to continue their behaviour.

Challenge
There have been lots of examples in recent years where people have committed very serious crimes – often mass murders – that have then been linked back to their use of media e.g. the internet, films, computer games. Use a number of different (and reliable) websites to write a **case study** of an individual where there is evidence that their criminal behaviour was a result of imitating what they had observed through the media.

Internalisation
The process whereby a behaviour becomes an integral part of an individual's personality due to continuous reinforcement.

Consequences
The result of something, usually negative. For example, the consequences of being ignored by your friends might be feeling depressed.

According to Social Learning Theory, if a behaviour is strengthened through continual reinforcement then there is a point at which it becomes internalised. **Internalisation** describes the process where the behaviour has become 'part' of a person, and does not necessarily have to be reinforced for it to continue. For example, people may start by imitating criminal behaviour for some form of reward, but after time reach a stage where the behaviour has become habitual. This means people have learned to engage in criminal behaviour regardless of the **consequences**.

The nature/nurture debate

In psychology, one of the key debates is whether how we think and behave is **innate**; are we born with predetermined abilities, or are we born a 'blank slate'?

Nature

Some of our physical features are inherited from our parents through our genes, such as our eye or hair colour. Some psychologists think that some of our behaviour and personality are also inherited. Additionally, part of our behaviour can be attributed to human nature and evolution.

Nurture

Other psychologists, such as behaviourist John Watson, believe that we are born a 'tabula rasa', meaning a 'blank slate', and so our behaviour and personality characteristics are developed through experience and interaction with our environment and the people around us.

Nature and nurture

Most psychologists today recognise that nature and nurture do not work independently of each other. For example, research shows that individuals are born with the potential to be intelligent, but this is also dependent on their upbringing, such as how supportive the child's parents are and what kind of **education** system they go through.

Criticisms of Social Learning Theory

- **Social Learning Theory only focuses on the role of nurture, ignoring the role of nature in explaining criminal behaviour.** Some psychologists have argued that there is a 'criminal gene', and that without an inherited tendency to commit crime, people cannot learn to be criminals. It might be that nature and nurture have to interact before someone becomes a criminal.
- **The theory does not explain how criminal behaviour starts in the first place.** Even if we accept that each generation of criminals has learned its behaviours from the previous generation, there has to be a point at which criminal behaviour first began. Social Learning Theory does not tell us about the origins of criminal behaviour. Why and how did the 'first wave' of criminals come to commit crimes?
- **The theory does not account for people who turn to crime, even though they have not been exposed to criminal role models.** Evidence suggests that there are individuals from law-abiding families with good upbringings who unexpectedly commit crimes. In some cases, this is better explained by nature; some of these offenders may have parts of the brain that do not function normally.
- **If Social Learning Theory is correct then it should be easier to reduce crime.** If criminal behaviour is strengthened through reinforcement, then it should be reduced by receiving punishment and seeing others being punished. However, many people still commit crimes despite seeing the negative consequences, or re-offend after they have been punished themselves. This might suggest that it is in their nature to be criminal; it is something that cannot be changed and therefore was not learned.

> **STUDY HINT**
> Look at the first criticism. This is an effective way of developing a point. You can identify a factor that is ignored by the theory, and then give evidence for the existence or effect of that particular factor.

Nature
Relates to behaviours that people are born with or develop naturally

Nurture
Refers to behaviours that people learn through experience.

Check your understanding

1. What distinguishes role models from other people?
2. Why might a crime be observed but not imitated?
3. What is the difference between vicarious reinforcement and direct reinforcement?
4. What is meant by internalisation, according to Social Learning Theory?
5. Where does Social Learning Theory stand in the nature versus nurture debate, and why?

Social Learning Research Study: Cooper & Mackie (1986) – a study into the transmission of aggression through imitation and aggressive models.

Background

Cooper & Mackie's study was partly a response to a comment made by C. Everett Koop, a leading paediatric surgeon. At a psychiatric conference, Koop had said that children 'are into the games, body and soul - everything is zapping the enemy. Children get to the point where when they see another child being molested by a third child, they just sit back.' (Infoworld, 1982, pg 14). Computer games were relatively new at the time, and so Cooper & Mackie were interested in investigating whether they really encouraged aggressive behaviour in children.

Cooper & Mackie quoted many studies that showed **aggression** on television could be responsible for violent behaviour. One theory was that audiences were imitating the aggressive behaviour displayed by role models on television. However, the researchers pointed out that watching television is a passive activity where viewers just sit and **observe**. In contrast, playing video games is much more active. Cooper & Mackie were interested in whether this would make a difference to how or what behaviours were imitated. They also wanted to explore whether there was any effect from watching someone else playing a video game rather than playing it yourself.

Cooper & Mackie also focused on gender in their study. They noted how previous research often showed that males were more affected by observing aggression than females – possibly because most aggressive models in the media are males, or because men and boys are more exposed to media violence than females. The researchers referred to the fact that males were more likely to go to video arcades, be in computer clubs and have a computer at home. However, they also made the point that characters in video games often did not have an obvious gender. As they put it, 'the protagonist in many video games is a computer-generated blip on the screen under the control of the player'.

> **Challenge**
>
> In groups, discuss whether Cooper & Mackie's comments about gender and computer games are now out of date. If so, in what ways? Make notes on the outcome of your discussion.

Hypothesis

The researchers started their investigation with a key **hypothesis**. They predicted that playing an aggressive video game compared to other types of games would lead to increased aggression in children.

> **For more information on hypotheses see page 170.**

Method

Design

The researchers used a **laboratory experiment** to carry out this study using an **independent measures design**. The **independent variable** was the type of game played or observed and the **dependent variable** measured aggression levels after the playing or observing the game.

Sample

The **target population** was a set of schools in the suburbs of New Jersey, USA. The **sample** was made up of 84 nine to eleven year olds whose parents had given **consent** for them to take part in the study. A week before the **experiment**, the children filled out a **questionnaire** to assess their experience of video games.

For this experiment, the children were put into pairs so they were the same sex and age. In each pair, one child was selected to play a game and the other would be told to observe (the second child could talk to the first about the game but was not allowed to actually play it).

Materials

- Missile Command® video game, Pac-man® video game, Star Wars™ and Tron® paper-and-pen maze games, warrior figure, basketball set, pinball machine, building blocks, buzzer, questionnaire for recording previous experience of video games, questionnaire for rating games played in the experiment.

> **Aggression**
> Spoken or physical behaviour that is threatening or involves harm to someone.
>
> **Randomly**
> To leave to chance.

Procedure

Participants were **randomly** allocated to one of three conditions:

Condition 1: Participants played or observed an aggressive video game called Missile Command®. Players had to destroy laser beams before they demolished cities. A different group of children had rated it as highly aggressive because it involved considerable violence towards both people and objects, and had lots of shooting in it.

Condition 2: Participants played or observed a non-aggressive video game called Pac-Man®. Players had to control the Pac-Man® character being chased around a maze by ghosts. Other children had given this a very low rating for violence.

Condition 3: Participants played or observed paper-and-pen maze games, based on Star Wars™ and Tron®, using a felt tip pen. This was the **control** condition.

> **Time for some maths**
> Outline how the 42 pairs of children could be randomly assigned to three conditions.

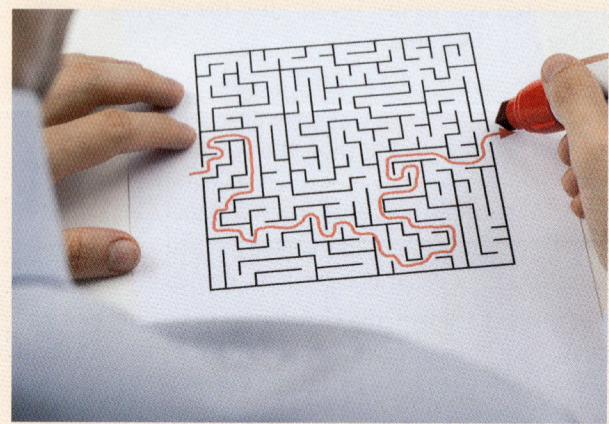

▲ The control condition in Cooper & Mackie's experiment was a paper and pen maze game.

As a way of controlling **extraneous variables**, all participants had eight minutes playing (or observing) the game they had been allocated. If participants didn't know the game, they had two minutes to familiarise themselves with it beforehand. After the eight minutes were up, the pairs of watchers and players were split up. One of each pair was taken to a playroom, while the other was taken to a room to do a test.

In the playroom, there was an aggressive toy (a warrior figure with a spring releasing fist and dart-firers), an active toy (a basketball set), a skill toy (a pinball machine) and a quiet toy (building blocks). There was an also an experimenter in the room who asked the participant to play by themselves and not disturb her because she had to 'work something out'. However, she was really recording which toys children played with, in what order, and for how long.

> **Control**
> A way of ensuring other variables do not affect the results of a study.

▲ There were four different types of toys that children could choose to play with in the Cooper & Mackie experiment.

> **Something to think about**
> Was it right for the experimenter to deceive the children by pretending to work on something when she was really observing them? Justify your answer.

In the test room, each participant performed an activity to measure their level of interpersonal aggression – how much aggression she or he felt towards another person. They were asked about how they would punish a child who had been caught behaving badly and how they would reward a child who had done something good. They were asked to press a buzzer to show the level of punishment or reward, and the experimenters timed how long they pressed for in each case. The difference between the duration of the punishment and reward buzzers was used to give the participant a score for interpersonal aggression.

> **STUDY HINT**
> You have a lot of information here on how Cooper & Mackie measured aggressive behaviour. If you are asked to describe the whole study in the exam, you will need to be able to briefly outline these measures. Plan ahead – what key points would you want to include? What can you afford to miss out while still clearly explaining how aggression was assessed?

After the observation and test had taken place, the participants were swapped around so the first one did the test and second was then observed playing. As a control, sometimes the participant who was the player was tested first and other times it was the participant who was the observer. This control is known as **counterbalancing.**

Observation method
A method of collecting data which involves watching and recording people's behaviours.

Counterbalancing
To even out trials/tasks so they do not occur in the same order each time.

> **Extension**
> Can you explain why counterbalancing was an important control in this study?

After being observed and tested, all participants were given one final task. They had to complete a questionnaire where they rated their experience of playing the game they had been given.

For more information on laboratory experiments see page 182.

For more information on target populations and samples see page 176.

For more information on consent see page 179.

For more information on questionnaires see page 184.

For more information on independent measures design and independent, dependent and extraneous variables see page 172.

For more information on rating scales see page 184.

Results
In the pre-experiment questionnaire, 61 per cent of all participants reported having a video game system at home, and this applied to more boys than girls. The researchers analysed the data to take into account the children who had not played the experiment's computer games before, but this made no significant difference to the results.

Participants in the aggressive game condition spent more time playing with the aggressive toy than participants in the other two conditions. However, this finding was down to the fact that girls who had played the Missile Command® game spent much more time playing with the aggressive toy than girls in the other conditions. Boys spent more time overall playing with the aggressive toy, but this time was hardly affected by which video game they had played.

> **Something to think about**
> Interestingly, the girls who played the most with the aggressive toy were those who thought they had performed badly in Missile Command®. Why do you think this was?

The **mean** amount of time in seconds spent playing with each type of toy by sex and by condition is shown in the table below.

▼ Table 1.1

	Maze game		Pac-Man®		Missile Command®	
	Female	Male	Female	Male	Female	Male
Aggressive toy	15.88	62.33	13.75	78.69	79.63	84.62
Skill toy	167.63	126.25	111.31	162.75	98.31	70.50
Active toy	69.50	110.50	41.94	72.50	121.00	117.13
Quiet toy	164.13	139.58	233.06	53.81	97.19	136.56

Source: Cooper, J & Mackie, D. 'Video Games and Aggression in Children' in Journal of Applied Social Psychology, November 1986, Volume 16 Issue 8, p. 748

> **Time for some maths**
> Using the table above, answer the following questions:
> 1 When females played the Pac-Man® game, which toy did they play with for the longest, on average?
> 2 In which condition did females play with the aggressive toy for the longest time, on average?
> 3 In which condition did females play with the active toy for a longer average time than males?
> 4 On average, which toy was played with for the longest across all conditions by males? Justify your answer.
> 5 Rewrite the table so that each mean is expressed to the nearest whole number.

The results showed that the type of game played had no effect on the participants' interpersonal aggression scores. The only significant effect was that the children had higher scores if they had actually played games rather than just observed then.

> **STUDY HINT**
> You don't need to learn lots of statistics for the exam. However, you need to look at the data provided here and identify some of the main patterns or trends in the results. This could gain you marks if you are asked to describe Cooper & Mackie's results in the exam.

The post-experiment questionnaire showed that participants rated the Missile Command® game as the most violent. When the researchers examined the children's scores in the games, they found that males had performed slightly better. However, the sex difference was significant only for Missile Command®, where boys scored an average of 8806.87 points and girls scored an average of 4993.75. The strongest difference in enjoyment of the games was also for Missile Command®, with girls giving it a mean rating of 3.3 and boys giving it a mean rating of 4.37. Similar patterns of results were found when researchers analysed how much children wanted to continue playing a game – boys wanted to keep playing much more than girls did, and again more in the Missile Command® condition than in the others.

> **Time for some maths**
> Using the paragraph above, answer the following questions:
> 1. What is the difference between the mean enjoyment ratings that boys and girls gave for the Missile Command® game?
> 2. Estimate the difference in the points that girls and boys scored on the Missile Command® game.

Conclusions

Cooper & Mackie concluded that playing or watching an aggressive video game had an impact on the aggressive behaviour of girls. They were more likely to choose to play with an aggressive toy afterwards.

The researchers suggested that because the girls were less experienced with violent video games (including the one used in the study) and less exposed to violence in general, they reacted to the aggressive video game with greater **arousal** than boys. This led them to imitate some of the behaviours they have witnessed. The researchers also suggested that allowing girls to play with aggressive games may have led to a **disinhibition** effect. This means that the girls felt it was socially acceptable to play with the aggressive toy because they had already been encouraged to play an aggressive video game.

> **Arousal**
> Activation of the nervous system making individuals awake, alert and attentive.
>
> **Disinhibition**
> When people have a lack of control over their own behaviour because they are not concerned about what is expected.

Cooper & Mackie also tried to explain why the aggressive video game had no impact on interpersonal aggression. They concluded that the study had ended up investigating two different types of aggressive behaviour. The buzzer pressing activity was clearly about aggression towards other people. In contrast, playing with the aggressive toy and shooting space ships in Missile Command® were more about aggression towards objects. This meant there was less of a clear link between the computer game and the buzzer pressing activity.

Overall, the study showed some evidence of children's play imitating the kinds of behaviours they had observed in the computer games, supporting the principles of Social Learning Theory.

> **Challenge**
> Revisit the Social Learning Theory of criminal behaviour and explain how this study can be used to support it. What kind of criminal behaviour does it relate to? Who are the role models? What is being observed and imitated? How is behaviour being reinforced?

Criticisms

- **The sample was biased and therefore it is difficult to make generalisations.** For example, the study only investigated a limited age range, which does not represent all children, yet alone adults. This is known as **age bias**. The sample can also be accused of being culturally biased. The impact of computer games may influenced by the cultural setting in which they are played. In addition, certain types of children may have been missing from the sample. For example, would a parent consent for their child to take part if he or she was already very aggressive? Or would a parent of a very passive and peaceful child want them potentially exposed to violent video games?
- **The study was in an artificial setting leading to low levels of ecological validity.** For example, are video games normally played under such strict time conditions, or with one person

watching who is not allowed to be physically involved in the game in any way? In general, playing games in a laboratory setting does not mirror game playing at home or in an arcade, where the effects may be stronger or weaker.

- **Aggressive behaviour was measured in a narrow way, leading to low levels of construct validity.** Although the researchers took two measures of aggression, they did not match; one showed the effects of aggressive video games, the other did not. This means there may be only one reliable measure of aggression. In both cases, they are very specific measures (i.e. how much aggressive toy is played with or how much a bad behaviour is punished). Both could be accused of taking a complex behaviour (aggression) and trying to narrow it down to a simple score.
- **There were a number of uncontrolled extraneous variables making it difficult to establish cause and effect.** For example, although the researchers accounted for whether children had experienced a game or not, they did not have a control for how much experience a child had had with a game. It may be that boys were less affected than girls by Missile Command® because they were more used to playing it; the initial effect may have happened already outside of the laboratory. Another extraneous variable is how much the child interacted with a game. Just because all children spent eight minutes on the game, it does not mean that they engaged with it in the same way.
- **Only the immediate effects of aggressive video games were tested.** In reality, video games may influence aggression over time, but the researchers expected it to happen straight away. If a child is playing violent video games in real life, it may be a while before they have the confidence or desire to imitate a behaviour they have observed. Even then, the internalisation process needs to happen over a period of time too.

Check your understanding

1. Which type of **experimental design** was used in Cooper & Mackie's study?
2. What were the three conditions in the experiment?
3. How was aggression measured in the experiment?
4. What were some of the main differences between genders shown in the results?
5. What were the limitations of using an experiment to investigate the effect of video games on aggression?

DIY

Psychologists sometimes carry out a content analysis. Rather than observing people directly, they observe what they have produced. In this sense, they are looking at **secondary data**.

Psychologists have carried out content analyses of violent computer games. This can be done by collecting **quantitative data** (e.g. counting the number of violent acts in a game or rating a platform for how violent it is) or by collecting **qualitative data** (e.g. describing the types of violence observed).

Design your own content analysis of a video game aimed at younger children. It is probably easier to plan an investigation that collects quantitative data. Decide how you are going to look for aggressive content in the computer game, and how you are going to score or measure it. You may even want to compare a number of different games to investigate which one is the most violent.

If you would rather not investigate computer games, then you can look for aggression in other types of media, for example children's cartoons or comics. You may even want to compare different types of media for violent content.

Eysenck's Criminal Personality Theories and the Biological Basis of Personality

Criminal personality
A set of relatively fixed traits associated with people who commit crimes.

In contrast to the Social Learning Theory, Eysenck's Criminal Personality Theories view criminal behaviour as being more fixed. It suggests that the impulse to behave in a criminal manner is something people are essentially born with.

OCR GCSE Psychology

Hans Eysenck was born in Germany in 1916. He spent most of his professional career in the UK, where he is best remembered for his work on **intelligence** and personality.

Eysenck's theory starts by identifying three personality traits: extraversion, neuroticism and psychoticism. Everyone is born with these traits, but to varying degrees, depending on **genetic inheritance**.

Eysenck devised questionnaires to score these three personality traits. For example, an individual with a high Extraversion score would be an extrovert, whereas an individual with a low score would be classed as an introvert. An individual with a high Neuroticism score would be classed as neurotic and an individual with a high Psychoticism score would be considered psychotic.

- **Extraversion:** People that score high on extraversion are out-going, sociable and confident. At the opposite end is introversion. Introverted people tend to be quiet, shy and unassertive. Of course, it is possible to be in between these two extremes.
- **Neuroticism:** People that score high on neuroticism are anxious, angry and prone to feeling guilt. At the opposite end is stability. Stable people tend to be calm, even-tempered and not easily stressed. Of course, it is possible to be in between these two extremes too.
- **Psychoticism:** People that score highly on psychoticism are impulsive, aggressive and selfish. At the opposite end is high impulse control. People in control of their impulses tend to be warm, considerate and conscientious. Again, people can be in between the extremes.

Genetic inheritance
When genetic information is passed on from parents to child through the pairing of chromosomes at conception.

Extraversion
A trait measuring how out-going an individual is.

Neuroticism
A trait measuring how anxious an individual is.

Psychoticism
A trait measuring how impulsive and aggressive an individual is.

Challenge
If you want to calculate your own E and N score, it is easy to find Eysenck's test online. Try searching for 'Eysenck's personality questionnaire'.

Evaluate the questionnaire. What do you think of the questions and the scoring system? How valid is it to use a questionnaire to measure someone's personality?

Time for some maths
When a **representative** sample's extraversion, neuroticism and psychoticism scores are calculated and plotted, they usually follow the patterns in the following graphs.

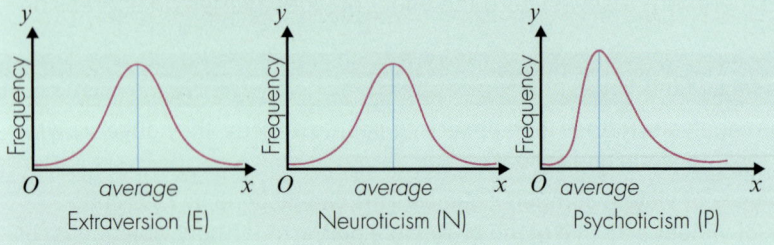

Using the graphs:
1. Name the distribution that E and N scores show.
2. What is the most common E and N score?
3. Estimate what **percentage** of a sample are more extrovert than introvert.
4. Which are the least common scores on the neuroticism scale?
5. Psychoticism scores show a **skewed distribution**. Describe the pattern of scores to indicate what this means.

According to Eysenck's theory, individuals with a **criminal personality** will score highly on each of his three scales: extraversion, neuroticism and psychoticism. For example, a neurotic extrovert is more likely to be a criminal than a stable extrovert.

- Criminals are often extroverts, as people with this trait need a lot of stimulation from the environment and are often thrill seekers. This excitement can be found through involvement in criminal activity.

▲ Note that the three traits that criminals score high on spell out the word PEN.

Chapter 1 Criminal Psychology

> **Challenge**
>
> Look again at the characteristics of psychoticism. Can you make links between these and more typical criminal behaviour?

Biological
Relating to brain and body.

Central nervous system
A system consisting of the brain and spinal cord, to which sensory impulses are transmitted and from which motor impulses pass out.

Reticular activation system
A neural network that mediates consciousness and alertness.

Cerebral cortex
The outer layer of the brain, which is important for conscious awareness.

Dopamine reward system
A neural network that is responsible for people experiencing pleasure.

Autonomic nervous system
The system responsible for unconscious control of the body's internal organs.

Limbic system
A neural network that controls emotional expression.

Dopaminergic neurons
Nerve cells that produce the neurotransmitter dopamine.

Synaptic transmission
The process where neurotransmitters are released by a presynaptic neuron and bind to and activate the receptors of postsynaptic neuron.

Conditioning
Learning by association and consequence.

Early socialisation
The process where young children are conditioned to accept the norms and values of their family and wider society.

- Criminals are also often neurotic; they can get stuck in patterns of behaviour to relieve their high anxiety levels, which can include criminal behaviour. Their high anxiety can also get in the way of attempts to punish criminal or anti-social behaviour, and as a result, they don't easily learn from previous mistakes.
- Criminals tend to be psychotics because the characteristics of these people are directly related to crime.
- Eysenck argued that there is a **biological** element to criminal behaviour by linking criminal personality traits to the **central nervous system (CNS)**. According to Eysenck, criminality can be linked to under-arousal in the CNS. The **reticular activation system (RAS)** is the part of the brain stem that links the brain and spinal cord and regulates the stimuli sent to the **cerebral cortex**. Eysenck argued that in extroverts the cerebral cortex is under-aroused because the stimuli is restricted by RAS. The cerebral cortex is 'hungry' for stimulation, which can be gained thorough risky, lawless behaviour. Extroverts also have a stronger **dopamine reward system**, which means they respond more positively to reinforcers like sex and money – to the point where they may need to acquire them illegally.
- Neuroticism is related to the activity of the **autonomic nervous system (ANS)**, which is activated during emotion-inducing situations and regulates the activity of the brain's **limbic system**. Eysenck argued that the ANS becomes over-aroused in neurotics, leading to higher levels of violence (a behaviour under the control of the limbic system).
- Eysenck suggested that psychoticism is the result of an excess of **dopaminergic neurons**, which cause over-production of **dopamine** by the **nervous system**. The excess dopamine leads to less inhibition of impulses in the brain during **synaptic transmission**.

> **Neuropsychology now**
>
> Note how Eysenck's theory considers different parts of the brain, and the nervous system generally, to explain the way that criminals think and act.

> **Challenge**
>
> Create a poster for the key terms listed in the paragraph above. Include definitions and consider how these terms relate to criminal behaviour.

High levels of extraversion and neuroticism, according to Eysenck, make people difficult to **condition**. People who are naturally stable and introverted learn the association between performing a criminal or anti-social act and its negative outcomes more easily, and so avoid committing crimes in the future. Since Eysenck believes children are born with their personality traits, he claims that those who score highly on E and N may be more resistant to **early socialisation** in terms of learning moral behaviour. It does not necessarily mean they are doomed to a life of crime, as nature and nurture interact. However, it does mean that parents and other agents of socialisation will have to work hard to divert their child away from the 'thrill' of crime. So extrovert, neurotic children will not necessarily become criminals, but they are likely to end up in occupations that match their personalities, such as politics or business. Politicians and business people have to make big decisions and take risks, which may feed their pleasure-seeking behaviour. Business people may relieve their anxiety by continually finding ways of making a profit.

Criticisms of Eysenck's theory of the criminal personality

- **Eysenck's theory is accused of ignoring individual differences.** Rather than emphasising the uniqueness of people, he tried to place them in broad categories. Critics argue it is wrong to 'lump together' neurotic extroverts (the most likely criminals) and assume they have similar reasons for turning to crime.
- **With such a range of crimes, it seems unlikely that criminals share a similar personality.** Even if we accept Eysenck's broad personality types, it is hard to accept that a person who spontaneously robs people in the street has the same kind of personality characteristics as the person who carefully plans to defraud others. In his later work, Eysenck himself suggested that violent people might be more stable than neurotic.
- **Eysenck's theory can be seen as being too deterministic.** The theory suggests that people are born with their personality type and therefore their chance of becoming criminals is mainly driven by biology. Critics say that this suggests crime is largely out of the control of the individual which does not help in terms of individuals taking responsibility for their actions.
- **Critics say that the concept of psychoticism is not useful.** Some psychologists do not accept that the trait of psychoticism *causes* criminal behaviour. Instead, they argue that psychoticism is simply a definition of criminal behaviour!
- **Although Eysenck considers both nature and nurture in his explanation, for some critics there is not enough emphasis on nurture.** Rather than saying that neurotic extroverts are naturally hard to condition, which puts the emphasis back on nature, critics say we should focus more on *how* we try to condition this personality type. In other words, with the right kind of environment, these people do not have to turn to crime as much as they do.

Something to think about
Why is a deterministic approach, like Eysenck's, not helpful when thinking about the rehabilitation of criminals?

Individual differences
How people are unique and different from one another.

For more information on rehabilitation see page 21.

For more information on determinism see page 78.

DIY
Carry out an investigation of your own to test the link between extraversion and crime.

Carry out an **interview** with someone you would identify as an extrovert and someone you would identify as an introvert, assessing their **attitudes** towards criminal behaviour.

Based on Eysenck's theory, you would predict that introverts respond less favourably to criminal behaviour than extroverts.

You need to decide whether you are going to use **structured** or **unstructured interviews**. Think carefully about the strengths of each and what best suits this study.

At the end of your investigation, try to make a conclusion about whether extroverts and introverts respond differently to criminal behaviour or not.

For more information on interviews see page 183.

Check your understanding
1. What three personality traits do criminals score highly on, according to Eysenck?
2. How is each trait associated with criminal behaviour?
3. What biological factors are involved in the criminal personality according to Eysenck?
4. In his theory, how does Eysenck consider both nature and nurture?
5. How can Eysenck be criticised for ignoring individual differences?

Chapter 1 Criminal Psychology

Criminal Personality Theory Research Study: Heaven (1996) – a study into delinquency, extraversion, psychoticism and self-esteem.

Background

Heaven's study recognised that there was strong evidence that personality variables were associated with criminal and anti-social behaviour, and he was particularly interested in exploring the traits identified by Eysenck. He challenged certain aspects of Eysenck's theory. For instance, research has shown that those who scored highly on neuroticism, but not extraversion, tended to be official offenders (those convicted and on record), whilst those who scored highly on extraversion, but not neuroticism, tended to score highly on self-report measures.

> For more information on self-report see page 183.

Hypothesis

The researcher predicted that measures of psychoticism, extroversion and self-esteem would be significant predictors for self-reported **delinquency**.

Method

Design

Heaven also noted that most previous research tended to be **cross-sectional** and his aim was to carry out a piece of **longitudinal** research, to investigate whether psychoticism, extraversion, and **self-esteem** at the start of the study (Time 1) were significant predictors of self-reported delinquency two years later (Time 2). Self-esteem, rather than neuroticism, was investigated for two reasons. Firstly, previous researchers had questioned the value of neuroticism in predicting self-reported delinquency. Additionally, low self-esteem is often seen as a feature of neuroticism, with several psychologists arguing that delinquent youths use anti-social behaviour as a way of compensating for their low self-esteem. For example, if a delinquent youth associates with a group of delinquent youths, the group is likely to approve of his or her behaviour, thus restoring his or her self-esteem.

> **Delinquency**
> Actions that go against accepted standards or laws.
>
> **Cross-sectional study**
> A study carried out at one point in time and comparing distinct groups of people.
>
> **Longitudinal study**
> A study carried out over a period of time looking at the same group of people.
>
> **Self-esteem**
> How much an individual values themselves.

Sample

The participants were 282 adolescents (146 females; 136 males) from two Catholic independent schools in New South Wales, Australia. Their ages ranged from thirteen to fifteen years old when the study began, with a **modal** age of fourteen years. All of the students were tested and although they had the option of withdrawing from the study, none chose to do so.

> For more information on mode see page 194.

Materials

At Times 1 and 2, students were provided with a test booklet which contained the following measures:

1) a set of questions, taken from Eysenck's questionnaire, to measure psychoticism and extraversion
2) a ten-item questionnaire to measure self-esteem
3) a questionnaire for self-reported delinquency that assessed two forms of delinquency: interpersonal violence and vandalism/theft, using a four point rating scale ranging from Never (scored 1) to Often (scored 4).

> For more information on questionnaires see page 184.

Procedure

All three questionnaires were checked for **internal reliability** and, apart from the psychoticism scale, scored well.

> For more information on internal reliability see page 201.

Participants were followed up after two years, with 80 per cent responding the second time around.

Questionnaires were completed anonymously and during class time and, although numbers were printed on questionnaires to allow for the follow-up, students were assured of the **confidentiality** of their responses and of the fact that individual responses would not be available to the school authorities.

> For more information on confidentiality see page 180.

> **Time for some maths**
> Look at the method section of Heaven's study to answer these questions:
> 1 What is meant by the statement that the sample had a modal age of fourteen?
> 2 How many participants were involved in the follow up questionnaires?

Results

The mean delinquency scores for males and females are shown in the table below.

▼ Table 1.2 Mean delinquency scores by gender

	Time 1	Time 2
Males	21.16	20.96
Females	18.71	19.58

Source: Patrick C.L. Heaven, 'Personality and Self-Reported Delinquency: A Longitudinal Analysis' in *The Journal of Child Psychology and Psychiatry*, Volume 37, Issue 6 September 1996, p. 748

This shows that males were more likely to engage in delinquency at Times 1 and 2.

The table below presents the **correlations** at Times 1 and 2 between delinquency and the personality variables tested.

▼ Table 1.3 Correlation coefficients for delinquency and each personality variable

	Delinquency Time 1	Delinquency Time 2
Psychoticism	0.43	0.51
Extraversion	-0.05	0.17
Self-Esteem	-0.11	-0.12

Source: Patrick C.L. Heaven, 'Personality and Self-Reported Delinquency: A Longitudinal Analysis' in *The Journal of Child Psychology and Psychiatry*, Volume 37, Issue 6 September 1996, p. 748

This showed a **positive correlation** between psychoticism and delinquency at Time 1 and Time 2. Extraversion correlated with delinquency only at Time 2 and was a weaker correlation. Generally, Heaven's results supported previous cross-sectional studies, which had shown strong associations between psychoticism and various forms of anti-social behaviour and criminality.

Data was analysed further to test the idea that psychoticism, extraversion and self-esteem at Time 1 significantly predicted delinquency at Time 2. The results suggested that psychoticism was the best predictor of delinquency at Times 1 and 2 but it was not as reliable as Heaven had hoped.

> **Time for some maths**
> Look at the results section of Heaven's study to answer these questions:
> 1 When was there a more significant difference between male and female delinquency scores – Time 1 or Time 2?
> 2 Rewrite the table of mean delinquency scores so that each mean is to one **decimal place**.
> 3 Which two variables showed the strongest positive correlation?
> 4 Which two variables showed the strongest **negative correlation**?
> 5 Which two variables showed the weakest correlation?

Conclusion

Heaven's study aligned with previous research, which showed that psychoticism is associated significantly with self-reported delinquency. It also supported Eysenck's idea that psychoticism is the 'linchpin' that explains the nature of delinquent behaviour. However, Heaven was keen to point out that the three independent factors tested in this study (psychoticism, extraversion and low self-esteem) explained only a modest percentage of the variance of delinquency. Evidence for their influence on delinquency over time was quite weak. Heaven therefore suggested that other psychological factors, such as peer pressure, parents' disciplinary styles and personality could determine whether or not some children engage in delinquent behaviour.

Criticisms

- **The sample used was culturally biased for a number of reasons.** The sample only used children from Roman Catholic schools, ignoring other religions or children without religion. Religion has a strong influence on children's moral behaviour. In addition, the children all attended a fee-paying school, meaning most would come from better off families. Again, income and crime are often linked, so it is a limitation that poorer children were missing from the study. Finally, the study may only represent patterns of behaviour in an Australian population; we cannot assume other cultures would have similar results.

- **The results may have been affected by age bias.** The participants' average ages were fourteen and then sixteen at the two times of measurement. It may be they were too old to properly establish the factors that lead to delinquency. This is because behaviours such as interpersonal violence, vandalism and theft almost definitely start much earlier than at fourteen or sixteen years for children who are going to get involved in delinquency.

- **The twenty per cent of participants who dropped out of the study by Time 2 may have biased the results.** Although Heaven did well to retain 80 per cent of his participants, the ones that dropped out may have represented particular types of people more than others. For example, this could include people that were engaged in lots of criminal activity by sixteen and did not want to report it or people whose self-esteem was so low they did not want to continue with the study. This would affect the overall **validity** of results.
- **The use of self-report can lead to invalid data.** Due to a **social desirability** bias, the participants may not have been honest about information, such as how much delinquency they were involved in, or how low their self-esteem was. Self-report methods also rely on people's insight; it might be the participants were not that aware of their personality traits when answering questions.
- **The use of closed questions can be criticised for their lack of construct validity.** Critics have said that the use of simple options and **rating scales** to measure complex constructs such as personality and delinquency is not appropriate. Using quantitative data hides the depth of the relationship between different factors.

▲ How much can psychologists trust self-report in a study into delinquency?

> **Something to think about**
> Which one of these criticisms is the most significant and which is the least? Compare your opinion with others.

For more information on cultural bias and age bias see page 204.

For more information on representativeness and generalisability see page 176.

For more information on self-report see page 183.

For more information on social desirability and construct validity see page 202.

For more information on closed questions see page 184.

For more information on quantitative data see page 192.

Check your understanding

1. Why is the Heaven study an example of a longitudinal study?
2. Who made up the original sample in the study?
3. How were each of the three traits investigated in the study measured?
4. How did Heaven's conclusions take into account both nature and nurture when explaining delinquency?
5. In what ways were Heaven's results potentially biased?

Application: the changing nature of punishment

If psychologists are able to establish the true cause of criminal and anti-social behaviour, whether it is more to do with nature or nurture, then there is a chance of preventing or reducing it. Of course, if it is in people's nature to be criminal then this is difficult to control. However, the way that psychological research is currently applied when dealing with crime does suggest that society believes criminal behaviour is learned and therefore is something that can be unlearned.

> **Something to think about**
> What if criminal behaviour is something people are born with and therefore part of their biology? What are the implications for controlling and reducing crime?

The effects of punishment and deterrents in reducing criminal/anti-social behaviour

When looking at Social Learning Theory earlier in this chapter, we considered the idea that criminal behaviour can be reinforced because it is rewarding. In contrast, if criminal behaviour is **punished**, then this should reduce the chance of it happening again; people generally want to avoid negative outcomes. **Prisons** have long been used as a way of punishing criminals. By taking away freedom, rights and privileges, criminals should learn to avoid criminal behaviour in the future. Prisons are also punishing because the living conditions are poor.

Fines are also used as a form of punishment, usually for more minor crimes, such as traffic offences, damage to property or failure to pay taxes. In the same way that money can be an incentive for committing certain types of crime, loss of funds has the opposite effect; it is a disincentive.

Community sentences are a more recent form of punishment. Offenders make some payment back to society, often by giving up their time to contribute to the community in some way. It is often made obvious to the public that they are doing community service, so the psychological punishments of shame and guilt are also part of the process.

> **Challenge**
> Use the internet to carry out research on community service orders. How many different types of jobs can you identify that could be part of a community sentence. A good starting point for your research is to search for 'community sentences' on the government's website.

Making punishment public, through community service, using the media to report imprisonments or issuing fines 'on the spot' can act as a **deterrent** for crime. Many people do not commit crimes in the first place and this is

Punishment
When negative consequences follow a certain behaviour and reduce the chance of that behaviour happening again.

Prison
A place where people are confined as a punishment.

Fine
A monetary charge imposed on an individual who has committed an offence.

Community sentence
Time that has to be given back to the community in the form of unpaid work.

Deterrent
Something that reduces the likelihood of a crime being committed.

Chapter 1 Criminal Psychology

because they want to avoid the negative consequences that they have seen others suffer. This can be seen in Social Learning Theory; if people imitate what they have seen being rewarded (vicarious reinforcement), then it makes sense that they will not want to imitate a behaviour that they have seen being punished.

> **Something to think about**
> Confidential surveys suggest that most of us have broken the law at some point, even if only a few of us are convicted. Does this mean that deterrents do not really work? If there are certain crimes that you would never commit, why is this? Are you deterred by the threat of punishment?

▲ The singer Boy George carried out community service in New York, in 2006. The red waistcoat is intended to draw attention to the fact that the offender has committed a crime, and is part of making them feel ashamed and guilty.

Rehabilitation
The process of reintegrating a convicted person back into society, with the aim that they will no longer want to commit crimes.

Pro-social behaviour
Behaviour that involves us being caring, helping and sharing. We may show pro-social behaviour because we are concerned about the well-being of others around us.

Restorative justice
A way of rehabilitating offenders by giving them the choice to be aware of the consequences of their actions.

> **Extension**
> Do some further research on Social Skills Training and/or Anger Management Programmes. Explain in more detail how these examples of rehabilitation make use of social learning and positive role models.

The role of rehabilitation in reducing criminal/anti-social behaviour and increasing pro-social behaviour

Psychologists were among the first to acknowledge that punishing offenders is not enough in itself to reduce crime. Offenders may need to unlearn their criminal ways, and learn how they should behave instead. This is the idea behind **rehabilitation**. Punishment is more about reducing criminal and anti-social behaviour, whereas rehabilitation is about promoting **pro-social behaviour**.

One way of rehabilitating offenders is through **restorative justice**. This approach actively involves the victim of the crime, to the point where often the victim will meet the person who has committed a crime against them. The idea is that the offender is held directly to account by facing their victim, so they are aware that their actions are against individuals and communities, not a faceless society. Offenders are encouraged to take responsibility for their actions and to repair the harm they've done, by apologising, returning stolen money, or doing community service. It brings them into the community, rather than allowing them to exclude themselves.

> **Challenge**
> Visit the website for the Restorative Justice Council at https://www.restorativejustice.org.uk. You will find some interesting case studies of how this scheme works. Can you spot any themes as you read the different case studies? Write these down to give a summary of how restorative justice works.

Another way of rehabilitating offenders is through the use of positive role models. Offenders need to be able to observe others behaving in pro-social ways, so that they have something to imitate. They need to see the behaviour as rewarding (e.g. it gains respect, trust, a job) and also need to believe that they can be 'good citizens'. Sometimes these role models are called mentors, and are matched with the offenders so that they are likely to identify with them. For example, they may be reformed criminals themselves or people from similar backgrounds as the offenders, but who have found success. Role models may also be professionals who lead a training programme, perhaps to improve offenders' social skills or to teach them how to manage their anger. They will demonstrate how to better deal with difficult situations and then get offenders to role play this.

> ### Check your understanding
> 1. What is the difference between punishment and rehabilitation when applied to criminal behaviour?
> 2. How do community sentences attempt to punish crime?
> 3. What is meant by restorative justice in relation to crime?
> 4. How can positive role models be used as part of a rehabilitation programme for criminals?

STUDY HINT
Although there are examples of rehabilitation that you have to know about, a broad exam question on rehabilitation will allow you to write about other examples that you may be aware of from elsewhere.

> **SUMMARY**
> This chapter has shown that psychologists need to be able to define and measure crime before they can begin to investigate it, and that this is not necessarily a straightforward process. Some psychologists look more towards the environment to explain crime, such as in Social Learning Theory. This idea is supported by studies like Cooper & Mackie's, which shows the potential effect of the media (one part of the environment) on aggressive behaviour (a common feature of crime).
>
> Other psychologists look more towards the biology of individuals to explain crime, such as Eysenck's Criminal Personality Theories. This idea of an innate criminal personality is supported by studies like Heaven's, who showed a link between psychoticism and extraversion and crime over time. However, Eysenck also recognised the role of early socialisation and other environmental factors.
>
> This combination of nature and nurture might be the best way to try to explain crime. Indeed, the role of nurture is considered important when it comes to trying to reduce crime and anti-social behaviour, as the main assumption is that such behaviour has been learned and so it can be unlearned and replaced with more pro-social behaviour. Using prisons, fines and community sentences to punish offences is seen as a way to unlearn criminal behaviour or even deter it in the first place. Meanwhile, rehabilitation programmes like restorative justice are a way of promoting pro-social behaviour in place of criminal behaviour.

Practice questions

The questions in this textbook have been written by the authors, Mark Billingham and Helen Kitching. They have not been produced or endorsed by OCR.

1. In a survey of 300 people, 95 per cent reported they had been a victim of acquisitive crime, 16 per cent reported they had been a victim of violent crime and 7 per cent reported they had been a victim of a sexual crime.

   According to the survey;

   a. What percentage of people had *not* been a victim of acquisitive crime? **[1 mark]**

   5 per cent

This is correct. (95 per cent reported being a victim so the remainder adds up to 5 per cent).

   b. How many people had been a victim of a sexual crime? Show your workings. **[2 marks]**

   7/100 × 300 = 0.7 × 300 = 7   Answer is 7

This answer earns one mark because although the final answer is wrong, the workings make sense.

   c. How many people had been a victim of violent crime? Express your answer as a fraction in its lowest form and show your workings. **[2 marks]**

   16/100 divided by 4 = 4/25   Answer is 4/25

This answer earns both marks because workings are present and the answer is right.

2. Outline **one** way in which crime can be measured. **[2 marks]**

   One way crime is measured is by looking at what different societies accept as normal or not. For example, homosexuality is no longer considered deviant in the UK so is not a crime, but in some, often more religious, countries it remains a crime.

This answer does not score anything. The candidate has misunderstood or misread the question, and focused on defining crime rather than measuring crime.

3. Explain how the central nervous system relates to the criminal personality. **[3 marks]**

   Eysenck says that extraversion is linked to the arousal of the central nervous system, including the reticular activating system, which is part of the brain stem. People who score highly on the extraversion scale are under-aroused and seek out risky behaviour to increase stimulation. The risky behaviour can be illegal, and so people become criminals.

There is enough to earn three marks here. The candidate outlines the role of the central nervous system (arousal) and links this to extraversion, which earns them two marks. They then go on to relate extraversion to criminal behaviour, which earns them a third mark.

4 Describe **one** criticism of Eysenck's theory of the criminal personality. [3 marks]

There are lots of different types of crimes so not everyone will have the same personality.

This point is made quite implicitly and is very brief. Although it is relevant, there is only enough detail to award one mark.

5 (a) Briefly describe the sample used in Heaven's (1996) study into the criminal personality. [2 marks]

There were nearly 300 teenagers, split relatively evenly between males and females. They came from two Australian Catholic schools. Their ages ranged from 13-15 years old at the start of the study.

This answer covers several features of the sample – the sample size, the sex and age of the participants, and where they are from. This easily earns two marks.

(b) Outline **one** criticism of the sample used in this study. [2 marks]

The sample was culturally biased because it only used students from Catholic schools and ignored other religions or children who did not come from a religious family. Religion can have a big effect on children's moral behaviour, so the sample is not generalisable.

This is a clear and well developed response that makes good use of appropriate terminology. It easily earns the two marks.

6 a Give **one** of the results from Cooper & Mackie's (1986) study into video games and aggression in children. [1 mark]

Participants in the highly aggressive game condition spent more time playing with the aggressive toy than participants in the other two conditions.

Although brief, this answer is enough for the one mark on offer.

b Suggest **one** way in which Cooper & Mackie's study could be improved. [2 marks]

One way of improving the study would be to do it in a natural setting so that the study is more realistic.

This suggestion is valid but not quite enough for two marks. The candidate needs to develop their response by putting it into the context of the study. In other words, what could be more realistic about the setting?

Chapter 1 Criminal Psychology

7

> **Serial Shoplifter**
> Leah has been caught shoplifting on a number of occasions. Up until now, she has been let off with a warning, but the police have recognised that this is not stopping her from reoffending.

Using the source, suggest how **both** rehabilitation **and** punishment could be used to try to stop Leah reoffending. **[6 marks]**

The police could use restorative justice to encourage Leah to stop shoplifting. She would have to go back to the shops that she had stolen from and apologise in person to the shop owner for what she had done. She would also have to return the stolen goods or pay for them. By facing up to what she has done, Leah would be taking responsibility. Maybe if she saw how upset the shop owner was, then she would think twice about stealing again in the future. Another way of stopping Leah from reoffending would be to punish her by sending her to prison. This would almost definitely stop her from doing it again.

This answer covers rehabilitation really well by applying both knowledge and understanding to Leah's case. However, the response is imbalanced, as the use of prisons is not adequately explained and therefore not fully applied. Overall, this response is worth four marks.

8 Use your knowledge and understanding from across the psychology course to explain how far you agree with the following viewpoint:

"Behaviours are learned and so can easily be unlearned."

In your answer you should refer to Social Learning Theory of criminal behaviour and at least **one** other area of psychology where you have studied the effects of learning.
[13 marks]

Social Learning Theory suggests that we learn our behaviour from other people. It assumes that our behaviour is all about nurture — our upbringing. It suggests that we learn criminal behaviour by observing peers, such as older siblings. If they are involved in criminal behaviour, we may see them as a role model and identify with them. We might observe them stealing something, for example. If we see them being rewarded, by having nice things that they couldn't otherwise afford to buy, then we will want to imitate their behaviour. If the behaviour is rewarded often enough then it becomes internalised.

However, if we can learn this behaviour, then according to this theory, we should be able to unlearn it by having role models who demonstrate the rewards of pro-social behaviour and by witnessing punishment for anti-social behaviour. However, many people still continue to commit crimes even when they are punished for their behaviour. As this theory is based only on nurture, it ignores the role of nature and how biology might have an effect on people's behaviour. For example, the idea that there may be a criminal gene. Eysenck believed that personality was innate and therefore that people were born with a criminal personality. This suggests that criminal behaviour cannot easily be unlearned.

Another learning theory, Mindsets, suggests that if we have a growth mindset, we are more likely to be motivated to succeed. Dweck says that children can be coached to have this type of mindset, and therefore we can help them to develop differently and to be successful in life. In contrast, Piaget believes that cognitive development is more related to biology and basically develops as a child gets older.

In conclusion, it might be that behaviours like crime and cognitive ability are a result of both nature and nurture interacting. For example, an individual may have a gene that makes them take risks. In some cases this may lead to them working in a job where they can take risks, but in the wrong kind of environment they could end up turning to crime. In a similar way, a child may have a natural tendency towards being intelligent, but this still needs to be nurtured through the right kind of environment.

This is a carefully thought-out response with some well-developed points. The Social Learning Theory of criminal behaviour is outlined accurately and clearly. Dweck's theory is given less attention, but is still an appropriate choice, which is fitted well with Social Learning Theory in the conclusion.

The evaluation of Social Learning Theory and the conclusion both earn AO3 marks. This answer earns six out of seven AO1 marks, and five out of six AO3 marks – getting eleven marks in total.

2 Development

Developmental psychologists are interested in how we change and develop across our lifetimes. Some psychologists, such as Jean Piaget, focus on how a child thinks, changes and develops from birth until adolescence. Researchers like Dweck look at how our thinking affects our ability to learn and progress at school. Neuropsychologists examine our brain and consider how it changes from the moment we are conceived until we die.

Development
How we change and mature across our lifetimes.

Pre-natal
From conception until birth.

Childhood
From birth to the age of twelve.

This chapter should enable you to:
- develop an awareness of the stages of development, from pre-natal to adulthood, including brain development, with reference to the nervous system, neurons and synapses
- understand IQ tests as a measure of intelligence
- be able to explain and evaluate Piaget's Theory of Cognitive Development, with reference to the four invariant stages of development, assimilation and accommodation, the concepts of object permanence, animism and egocentrism, the processes of decentration, reversibility and conservation, and the reductionism/holism debate as part of criticisms of the theory
- describe and evaluate Piaget's (1952) study into the conservation of number
- explain and evaluate learning theories of development with reference to Dweck's ideas about Fixed and Growth Mindsets and Praise for Effort, and Willingham's ideas about the Myth of Learning Styles and the Importance of Meaning for Learning, and the Nature/Nurture Debate as part of the criticisms of the theories
- describe and evaluate Blackwell *et al.* (2007) study into fixed and growth mindsets
- explain how Piaget's ideas have been applied to education through the use of key stages, readiness, active learning and the concept of intelligence
- explain how learning theories apply to the development of intelligence through growth mindsets and teaching through meaning.

Stages of development

- **Pre-natal:** The pre-natal stage is the time from when a baby is conceived to when it is born.
- **Childhood:** This is the period from birth through to the age of twelve. Children at the start of this stage are totally reliant on their parents/caregivers, who they bond with in order to gain self-confidence and independence. As they move through the stage, they rapidly gain skills, such as walking and talking, and start to be more autonomous.

- **Adolescence:** This stage runs from thirteen to nineteen years old and is the transitional stage from childhood to adulthood. The body undergoes significant changes during this period as it matures sexually. Individuals going through this stage begin to think, act and feel differently.
- **Adulthood:** From the age of twenty until death, an individual enters adulthood. This is a time of taking on new responsibilities such as intimate relationships, parenthood and careers.

The nervous system, neurons and synapses

The **nervous system** acts as the body's control centre. It interprets the sensory information that enters the body via the senses like touch and taste, and sends information through to the glands and muscles with orders for how they should react.

The **central nervous system** includes the brain and the spinal cord, and the peripheral nervous system consists of the nerves that branch out from the brain and spinal cord throughout your body.

The nervous system is made up of **neurons**. Each neuron has a cell body. The cell body is covered in dendrites, which look a bit like fingers, and an axon, which looks like its tail. The dendrites receive information from other neurons and transmit this information via an electrical impulse to the cell body. The impulse is then transmitted to another neuron by the axon.

The **synapse** is located at the end of the axon. As the electrical impulse travels along the axon, it triggers the release of **neurotransmitters**, which are chemical messengers. Once they reach the synapse, the neurotransmitters diffuse across the synapse, which is the gap between two neurons. When they reach the other side, the neurotransmitters will then bind with **receptors** on the next neuron. There are different kinds of receptors, and the neurotransmitters will only bind with the receptors that are designed specifically to receive them, like a key going into a lock. The message is then passed along that neuron to the next one in the same way.

Brain development
Stages of brain development
Pre-natal

In the first trimester, sixteen days after fertilisation, the human embryo develops a neural tube. This is what will become its brain and spinal cord. Cell are created from around 6 weeks gestation until around 20 weeks gestation. These then follow a process called 'migration' where they move to their correct location in the brain where they become neurons and begin to form the nervous system. This process of migration starts around eight weeks gestation and is complete by around 29 weeks gestation. When the **foetus** is around two months of gestation, the neural tube divides into brain cells and nerve cells. The **cerebral cortex** is formed. This part of the brain is responsible for how we think and act, as well as our memories and our intelligence. It is divided into four different sections: the **frontal lobe**, the **temporal lobe**, the parietal lobe and the occipital lobe.

Adolescence
From age thirteen to nineteen years.

Adulthood
From twenty years until death.

> **Neuropsychology now**
> Psychologists are interested in how the brain develops and changes across time and how these brain changes can affect our behaviour, such as in adolescence where a less mature brain is thought to have an effect on risk-taking behaviour.

Nervous system
A network of nerve cells and fibres that transmits impulses between parts of the body. The body's control centre.

Neuron
A cell that transmits nerve impulses to send messages between the brain and other parts of the body.

Synapse
The gap between two neurons.

Receptors
Parts of the neuron that accept the neurotransmitter from another neuron. They help transmit the message between the neurons.

Foetus
The name given to the developing baby during pregnancy, when it has reached eight weeks after conception (and all the major structures have been formed) until birth.

At four to six months, the pregnancy enters the second trimester and the brain becomes fully developed, although it is not yet grown to its full size. At this point, the majority of the 100 billion neurons have formed. At around 20 weeks gestation, the neurons start to develop, including the axon and the dendrites. By the fifth month, simple synapses have formed allowing the neurons to communicate with each other. By the end of the second trimester, the nervous system has developed enough that the foetus can react to loud noises outside the womb – for example if the mother plays loud music or walks past someone drilling a hole in the road!

In the third and final trimester of pregnancy, the brain continues to grow.

The brain development can be affected by what the mother consumes during pregnancy. For example, if she drinks a lot of alcohol, the baby may be born with a condition called Foetal Alcohol Syndrome. The alcohol disrupts the nerve connections in the baby's brain and this can result in learning difficulties when they are born, such as problems with memory, speech and thinking.

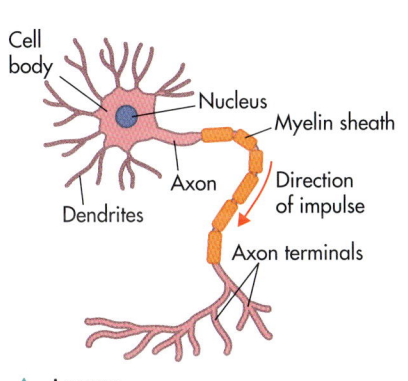

▲ A neuron

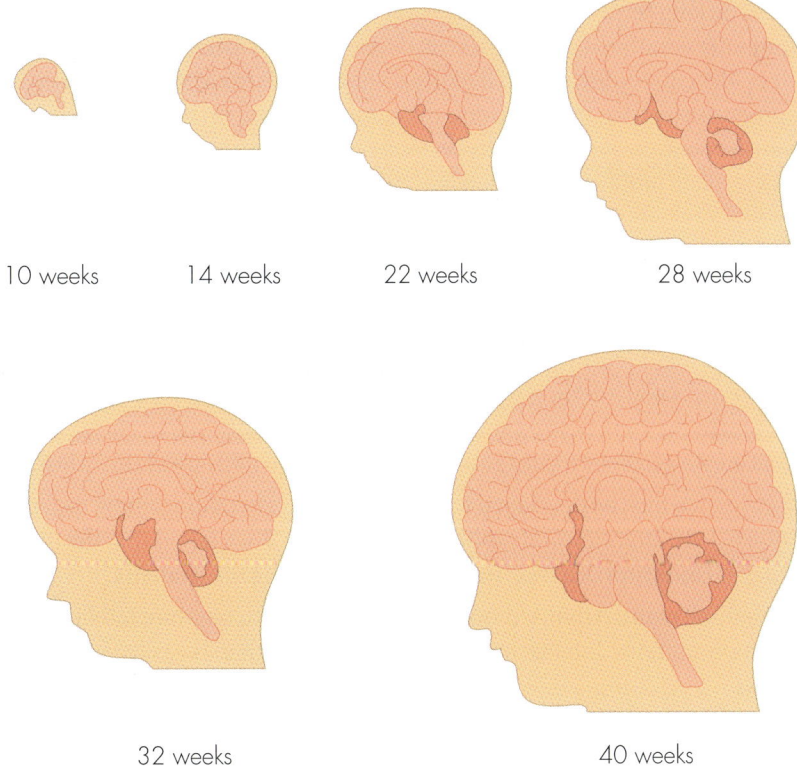

▲ The developing brain of the foetus during pregnancy.

Childhood

After the child is born, the brain develops many new neural connections (approximately 1,000 per second). For example, in the visual cortex, the number of synapses nearly doubles up to the age of four months. When a baby is born, its ability to see clearly is limited. By the time it is five months old, the new synapses allow it to see in 3D and it will have gained the ability to see in colour as well. Around the age of three, the density of synapses in the **prefrontal cortex** is at its peak. This allows the child to start to use their past experiences to understand their present. They also start

Challenge

Make your own model of a neuron out of plasticine or sweets. Spend three minutes memorising the diagram and then see if you can label it without looking. Write your labels on paper and place them around the model with arrows pointing to the correct section. Don't forget to take a photo of your model after you have checked that your labelling is correct.

Prefrontal cortex
The part of the brain that is located behind the forehead and is associated with making moral decisions.

to understand **cause and effect**. During later childhood, these connections are then 'pruned', meaning that we get rid of the neural connections that we do not use.

Adolescence

During adolescence, the brain undergoes some significant changes. The grey matter, which is found on the surface of the brain and is composed of the cell bodies of neurons, nerve fibres and support cells, reaches its maximum density.

Areas of the brain like the limbic system are the first to mature. The limbic system regulates emotion and helps form new memories. The prefrontal cortex is last to mature. This regulates decision making and moderates social behaviour. The differences in time taken to mature between the limbic system and the prefrontal cortex are thought to explain behaviour in adolescence, such as risk taking. The frontal lobes continue to develop during adolescence and reach maturity around the age of 16.

Adulthood

At around the age of 25 the prefrontal cortex, the 'rational' part of the brain, finally matures. This part of the brain helps people make rational decisions and be able to focus on long-term **consequences** of actions. This reduces impulsiveness. During later adulthood, individuals can develop neurodegenerative disorders such as Alzheimer's disease and Parkinson's disease. Neurodegenerative diseases are progressive in that they get worse over time and result in the death of neurons within the brain. In Alzheimer's disease, scientists believe that changes in the cortex result in problems with thinking and memory.

IQ tests as a measure of intelligence

Alfred Binet was one of the first psychologists to develop a test to measure **intelligence**, known as the IQ (intelligence quotient) test. In the early 1900s, he was asked by the French government to find a way to identify which school children were at greatest risk of struggling at school so that they could provide extra help.

The **IQ test**, which he developed with his colleague Theodore Simon, tested memory skills, attention and problem-solving skills. They found that the test was a good indicator of a wide range of abilities among the students.

Binet himself realised that, although the test was able to measure intelligence, it had its limitations. Intelligence is far more complex than is easily measurable by a test.

The test was used as the basis for an IQ test that is still used today: the Stanford-Binet Intelligence Scales test. It was developed by a psychologist called Lewis Terman at Stanford University in the USA.

Today, IQ tests are generally used to identify the children who have either very high or low intelligence. For those children who are identified as having low intelligence, then extra support can be provided. They are also used to see who has the highest intelligence quotient in the country. Those who score really highly can join an organisation called Mensa®. Those children who are tested and found to have very high IQs can then be appropriately stretched and challenged within their school to ensure that they are able to meet their potential.

One of the most widely used IQ tests for children is the Wechsler Intelligence Scale for Children. It is used with children aged 6 to 16 years. It is also sometimes

Intelligence
Our ability and potential to learn, think and problem solve.

IQ test
Intelligence Quotient test which is designed to measure people's intelligence.

used as part of a wider range of tests, for example, to see if children have dyslexia or dyscalculia or attention-deficit hyperactivity disorder (ADHD).

Psychological testing as a form of social control

Read the following information. Discuss how this relates to the key idea of cultural **bias**.

Although IQ tests have been used in a positive way to identify students who need support, they also represent a dark period in the history of psychology. During the First World War, in the USA, an American psychologist named Yerkes developed three IQ tests to screen recruits for the US army, some of whom were recent immigrants to the country and knew little about American **culture** and may not have spoken English. One test (Alpha) was a written test for literate recruits. Another test (The Beta) was a seven-part picture completion task, and was given to illiterate recruits. The third test was a spoken examination for those men who failed the Beta test. These tests were designed so that large numbers of recruits could be tested in one go, and allowed the army to identify who would make good officers and leaders.

Over 1.75 million recruits were tested. Yerkes believed that his tests were reliable and were not influenced by how much or little **education** someone had received or their cultural background.

Criticisms

- There were a significant number of issues with the tests that affected both their **reliability** and **validity**. Some of the pictures were culturally specific. Also a number of the questions required a level of cultural knowledge, such as: 'Crisco° is a: patent medicine; disinfectant; toothpaste; food product'. If you don't know, Crisco° is the brand name of a food product, used like margarine in baking cakes and biscuits. However, if you have never lived in America, you are unlikely to know this. Imagine you had just arrived in America from Europe. Would this type of question be a fair test of your intelligence?

- There were also problems with the Beta test as far too many recruits were illiterate which meant many of them were given the Alpha test as it was far easier and quicker to run. This meant those who could not read or write were hugely disadvantaged.

- The results of the tests showed that the average mental age of white American males was just thirteen. Those people who were immigrants from Southern and Eastern Europe were found to be 'less intelligent' than people from Northern and Western Europe. Black people had the lowest mental age of 10.41. However, it was not recognised that there were problems with the tests or that many of those tested had only recently arrived in America and were consequently not fluent in English. The test also did not consider those who had not had the opportunity to go to school as children.

- The results were also used as 'evidence' to support an argument that people of low intelligence should not be allowed to immigrate to the USA. This had a huge impact during the Second World War: based on these results, many people from Eastern and Southern Europe were prevented from fleeing persecution from the Nazis, as the American 1924 Immigration Act barred entry to those who had scored poorly on the IQ tests (an example of this is Anne Frank who was denied a visa to enter America).

Education
A system of teaching, learning and assessment associated with schools, colleges and universities.

Something to think about
Look online at some IQ tests. Try www.mensa.org.uk. What sort of skills/abilities do they not test for?

Extension
For more detailed information on what Yerkes did, read the research study *A Nation of Morons* by Gould (1982). You can search for this online.

Check your understanding
1. What is the role of the central nervous system?
2. Name two key things that happen to the brain during the pre-natal phase of development.
3. What is the name of the gap between two neurons?
4. What does IQ stand for?
5. Why were IQ tests first developed?

Theories of development
Piaget's Theory of Cognitive Development

Jean Piaget was a Swiss psychologist, born in 1896. Whilst standardising IQ tests at the Alfred Binet laboratory in Paris, he became interested in the ways children learn. Although children often gave incorrect answers to the IQ tests, when Piaget asked them to explain their answer, he discovered they often used their imagination when they didn't possess the necessary knowledge. He found that the way children thought changed as they grew older. This inspired him to observe his own children and their friends, looking at how they played and how they learnt. He was interested in how their thinking changed over time. Piaget used his results as a basis for his Theory of **Cognitive Development**.

Key features of Piaget's theory (1936)

It has four stages.

- The stages are **invariant** – this means they do not change and children pass through each stage in the same order.
- The stages are **universal** – they are the same for all children.
- Piaget viewed children as 'little scientists' who, from the moment they are born, are actively trying to understand their environment.
- **Schemas** – Piaget believed that children had mental pictures of their world, called schemas, which help them to understand how to react to the world around them. For example, a simple schema for a very young child might be the knowledge of how to get food into his or her mouth using a spoon. In other words, the schema for feeding themselves.
- **Assimilation** – This is where new information that the child encounters is merged into an existing schema. For example, a child might have a schema that 'all deer have antlers', but they might see some deer that don't have antlers, so the deer schema is expanded to include 'some deer have no antlers, but they are still deer'.
- **Accommodation** – This is where a child encounters new information which results in either a new schema being formed **or** an existing schema being altered in some way. For example, if a child thinks that all vehicles with four wheels are cars, but then encounters a camper van and learns that you can live in it, then the schema that 'all vehicles with four wheels are cars' needs to be altered.

For more information on schemas see page 134.

The stages of cognitive development

1. Sensori-motor stage: 0–2 years

During the **sensori-motor** stage of development, babies learn about the world through their senses: touching, tasting, seeing and hearing (sensori); and by moving around their environment and doing things (motor).

Key features of the stage include:

- **Object permanence** – At the start of the sensori-motor stage, if a toy is hidden from the baby, they will not search for it. Once the toy is out of sight it ceases to exist in the baby's mind, because the baby lacks object permanence. Before the end of the sensori-motor stage (around twelve months), the child will have developed object permanence and so if a toy is hidden from their view, they will actively look for it.

Cognitive development
How our thought processes change over time throughout childhood. This includes language, memory and perception.

Invariant
Something that does not change or vary.

Universal
The same for everyone.

Assimilation
New information is incorporated into an existing schema.

Accommodation
New information is used to either alter an existing schema or create a new one.

Cognitive
Mental processes of memory, perception, judgement and reasoning.

Sensori-motor
The first stage of Piaget's Theory of Cognitive Development in which babies start to learn about their environment using their senses.

Object permanence
The idea that something still exists, even if it is hidden from view.

▲ If you have trouble remembering the four stages of development, try using this mnemonic: '**S**ee **P**retty **C**ows **F**ly'.

Chapter 2 Development

Animism
Giving thoughts and feelings to inanimate objects.

Pre-operational
The second stage of Piaget's Theory of Cognitive Development in which children start to learn to talk. Children in this stage are still egocentric.

Egocentrism
If a child is egocentric, they will assume that everyone views the world in the same way that they do.

Reversibility
The ability to be able to think about things in reverse order.

Conservation
The ability to understand that even though something might change it's shape or form, it's volume, mass or length remain the same.

Concrete operational
The third stage of Piaget's Theory of Cognitive Development. Children in this stage achieve the ability to conserve.

Formal operational
Piaget's fourth and final stage of cognitive development. During this stage, children develop abstract thinking.

> **STUDY HINT**
> Remember that Piaget's three mountains **experiment** is just given as an example of egocentrism. This is *not* the Piaget study that you need to know in detail for the exam.

> **For more information on Piaget's conservation of number experiments see page 36.**

2. Pre-operational stage: 2–7 years

During this stage, children will start school and they continue to develop their skills.

Key features of the stage include:

- **Animism** – Children in the **pre-operational** stage believe that inanimate objects have feelings. For example, if they see a wilting flower, they might say it is 'sad'. They will also treat their toys as though they are alive and have conversations with them.

- **Egocentrism** – Children at this stage can lack empathy because they think that everyone sees the world in the same way that they do. They cannot understand that different people, such as their parents or siblings, can be feeling or thinking different things to them.

- **Reversibility** – During the pre-operational stage, children are unable to think about things in reverse order. They are also unable to understand that if you add or take something away from an object, that you can return it to its original state. For example, if a ball of plasticine is squashed into a flat disc, it can be changed back into a ball again.

Piaget used his experiment called the 'Three Mountain Problem' as evidence to support the idea of egocentrism. In the task, children were shown a model of three mountains. They were seated on one side of the model, and a doll was placed on the other side. The child was shown ten cards with different views of the three mountains model and asked to choose the card which showed the doll's view of the model. Most of the children in the pre-operational stage chose the card which showed their view of the mountains. Piaget said that this was evidence that they were egocentric.

▲ Piaget's three mountains task.

3. Concrete operational stage: 7–11 years

Key features of the stage include:

- **Conservation** – Once children enter the **concrete operational** stage, they gain the ability to conserve. This means that if they see a substance such as liquid or clay, or an object such as a piece of string, change its shape, they realise that the volume, mass or length do not change. For example, if they are shown some juice that is in a short, wide glass and see it poured into another glass that is tall and thin, those children who can 'conserve' will know that although it looks different, the volume has not changed. On the other hand, children who are in the pre-operational stage might say that that there is more juice once it has been poured into the tall glass because it looks like there is more. Piaget tested this theory using his 'conservation' experiments.

OCR GCSE Psychology

- **Decentration** – In this stage, children are able to focus on more than one aspect of a situation. This is important when learning to read. A child who has not decentred would look at the individual letters and be able to understand them but would not be able to put them together to make words or sentences. Children who have entered the concrete operational stage and have decentred are able to read.
- **Seriation** – Children in this stage are able to put things into rank order, for example, putting coins in order from the smallest amount to the largest.
- **Linguistic humour** – Children gain the ability to use language to creates jokes. For example, they might say 'Knock knock...who's there? Stop watch... Stop watch who?... Stop what you're doing and come and play!'

▲ Coins arranged in order of value.

4. Formal operational stage: 11+

Children who have reached the **formal operational** stage will be able to demonstrate abstract thinking. They also start to think more logically and can compare and contrast different theories or sides of a debate. They can mentally manipulate ideas: for example, a child who is still in the concrete operational stage would be able to put coins in order of size if they have the coins in front of them. A child in the formal operational stage would be able to tell a teacher the order of the coins from smallest to largest without actually seeing the coins.

- **Hypothetical thinking** – Children are able to think about abstract ideas once they reach this stage. For example, they should be able to imagine what is was like for children living in extreme poverty in Victorian England, even though they may have never experienced poverty themselves.

Decentration
This is the ability to be able to focus on more than one aspect of a situation. For example, putting individual letters together to make a word.

Seriation
The ability to be able to rank things in order.

Linguistic humour
Playing with words to create jokes or humour.

DIY

Find some clear bottles of different shapes and sizes in the recycling, making sure to check they don't contain anything harmful first! Rinse them out and, using a measuring jug, fill all but one with exactly the same amount of water. For the final bottle, add a smaller amount of water. Make sure you have labelled the bottom of the bottles with a permanent marker to identify which contain the same and which is different. Then test your classmates to see if they tell which bottles contain the same amount and which has less in it, without seeing you pouring the liquid in from the measuring jug. You can use this test to check that your classmate can conserve – as they should be able to at their age!

Reductionism/holism

Reductionism

Reductionism views human behaviour from a simple perspective: it fails to take into account the 'bigger picture'. Human behaviour is complex, so by trying to explain it in simple terms we are ignoring all the other important factors that contribute to how we think and how we behave, such as the influence of others around us. However, looking at specific parts of behaviour allows us to test behaviours scientifically and make predictions about how people will behave in similar situations.

Holism

Holism 'The whole is greater than the sum of its parts'. Holism recognises the importance of seeing people as individuals and that one approach or theory cannot fully explain human behaviour. An example of an approach which takes a holist view is Humanistic psychology, which views us as individuals and how we are each unique. We are products of many different factors interacting with each other. The problem with the holistic approach is that if we assume everyone is different and unique, it makes it very hard to test behaviour and make predictions about how people will act in certain situations.

STUDY HINT

If you are having trouble understanding the concepts of reductionism and holism, imagine you ask a dairy farmer what ingredients you need to make a chocolate cake. She might say 'butter'. You know that it's true, but you also need other ingredients to make the cake. But to the dairy farmer, butter is what she makes and sells and that is what is important to her. The dairy farmer is being reductionist.

However, if you asked a baker, he would give you all the ingredients, because he knows that alone, the ingredients are not particularly tasty, but mixed together they make a very delicious cake. The baker is being holistic.

Extension

Recreate Piaget's experiment. Create a simple 3D model of Piaget's three mountains. Take ten photos of different views around the mountains, print them out and place a doll in the mountain scene. Try conducting the experiment with other members of your class. How easy is it to work out which is the doll's perspective? Can you dramatically recreate it with students pretending to be children in different stages of cognitive development? Make sure the responses are appropriate for the age of the child you are pretending to be. Think about how hard this would have been for young children to work out. How easy do you find it?
Remember: this is not the study you need to know in detail for your exam!

Criticisms of the theory

- **Piaget has been criticised for underestimating the age at which children can achieve different parts of the stages.** For example, psychologists have argued that young children may have object permanence but may lack the skills or motivation to find the missing toy.
- **Researchers have shown that only around half of adults actually reach the formal operational stage with many not being capable of abstract thinking.** Piaget failed to realise that not everyone reaches the final stage of cognitive development, therefore the theory is not universal.
- **Piaget describes the different stages but doesn't explain how these stages actually occur and what changes the child's thinking.** Therefore, although we have an idea of what happens, we don't know why and what actually prompts the changes.
- **Some of Piaget's research has been criticised for being too complicated for the children to understand.** For example, when young children are given a simplified version of the three mountains task, they are able to see things from the doll's perspective, suggesting that they are not egocentric.
- **Piaget's theory can be considered reductionist because he didn't take into account the important role teachers have in children's learning.** He viewed children as independent and 'little scientists' who are exploring the world without the need for support from teachers. Piaget stated that children must reach certain stages in their development before they can continue their learning. However, another psychologist working around the same time as Vygotsky recognised that learning is a key aspect of development, and if teachers 'scaffold' that learning and support students, then they can continue to learn effectively.

Check your understanding

1. What are the key features of the concrete operational stage?
2. What is meant by object permanence?
3. What does egocentrism mean?
4. How might a child demonstrate abstract thinking?
5. What are the main criticisms of Piaget's Theory of Cognitive Development?

Cognitive Development Research Study: Piaget (1952) – a study into the conservation of number.

Background

According to Piaget, conservation is one of the skills that children acquire as part of their cognitive development. It is the understanding that even if the appearance of an object or liquid changes or is 'transformed', its physical properties remain the same. This means that if you take a ball of plasticine and flatten it into a disc, its appearance will have changed but its mass will not. Similarly, if you take a glass of water and pour it into a different shaped glass, the amount of water might look different but its volume will remain the same.

The ability to conserve develops during the concrete operational stage. According to Piaget, conservation of number is the first to be acquired, followed by mass and finally volume.

Piaget created many tasks to test conservation. This study describes how Piaget tested the conservation of number.

Aim

The aim was to demonstrate that children in the concrete operational stage are more likely to be able to conserve than children in the pre-operational stage.

Hypothesis

Children in the concrete operational stage will be able to conserve, whereas children in the pre-operational stage will not.

Method

Research method/design

The study was a **natural experiment**, as the **independent variable** (IV) was naturally occurring (the age of the children).

The **dependent variable** (DV) was the ability to conserve number.

It is a **cross-sectional study** because Piaget tested different children of different ages.

The design is **independent measures** as each age group represents a different condition of the IV.

For more information on cross-sectional studies see page 17.

For more information on natural experiments see page 182.

Sample

- The actual size of his **sample** is not known as he did not report it.
- It consisted of a relatively small sample of Swiss school children from Geneva.
- The sample included his own three children.

Materials

- Counters

Procedure

Each child was tested individually. They were shown two rows of counters that were lined up side by side. Each counter in each row was lined up directly opposite the counter in the next row so that both rows were equally matched.

The child was then asked 'Is there the same number of counters in each row?'

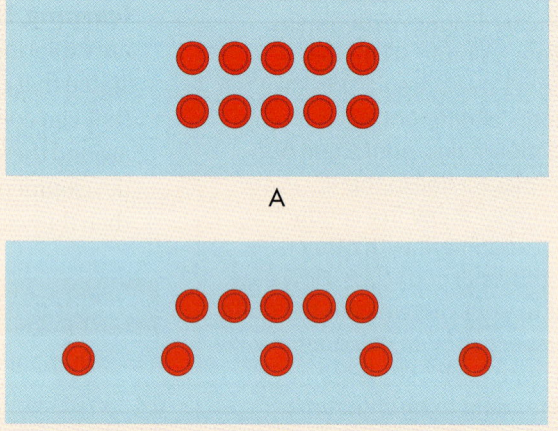

▲ How the counters were lined up in the study.

The experimenter then spread out one of the rows of counters in front of the child, so that they could see the transformation process. The row was changed so that it either looked longer or shorter compared to the other row of counters.

The child was then asked the same question again 'Is there the same number of counters in each row?'

Results

- Three to four year olds, who were still in the pre-operational stage, typically stated that there were more in the longer row that had been transformed.

- A few children who were near the end of the pre-operational stage (aged around five to six) were able to state that the number of counters remained the same. However, they were generally unable to justify their answer correctly; they were not able to say 'although the length of the row has changed, the number of counters remains the same'.
- Many of the children in the concrete operational stage were able to recognise that both rows still contained the same number of counters, despite the transformation of one of the rows. They were also able to correctly explain why they had made this judgement.

Conclusions

Piaget supported his hypothesis as he found that children in the concrete operational stage were more likely to be able to conserve number than children in the pre-operational stage. They were also more likely to be able to justify their answer.

Criticisms

- **Piaget's research has been criticised for having methodological problems.** The fact that the children were asked the same question twice, before and after transformation, might have confused the younger children. Rather than being unable to conserve, they were actually showing demand characteristics, in that they thought that they were expected to give a different answer because they had been asked the same question twice. Researchers Rose and Blank (1974) and Samuel and Bryant (1984) addressed this issue by replicating the research but only asking the question once, post-transformation. They found that when younger children in the pre-operational stage were only asked the question once, many more of them showed the ability to conserve number.
- **This study has also been criticised for being artificial.** For example, the adult deliberately moving the counters in front of the children might have made the younger ones think that something must have changed because the adult did something. McGarrigle and Donaldson (1974) addressed this issue by using a 'naughty teddy' who comes along and messes up the counters and makes one row shorter by moving the counters together. When the researcher asks the question a second time the focus of the transformation has been taken away from the researcher. They found that significantly more children in the pre-operational stage said that the number of counters had not changed and therefore demonstrated they were able to conserve.
- **The study was culturally biased.** It was only conducted on Swiss school children. The ability to conserve may be affected by education and upbringing, therefore the results may not represent all children in different countries. In psychological research, results can be generalised but this may not be appropriate for all cultures, as people or children may act differently simply because of their upbringing or background. This does not mean that one culture is necessarily better than another but simply that they are different.

Challenge

Try to think of different ways that you could test Piaget's study of conservation. Would you have the same methodological issues that Piaget had? How could you improve on his design?

For more information on ethics and informed consent see page 179.

> **Challenge**
>
> Evaluate the research method, sample and **experimental design** of Piaget's study into the conservation of number for both strengths and weaknesses. Use the table below to help you. Some of it has been filled out to give you a head start.

▼ Table 2.1 Evaluation of Piaget's study into the conservation of number.

	Research method	Sample	Experimental design
Strengths		The sample size was relatively small and consisted of children from a school in Switzerland. The results cannot therefore be generalised to children in other countries as the different education systems might have an effect on their cognitive development.	
Weaknesses			The design is an unusual one in that the independent variable is the children themselves, in the different age groups. This could be seen as a weakness because there may be individual differences among the children in the different groups. It might have been better to follow the same children over a number of years and see how their performance on the task changes as they get older.

STUDY HINT

When evaluating a study, it is really important to contextualise your answer. This means explaining the strength or weakness of the **sampling method** of that study in particular, and not just giving a general answer about weaknesses.

> **Check your understanding**
>
> 1. What research method did Piaget use?
> 2. Where did he conduct his research?
> 3. What was the question that the participants were asked twice?
> 4. What were his results?

Chapter 2 Development

Learning theories of development
Dweck's ideas on fixed and growth mindsets

Mindset
How a person thinks or their attitudes. People can have either growth or fixed mindsets.

Fixed mindset
Where people think their intelligence is innate and cannot be changed.

Growth mindset
Where people think that they can develop their intelligence over time.

Innate
Something you are born with.

Carol Dweck, a famous psychologist from Stanford University in the USA, has spent many years researching what affects people's achievement. Much of her research has taken place in schools, investigating what motivates children and adolescents to succeed and what the differences are in thought processes between students who do well and students who fail to achieve their potential. Dweck's is a learning theory because she focuses on how children learn in the classroom and what influences their ability to succeed.

Dweck suggests that people have one of two types of **mindset**:

1. **Fixed**, which means they think their intelligence is **innate** and therefore cannot be changed.
2. **Growth**, which means they can develop their intelligence over time.

Someone with a growth mindset realises that not everyone has the same potential. For example, not everyone can be as talented as Mo Farah or Laura Kenny. However, there is also the understanding that Mo and Laura would not have been as successful without dedication, practice and constantly challenging themselves to improve. At the 2016 Olympics in Rio, Mo Farah even managed to win a race after tripping over and falling to the ground. This demonstrates his positive belief in his ability to achieve.

Dweck suggests that nearly every successful athlete and musician, for example, has a growth mindset which allows them to see failure as a challenge to improve, having the resilience to cope with setbacks and have a positive **attitude** towards working hard and practising their craft. Talented people who have a fixed mindset can be at a disadvantage. For example, a talented swimmer might initially beat all the others in their class, but if they have a fixed mindset they won't see the need to practise and try to improve. They might then find that the students who were less naturally talented, but who have a growth mindset, could win as a result of hard work and determination.

▲ Laura Kenny winning gold at the 2016 Olympics.

▲ Mo Farah went on to win at the Olympics, even after tripping over during the race. Setbacks along the way do not necessarily mean you have failed.

Effort
Determined attempt to do something.

Mindset in school

According to Dweck, students who have a fixed mindset are most concerned with looking intelligent. They avoid doing things that they could potentially fail at, instead of seeing them as learning opportunities. Failure can affect their **self-esteem**, making them believe they are not as intelligent as they originally thought. Students with fixed mindsets do not like making an **effort** as they believe that ability is innate and they therefore shouldn't need to practise.

Students who have a growth mindset believe that with effort and practice, they can improve. They view setbacks as challenges and opportunities to learn from their mistakes.

Dweck suggests that teachers should encourage their students to take their time to become proficient at new skills and teach the idea that being able to do something quickly is not necessarily a good thing, as it suggests the skill has not been deeply learnt. The key is understanding that it is not how quickly students are able to learn new skills, but that with practice and effort they can improve.

Having more than one mindset

Dweck states that individuals can hold different mindsets for different abilities. For example, someone might have a fixed mindset for maths ('no matter how hard I try, I won't improve because I'm just not good at maths'), but have a growth mindset for music ('I've only just started playing the piano but I know that if I practise I will improve').

Reducing bullying

A growth mindset has been found to have other benefits. For example, Yeager, Trzesniewski, and Dweck (2013) investigated the benefits of a growth mindset on reducing **aggression** and bullying. They found that students in the incremental theory intervention group (the growth mindset group where students were taught that they had the potential to change their behaviour) behaved less aggressively and demonstrated more **pro-social behaviour** than the **control group**.

> For more information on the nature/nurture debate see page 8.

Dweck's ideas on praise for effort

Mueller and Dweck (1998) have also investigated the effect of **praise** on achievement, examining the effects of praising intelligence versus praising effort. They found that children who were praised for their intelligence, when they had succeeded in a task, often then chose problem-solving tasks that allowed them to continue to succeed rather than choosing ones that would challenge them. Dweck calls this a 'performance goal'. Children who were praised for working hard chose problem-solving tasks that would increase their learning.

They concluded that children who are praised for intelligence value performance. They are focused on both their own performance and comparing themselves to others. When they are faced with failure, they tend to attribute it to their intelligence, rather than the lack of effort that they have put into it.

Children who are praised for effort demonstrated more value for learning opportunities. They tend to attribute failure to lack of effort rather than lack of ability. According to Dweck, praise for effort leads to growth mindset and praise for intelligence leads to fixed mindset. When intelligence is praised there is a ceiling. A child will think that if they have reached the limit of their intelligence then they won't be able to develop any more. If they think their intelligence is limited then they will think that they cannot develop at all. This can result in problems for young people who have not found GCSEs challenging but don't know what to do when confronted by the much tougher A levels.

Criticisms

- **Alfie Kohn (2012) criticises Dweck's view, suggesting that it conveys the message to children that they are not very good at what they are doing.** 'If I'm being praised for my effort then I mustn't have done very well, otherwise I would be praised for how much I've achieved.' He suggests that teachers should avoid using praise at all.
- **One of the problems with the theory is that it places failure very firmly on the student.** If they fail to achieve, it is because they have a fixed mindset or they didn't try hard enough. This doesn't take into account other factors for failure, such as personal circumstances like bullying, which may be affecting their ability to learn or concentrate. The emphasis on fixing the blame on the mindset of the child could have a detrimental effect on their self-esteem and mental health.
- **The theory was challenged by a large scale study.** The Education Endowment Foundation (EEF) (2015) funded research into growth mindsets in schools in the UK. Children in 30 schools were given an intervention

---

Challenge

You can test your own mindset online. Try searching 'Dweck's growth mindset questionnaire' online to find out!

Extension

Go to https://www.mindsetworks.com/Science/Changing-Mindsets and click on the 'Science' tab at the top. Read some of the research that supports the idea of growth mindset. What do you think of the research? Do you think it offers strong support for Dweck's theory?
There are also case studies to look at. Does your school promote growth mindset?

Praise
Expressing approval of something.

Check your understanding

1. What is the difference between a fixed mindset and a growth mindset?
2. What does Dweck believe about intelligence?
3. Why does Dweck believe that praise for intelligence can have a negative effect on children?
4. How does having a growth mindset help children learn at school?

Chapter 2 Development

STUDY HINT
If asked to write about learning theories you will need to refer to both Dweck and Willingham's theories. If asked to write about one learning theory, you can choose either.

Extension
It is possible that there is more research that has failed to find significant evidence that mindsets work. However, in psychology, it tends to only be research that has found significant results that is published, giving an unrealistic view about the extent to which a theory is supported by significant research results. Therefore, as Dweck suggests, teaching children to have a Growth Mindset may not have as big an impact on learning as the theory would suggest.

Learning styles
The theory that students have different ways of learning and they would learn better if taught in the style that suits them.

Myth
A widely held but false belief.

that taught them about growth mindset. Results showed that there was no significant difference in progress in maths and English compared to the control group. This research, therefore, does not support Dweck's theory.

- **It is possible that there is more research that has failed to find significant evidence that mindsets work.** However, in psychology, it tends to only be research that has found significant results that is published, giving an unrealistic view about the extent to which a theory is supported by significant research results. Therefore, as Dweck suggests, teaching children to have a Growth Mindset may not have as big an impact on learning as the theory would suggest.

- **Nurture is a key aspect of this theory as it assumes that the child can make the changes themselves, but this can have a negative impact on their self-esteem if they fail to succeed.** It might be that innate traits have a greater impact on a person's ability to succeed than Dweck recognises.

Willingham's ideas on the myth of learning styles

Learning styles have been used in education for many years and make the assumption that students have different learning styles and would learn better if the teacher created lessons tailored to each preferred style.

Learning styles include **visual** learners who might learn best from reading a textbook, **auditory** learners who might learn best from listening to teachers or podcasts for example, and kinaesthetic learners who might learn best from actually having a physical 'hands on' approach.

Daniel Willingham is a cognitive psychologist from the University of Virginia and a fierce critic of learning styles. Willingham argues that although learners may express a preference for the way that they learn, when this is tested under experimental conditions, it makes no difference to their learning. He also observes that although people may state a preferred learning style, if they are asked how they would like to learn something, people want to know what it is they are going to learn first, suggesting that the learning objective is more important than the learning style.

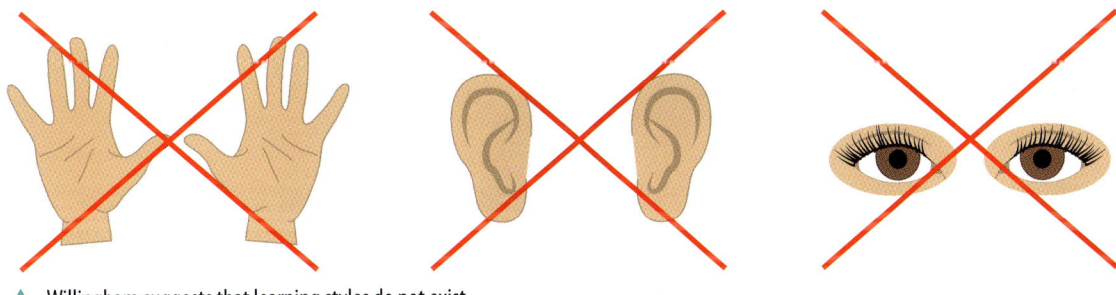

▲ Willingham suggests that learning styles do not exist.

> **Something to think about**
> Have you ever been tested to see what your learning style is? If so, did you agree with the results? Is Willingham right to question learning styles?

Willingham suggests that the confusion arises from the fact that different people have different abilities. For example, Orla might be excellent at processing visual information and Joshua might be skilled at processing auditory information. If you show Orla and Joshua a map of Venice and then put them in the city, Orla will be much better at orientating herself while Joshua gets lost. However, if Joshua hears a new song once on the radio, he will be able to sing the song word for word the next day. This doesn't mean that Orla would learn better by reading a book and Joshua by listening to a podcast. Nor does it mean that Orla, for example, would learn a new cooking technique better by reading about it instead of practising it.

Pashler, McDaniel, Rohrer and Bjork (2008) conducted a comprehensive review of the research into the effectiveness of students being taught by their preferred learning style. They found that although there was a vast amount of research, most of it did not follow experimental procedures and was therefore not able to effectively test the validity of the learning styles. For example, after determining the preferred learning style, participants should have been **randomly** assigned to groups receiving different ways of learning the same information, then all be tested on their learning in the same way. Most of the studies did not do this. Those studies which did use appropriate research methods failed to find evidence that using people's preferred learning styles improved performance. Willingham also suggests that a person's ability, background knowledge and interest in a subject has a more influential effect on learning than learning styles. Willingham believes that the idea of learning styles has persisted for so long because people don't distinguish between learning styles and people's ability.

He also suggests that the idea has persisted because of something called 'confirmation bias'. Willingham explains that when we are evaluating our beliefs, we tend to take notice of information that supports our views and ignore information that contradicts it, even if there is a lot of contradictory evidence.

Willingham states that teachers should be more concerned whether the method of teaching best fits the content rather than concerning themselves with using a video for visual learners or podcast for auditory learners.

Willingham's ideas on the importance of meaning for learning

In Willingham's book, *Why Don't Students Like School?* (2010), he suggests that knowledge must be 'meaningful'. He recommends that teachers ensure that when teaching knowledge or facts to students that they create links between the information, rather than just giving students lists of facts to memorise.

> **Something to think about**
> Sometimes teachers are told how they should teach their classes by the senior leaders in the school. Why do you think that teachers might not want to use individual learning styles when teaching?

Meaning for learning
The idea students should understand the meaning of what they are being taught, rather than just being drilled information.

▲ Willingham suggests that 'drilling' information into children leads to boredom in the classroom.

Chapter 2 Development

> **DIY**
>
> Carry out an experiment to test the idea that knowledge must be meaningful. Using an independent groups design, divide a group of participants into two. Give both groups the same list of 20 words. Ask one group to repeat each word three times and then test their recall of the words at the end. Ask the other group to choose a word with the same meaning as each of the words in the list (so they are thinking about meaningfulness). Test their recall of words after they have completed the task. Which group would Willingham predict would do better? Do your results support Willingham's theory?

> **Challenge**
>
> See if you can condense Willingham's thoughts on the myth of learning styles into about 60 words. Can you then condense those 60 words into just one sentence? Once you have done this, get everyone to read theirs aloud. Have you all got the same information? Who do you think had the best description?

For example, instead of just giving students a list of Kings and Queens of England to learn, teachers should explain to students the reasons why and how each monarch came to the throne. What is most important for learning is thinking about the meaning of the material. This is much more important than trying to teach a child using their preferred 'learning style'. This means that students will learn the information more deeply and be more likely to recall it from **long-term memory**. Willingham believes that 'drilling' information is damaging for students as it is boring and makes them dislike learning and school. He also suggests that teachers should be very careful about what they set for homework and consider whether it will actually benefit the students, as it will affect what they remember.

Although Willingham argues that knowledge should be meaningful and engage learners, teachers should not worry about trying to make the information relevant to the students' personal interests as it doesn't improve learning.

He also suggests the students are unable to think like actual scientists or historians as this, according to Willingham, is only possible after many years of study. Therefore, Willingham recommends that teachers think very carefully about what benefit there is for students to conduct scientific experiments.

Criticisms

- **Many teachers and lecturers at universities would disagree with Willingham's views about there being little benefit in students trying to be like actual scientists or historians.** They argue that it is very important for students to conduct experiments themselves for the exact reason that they start to learn the issues involved in conducting research themselves, such as the difficulties in ensuring research is replicable and **controlling** for **extraneous variables** that can affect the outcome of the research.
- **Certain things might benefit from being drilled.** For example, learning times tables by rote (chanting them). If students are able to access and recall their tables this way, it will help them with their mental arithmetic at school and in the future. While it might not suit every learner, many students would benefit from it.
- **In general, both Dweck and Willingham's theories favour the idea of nurture over nature as they are learning theories.** Willingham states that if the method of teaching best fits the content, then learners will do well. However, by ignoring the influence of innate factors on children's development – for example, some children's brains may be wired differently – he may be discounting the fact that those children might need to be taught in a specific way to assist their learning, regardless of the content.
- **Although Willingham's theory favours nurture, he ignores the fact that some children are kinaesthetic learners because this is how they were taught at school when they were very young.** Therefore, having been conditioned to learn in that way, children may do better continuing to learn kinesthetically as they grow older.

> **Check your understanding**
>
> 1 What are learning styles?
> 2 What evidence is there that learning styles do not improve learning?
> 3 According to Willingham, why is learning the meaning of things important?
> 4 What is the difference between ability and learning styles?

Blackwell, Trzesniewski, and Dweck, (2007) Implicit theories of intelligence predict achievement across an adolescent transition: A longitudinal study and an intervention.

Background

There are many changes during adolescence, including physical maturation, changing demands from society, relationships becoming increasingly complex and new academic expectations.

In the USA, the transition from elementary school to junior high at the age of around twelve years presents many challenges, such as a significantly more competitive environment and social comparison. There is also a decrease in choice and decision-making at a time when adolescents are aiming for more control.

The motivational model of achievement has been developed to help us understand why some students succeed under pressure at school while others do not.

Dweck and Leggat (1988) suggest that students may hold different beliefs about their intelligence. Some think that intelligence is 'fixed' and so is unchangeable, regardless of how hard you work (entity theory). Others believe that intelligence is flexible and with work, can be developed (incremental theory).

Henderson and Dweck (1990) found that students who believed that intelligence is flexible gained significantly higher grades during the first year of junior high school than those students who believed that their intelligence was fixed. In another study, researchers Good, Aronson and Inzlicht (2003) found that by using an intervention that taught students that intelligence can be changed, it led to a significant improvement in test scores, compared to a control group.

This study was designed to look at whether students' theories of intelligence have a lasting effect across junior high school.

> **STUDY HINT**
> The theories of intelligence that are being investigated in this study are Dweck's ideas on Fixed and Growth Mindsets.

STUDY 1

Aim

To see whether theories of intelligence correlate with academic achievement in mathematics and to test the impact of academic intervention.

Hypothesis

There will be a relationship between 7th grade students' theories of intelligence (fixed or growth mindset) and their achievement grades on a standardised mathematics test.

Method

Research method/design

Study 1 was a **longitudinal study** that took place over five years. It was a **correlational field study** and it investigated students' theories of intelligence and achievement-related beliefs, as well as their achievement in mathematics as they progressed through the seventh and eighth grades. It took place in a natural setting, their school in New York.

Therefore, the variables studied were:

1. Students' theories of intelligence
2. Students' achievement-related beliefs
3. Maths achievement in the seventh and eighth grade.

Sample

- 373 students (198 females and 175 males) from four successive seventh grade classes at a public secondary school in New York City.
- The data from the four cohorts of students was combined for the presentation of their results.
- The sample was varied in **ethnicity**, achievement and socioeconomic status (SES).
- 205 were African American, 101 were South Asian, 56 were Hispanic, and 11 were East Asian and European American.

> **Time for some maths**
> Change the number of students in each of the ethnic groups into **percentages** then create a **bar chart** using these percentages. Remember to round up your percentage to the nearest whole number. To calculate the percentage, divide the number of students in the ethnic minority group by the total sample size and multiply by 100.

Materials

- Scores on a standardised mathematics achievement test, which was taken in the spring term of sixth grade, while they were still at elementary school. These were used as a baseline to compare the later scores on mathematics tests.
- A standardised mathematics test to measure achievement in the autumn and spring terms of both seventh and eighth grades.

- A motivational questionnaire which was scored on a 6-point Likert scale from 1 (Agree strongly) to 6 (Disagree strongly) which assessed:
  1. **Theory of intelligence** with statements such as 'You have certain amount of intelligence and you really can't do much to change it' and 'You can always greatly change how intelligent you are'
  2. **Learning goals,** for example 'An important reason why I do my school work is because I like to learn new things'
  3. **Effort beliefs,** for example 'The harder you work at something, the better you will be at it' and 'To tell the truth, when I work hard at my schoolwork, it makes me feel like I am not very smart'
  4. **Helpless responses to failure.** Participants were given a scenario and asked to report what they thought they would think and do in that situation.

> **Something to think about**
>
> This is the scenario that participants were presented with:
>
> 'You start a new class at the beginning of the year and you really like the subject and the teacher. You think you know the subject pretty well, so you study a medium amount for the first quiz. Afterward, you think you did okay, even though there were some questions you didn't know the answer for. Then the class gets their quizzes back and you find out your score: you only got a 54, and that's an F'.
>
> Imagine this scenario happened to you. How would you react? How would you justify your grade?
>
> Source: Blackwell, L., Trzesniewski, K., and Dweck, C., 'Implicit Theories of Intelligence Predict Achievement Across an Adolescent Transition: A Longitudinal Study and an Intervention', in *Child Development*, Volume 78, no. 1, 2007, p. 250

Procedure

- Informed consent was obtained from both parents and students. They were made aware that their participation was entirely voluntary and they had the right to withdraw from the study at any time without penalty.
- At the beginning of the seventh grade, participants completed the motivational questionnaire.
- The questionnaires were given by trained research assistants during normal lesson time. Permission to do this was given by the teacher.
- Participants had only one teacher during seventh grade and one teacher during eighth grade. The mathematics teaching was not unusual compared to other schools.

Results

- There was no significant correlation between theory of intelligence (fixed or growth mindset) and other motivational scores and maths test scores when measured at the start of the seventh grade.
- However, when participants were tested in the autumn term of seventh grade and spring term of eighth grade, theory of intelligence (fixed or growth mindset) became a significant predictor of maths achievement.
- This means that those participants who held the belief that they had the ability to change their intelligence showed greater improvement on the maths test than those who thought their IQ was fixed at birth.

STUDY 2

Hypothesis

Students who are taught to think intelligence is malleable display more positive motivation in the classroom and achieve more highly than students who were not taught that intelligence is malleable.

Method

Research design/method

Study 2 is a correlational field study with an experimental section. The research took place in a public secondary school in New York City. It was an independent measures design.

The independent variable (IV) of the experimental section was whether the participant was in the incremental theory intervention group or the control group who were not given the intervention.

The dependent variables (DVs – what was measured) were levels of motivation and achievement on mathematics assessment.

Participants

- There were 99 participants (49 female, 50 male) from a seventh grade class.
- The participants came from varied socioeconomic status and ethnicity.
- Participation was voluntary and consent was obtained in advance from both the students themselves and their parents.

- Of the 99 who took part in the questionnaire study, 91 continued to the intervention study (48 in the **experimental group** and 43 in the control group).

> **Time for some maths**
> Work out the percentage of participants who were male and female. What percentage of males and females went through to the intervention stage?

Materials
- Sixth grade mathematics grades were used as a baseline.
- Motivational questionnaire (Theory of Intelligence) – same as used in Study 1.

Procedure
Participants completed the motivational questionnaire at the start of the autumn term of seventh grade.

Participants were randomly assigned to either the intervention group (incremental theory training) or the control group.

Both groups were told that they had the opportunity to take part in an eight-week voluntary workshop on the brain that would help them with their study skills.

The intervention group were taught a key message that 'learning changes the brain by forming new connections, and that students are in charge of this process'.

The control group had a lesson on memory and discussed various, relevant areas of academic interest.

Sixteen undergraduate students were recruited and trained as mentors for the participants. Some were trained to teach one of the motivational workshops. Others mentored the control group and were trained to teach an alternative workshop on the structure of memory.

At the end of the eight-week course, students in both the experimental and control groups were given a multiple-choice quiz on the content of the workshops.

Three weeks after the last of the eight sessions, participants were given the motivational questionnaire to complete again.

The maths teacher was asked to write a report on any students who had shown changes in their motivational behaviour. The comments were coded as to whether the change recorded was a positive one; the researchers doing the coding did not know which group the participants had been assigned to.

The teacher did not know that the students had been placed in two different groups so did not know which students had received the intervention.

Participants' maths grades were recorded in the autumn term of seventh grade and the spring term of eighth grade.

Results
Multiple-choice quiz
- There was no difference in recall on the multiple choice quiz between the two groups on general content that was taught to both groups.
- The experimental groups scored significantly higher than the control groups on questions that tested the incremental theory content.

Motivational (Theory of Intelligence) questionnaire
- The participants who had been in the intervention group showed that they had changed significantly in their theory of intelligence and showed more positive mindsets. There was no change for participants in the control group.

Teacher report
- 27 per cent of students in the intervention (experimental) group were reported as showing more positive motivation compared to only nine per cent of the control group.

Mathematics grades
- Participants in the intervention group gained significantly higher grades in their autumn and spring maths assessments than those in the control group.
- They also showed no decline in grades, which was found before the intervention and in the participants who were in the control group.

Conclusions
A positive effect on motivation is seen for students with a growth mindset, and they hold more positive beliefs about effort too. They also choose more positive, effort-based strategies in response to failure compared to a fixed mindset.

Teaching students that intelligence is flexible has a positive effect on their motivation and achievement in mathematics during the transition period to junior high school.

This research provides compelling evidence for schools to endorse the incremental theory, in order to help students reach their full potential.

Criticisms

- **The study is culturally biased.** The results might not be **representative** of children in different states in America or in different countries. Studies 1 and 2 each took place in a separate school in New York City. It might be that something in the specific education system in New York City had an effect on the results. The study would need to be replicated in different states/countries before it can be reliably stated that the growth mindset has a positive effect on achievement.

- **In Study 2, participants in the experimental group received more anti-stereotyping training than the control group.** By being taught how the terms 'stupid' and 'dumb' are forms of stereotyping, this extra instruction could have affected the participants' motivation by creating a sense of unity within the class. This could have acted as a confounding variable.

- **Although there were significant differences between the groups, the impact of the actual effect was relatively small.** However, the researchers argue that even small effects on motivation and attainment can have a significant impact over time.

- **The study was reductionist as it only focused on the students' mindsets.** The researchers recognise that if both the parents and teachers held the belief that intelligence is not fixed that they might reinforce the belief in the students.

Challenge

Evaluate the research method, sample and experimental design of Study 1 for both strengths and weaknesses. Use this table to help you. Some of it has already been filled in for you. Note: the study used more than one research method. Field study is given as the example here. Can you create another table to evaluate the other method used?

	Research method	**Sample**	**Experimental design**
Strengths	As this was a field study, students learnt in their own school environment and this means that the study is high in **ecological validity**, meaning it reflects the students' normal learning atmosphere in school.		
Weaknesses		The schools chosen were also from New York City, so the students' life experiences and educational backgrounds might be different to students in schools in the UK or Siberia or China. Therefore, we must be careful about generalising the results to other cultures.	

Check your understanding

1. What was the difference between the samples in the two studies?
2. What other factors could have increased the children's maths ability apart from having a growth mindset?
3. What was the purpose of some of the controls used in Blackwell *et al.*'s research?

Application: the changing role of education

How Piaget's ideas have been applied to education through the use of key stages, readiness, active learning and the concept of intelligence

Piaget's theories were applied to the 1967 Plowden report on primary education, which explained to educators how his invariant stages of development work and how children all go through the same stages. Piaget's ideas have been used in a practical sense within the classroom for many years since the Plowden report and teachers still adapt their teaching based on his theories, where his stages of development are linked to the different **key stages**.

Readiness
The idea of **readiness** is linked to Piaget's stages of cognitive development. The idea is that children are not ready to learn in certain ways until they have reached the relevant developmental stage. For example, if you asked a child who was still in the concrete operational stage to work out a maths question in their head, they would be unable to do it because they have not reached the stage where they can use abstract thinking. As a result, teachers need to ensure that they ask students questions in a way which mirrors their developmental stage.

Sensori-motor stage
A child in this stage should be given simple toys to explore such a a rattle. So that the child can learn to grasp it, then shake it and in doing so learn that it makes a sound.

Pre-operational stage
Children in the pre-operational stage could be given dressing-up clothes for role playing to help them develop their **symbolic play**.

Concrete operational
Children in this stage start to learn to conserve. Learning to cook could help them develop this skill by using measurements and pouring ingredients into different containers for mixing and baking.

Formal operational
Children who reach this stage could be given hypothetical situations to debate to help them develop their hypothetical thinking.

Active learning
Piaget suggests that children need to be active learners, like 'little scientists'. This idea is used in the classroom today and is called 'discovery learning'. Play is an important part of **active learning** and children's progress should not only be assessed by what is measurable. For example, if a child is given mud to play with to make 'cakes', their teacher could measure how well they have made a 'cake' out of mud, but equally, the child may also have learnt about the texture of mud, how much water is needed to make it stick together and how it feels on their fingers. They are learning how to solve problems and think creatively, none of which is easily measurable but is still important.

STUDY HINT
Be prepared to answer questions on specific applications, such as key stages, readiness and active learning as well as broader questions about how Piaget's ideas have been applied to education.

Key stages
Age related stages of development used to organise the education of children.

Readiness
The idea that children are not ready to learn certain things until they have reached a particular stage of cognitive development.

Symbolic play
This is where children play 'make believe', where a coat might be a Superhero cape, for example.

Active learning
The idea that children should not just be sat at a desk and given information but should be actively engaging with their environment to learn from it.

Challenge
Create an advice sheet for new teachers suggesting ideas of different learning activities that children could do in each of Piaget's four stages.

Chapter 2 Development

▲ Discovery learning allows children to learn beyond the curriculum.

> **Challenge**
>
> Think of an area of psychology that you are studying and suggest ways in which you could learn for meaning. What links could you make between the different sections of study? For example, how can you link the information that you are learning in the research methods section to the core studies in each chapter?

> **STUDY HINT**
>
> Think about your own experiences of being in the classroom to help you to understand and recall the details of how research can be applied to education. You may even end up using your own experiences as part of an answer to a question. This is acceptable as long as it is relevant.

The concept of intelligence

How Piaget viewed the concept of the intelligence and how it can change.

Piaget believed that intelligence was innate and that it developed naturally as children interacted with their environment and accommodated and assimilated new information into their schemas. Piaget suggested that a child's intelligence matures as they pass through four stages of cognitive development. Therefore, it was important that teachers understand which stage of cognitive development the child is in, and base their lessons on the child's abilities at that stage.

How learning theories apply to the development of education intelligence through growth mindsets and teaching through meaning not learning styles

Growth mindsets

Growth mindsets applied to education

Educators should learn from Dweck's theory that making assumptions about students' ability through their IQ scores does not support them to reach their potential. This has shifted the view of education from seeing children's IQ as a fixed, unchangeable thing to something that can be grown, given the right mindset.

Teachers can focus on setting small but doable tasks for students so they feel that they are making progress. If they feel like they are achieving, then this would encourage them to have a growth mindset.

While encouraging students to try hard, teachers must ensure that students are also given the strategies and tools to succeed. Otherwise, asking students to simply work harder won't create a growth mindset.

Teachers should praise students for their effort and not for their intelligence, as this also helps develop a growth mindset.

Meaning not learning styles

For many years, schools have focused on the idea of learning styles. However, current evidence points to the fact that learning styles do not work. This means that key educators need to ensure that teachers are no longer differentiating lessons to suit different learning styles, but are using methods that are more effective in supporting students' progress.

Willingham suggests that teachers focus on supporting students to think about the meaning of information, rather than teaching them in a way that fits their learning styles.

For example, if a teacher is trying to get her students to understand research methods, instead of just teaching a list of words and definitions, she could give the students different research studies to look at, that all investigate the same thing. The students would have to explain how the different research methods relate to each study and compare and contrast how effective those methods were in explaining the behaviour that was being studied.

Check your understanding

1. Explain what is meant by 'readiness'.
2. Give an example of 'active' learning.
3. How can teachers encourage a growth mindset?
4. How could a teacher encourage children to think about the meaning of what they are learning?

SUMMARY

In this chapter, we have seen how children's thinking develops over time and how educators use this information to plan age-appropriate lessons for their children. We've looked at Piaget's study on conservation, and have seen that children's ability to conserve depends upon which stage of development they are in. We have also learnt that having a fixed mindset can hinder learning as it can prevent learners from trying new things for fear that they will not perform as well. However, the theory does also place the blame on the student if they do not progress, suggesting that they somehow are not working hard enough. While this sometimes might be the case, it does not take into account individual circumstances of the students. We've also learnt about Blackwell *et al.*'s research, which showed that having a growth mindset has a positive effect on motivation. We've also seen Willingham discuss that learning styles are not supported by research evidence and that a student's interest and motivation in a subject is far more important. Finally, we've seen that thinking about the meaning of what we are learning is really important, especially if we can make links between the different things that we are learning.

Chapter 2 Development

Practice questions

The questions in this textbook have been written by the authors, Mark Billingham and Helen Kitching. They have not been produced or endorsed by OCR.

1 a Identify what Dweck and Willingham's theories have in common.

A Cognitive theories

B Evolutionary theories

C Learning theories

D Psychodynamic theories [1 mark]

Your answer ☐ C ☐

Correct. One mark.

1 b Identify what Dweck said children should be praised for.

A effort

B energy

C engagement

D enthusiasm [1 mark]

Your answer ☐ A ☐

Correct. One mark.

1 c Identify what Willingham said was a myth.

A assessment styles

B learning styles

C management styles

D teaching styles [1 mark]

Your answer ☐ D ☐

Incorrect. No mark.

2

> **Children at Different Stages**
>
> Chloe likes to play with her teddies. She often has conversations with them and looks after them when they are 'feeling ill'. Aysha enjoys science at school. She likes to think about new ideas and plan experiments to test out her theories.

Using the source:

a Name the stage of cognitive development Chloe is in according to Piaget's theory. [1 mark]

Pre-operational stage.

Correct. One mark.

b Name the stage of cognitive development Aysha is in according to Piaget's theory. [1 mark]

Form.

The answer needs to say 'formal operational' to secure the mark.

c Identify the concept that Chloe is demonstrating. [1 mark]

Aminism.

Although this is misspelt, it is obvious what the candidate means, so the mark is given.

3 Outline **one** criticism of Piaget's Theory of Cognitive Development with reference to the reductionism/holism debate. [3 marks]

Piaget's theory is too reductionist, as it essentially reduces cognitive development down to biological maturation. In doing so, it ignores the idea that emotional and social factors may interact and influence development.

This response scores three marks. A mark is awarded for recognising that Piaget's theory is reductionist rather than holistic. A further mark is awarded for applying the idea of reductionism to the theory. A final mark is awarded for the explanation of why reductionism is a limitation for the theory.

4 Explain how Piaget's ideas have been applied to education with reference to **either** readiness **or** active learning. [4 marks]

Piaget would suggest that teachers should make their lessons appropriate to their students' stage of development. Therefore, if a child is still in the pre-operational stage, they should not be given tasks that only a child in the concrete operational stage would be able to do. This is because it could make them think they were not capable, when really they are just not ready for that type of learning yet.

Although not identified, this answer appears to be focusing on readiness. The student shows some understanding of what the concept is and how it impacts on a child's education. However, the response is not detailed enough for the four marks on offer. It may have been useful to include an example of the effective use of readiness.

5 Describe and evaluate Dweck's ideas on fixed and growth mindsets. [8 marks]

Dweck suggests that people have one of two different types of mindset: fixed or growth. People with a fixed mindset think that they are born with an innate intelligence that cannot be changed. People who have a growth mindset realise that they can develop their intelligence over time. Someone with a growth mindset understands that not everyone has the same potential — not everyone can be Einstein, but with work and motivation people can improve. Even high-flying people, who others might think were born with their talent, still have to work very hard to improve and be the best. Dweck says that people with a growth mindset see failure as a challenge to improve and have a positive attitude to working hard.

Dweck thinks that people with a fixed mindset who are born with a particular talent are disadvantaged because they think that they don't need to practise their talent as it is innate. While they may be the best at first, someone with a growth mindset who is born with less natural talent might end up being better than them. People with a fixed mindset are more interested in looking intelligent and might avoid more challenging tasks because they have a fear of failing. In conclusion, a growth mindset is an advantage over a fixed mindset.

One criticism of this theory is that it places the blame on the student if they don't succeed, which may not be good for self-esteem. It doesn't take into account other reasons why a student might not be improving. For example, they might be being bullied or having problems at home, which could be affecting how well they focus in lessons. Or in more simple terms, they also might just not like a subject or task, and not feel motivated to learn. Blaming a student for not improving could make them feel even worse.

Psychologists did a large piece of research looking at children in 30 schools. Those children who had the intervention about growth mindset showed no improvement in maths and English compared to the control group, showing that learning about growth mindset doesn't necessarily improve students' achievement. However, other research (such as Blackwell's) suggests that it does make a difference. This contradiction means that the theory is not yet reliable enough to be applied more widely.

This response gives a thorough description of the two types of mindset and demonstrates good understanding. The description earns all four AO1 marks for coherency. The evaluation provides both breadth and depth, with a number of points clearly made. This earns all four AO3 marks on offer. Overall, the candidate has provided a strong full-mark response.

3 Psychological problems

It is quite common for most, if not all people, to encounter psychological problems at some point in their lives. For example, it is quite typical to experience stress around exam time, or to feel low after breaking up with someone. However, sometimes people's thoughts and behaviour may be more unusual, such as experiencing stress following a minor event or being depressed for longer than expected. When psychological problems are more extreme and a person is finding it difficult to cope, this is when we may decide that someone has a mental health issue. In these cases, psychologists and other professionals may need to intervene and offer some form of treatment.

Sexual orientation
Describes the sex or gender that person is attracted to.

Dopamine hypothesis
The theory that an excess of dopamine causes schizophrenia.

Brain volume
The amount of space the brain occupies measured in 3D.

This chapter should enable you to:
- develop awareness of ways of defining mental health (including the mental health continuum), the current prevalence of mental health problems (referring to age, gender and sexual orientation), the incidence of significant mental health problems over time, and changes in attitudes towards mental health
- develop understanding of the effects of significant mental health problems on the individual and wider society, including the effects of stigma and discrimination, and impact on community care
- know the clinical characteristics of schizophrenia and key statistics associated with this disorder
- be able to explain and evaluate the social drift theory of schizophrenia, with specific reference to rejection by society, disengagement of individuals, and problems establishing cause and effect
- be able to explain and evaluate the biological theory of schizophrenia with specific reference to the dopamine hypothesis, brain dysfunction in relation to brain volume and the frontal lobes, temporal lobes and hippocampus, and the nature vs nurture debate
- be able to describe and evaluate the Daniel, Weinberger, Jones et al.'s (1991) study into the effect of amphetamine on regional cerebral blood flow during cognitive activation in schizophrenia
- know the clinical characteristics of clinical depression and key statistics associated with this disorder
- be able to explain and evaluate the social rank theory of clinical depression with specific reference to the evolutionary function of depression, the role of a lower rank in reducing conflict, and the reductionism/holism debate
- be able to describe and evaluate Tandoc et al.'s (2015) study into Facebook use, envy, and depression among college students
- be able to explain and evaluate the ABC model of clinical depression, with specific reference to rational vs irrational beliefs, the roles of activating events, beliefs and consequences, and the free will/determinism debate
- understand the use of anti-psychotics and anti-depressants to treat schizophrenia and depression respectively through changing the actions of the brain and how they improve mental health
- understand the use of psychotherapy for treating schizophrenia and clinical depression and how it improves mental health
- understand the development of neuropsychology for studying schizophrenia and clinical depression, including neuropsychological tests and brain imaging techniques.

An introduction to mental health
Ways of defining mental health

The fact that there are different ways of defining mental health tells us that it is not a straightforward concept. This is partly because mental health can be seen as a very **subjective** and personal experience that cannot be viewed and judged objectively outside of the person.

Mental health problems are often seen as abnormal, which would suggest they do not affect that many people. But does this mean that being in good mental health is the normal state of being? How many of us could confidently say that we feel fully mentally healthy most of the time?

Some psychologists recognise that good mental health is an ideal that many of us may not reach very often. For example, Jahoda (1958) suggested it can involve:

- having high **self-esteem**
- personal growth and self-actualisation
- integration
- autonomy
- an accurate perception of reality
- mastery of the environment.

As it can be hard to achieve all of these things, this definition can be seen as quite pessimistic. People like to think that good mental health is more achievable than this.

Rather than talking about whether an individual is mentally healthy or not, some psychologists have found it useful to define mental health using a **mental health continuum**. This relates to the idea that there are degrees of mental health:

Although 'Reacting' is a sign of mental health problems, people are still at a stage where taking care of themselves and using social support networks (friends, family) should be good enough to cope. However, if people move along the continuum towards 'injured' and 'ill' then it is likely that they will need to seek out professional care. They may even get directed towards it if they are particularly ill e.g. referred by a family member or sectioned by a health care worker.

Mental health continuum

A way of defining mental health by looking at it on a scale; individuals may feel more or less mentally healthy, rather than being mentally healthy or not, at different times and in different situations.

> **STUDY HINT**
> The mental health continuum is the only definition of mental health you have to know specifically, but make sure you know at least one other definition (e.g. Jahoda's) so you can write about different ways of defining mental health.

The current prevalence of mental health problems

Prevalence measures the number of people with a mental health problem at any one point of time. Current statistics show the following about the prevalence of mental health problems today:

- one in four British adults report having been diagnosed with a mental health disorder
- each year, one in ten British children (aged five to sixteen years) have a clinically diagnosed mental health disorder
- the WHO estimates about 450 million people worldwide suffer some form of mental health problem.

Every seven years the Adult Psychiatric Morbidity Survey (APMS) is carried out to measure the number of adults in England who have different types of mental health problem at that point in time. The following figures were published in 2016.

▼ Table 3.1 Mental health disorders by percentage of population diagnosed

Disorder	Percent of population diagnosed in the past year
Depression	8.6
Nervous Breakdown	0.5
Obsessive Compulsive Disorder	0.8
Panic Attacks	2.5
Phobia	0.7
Post Traumatic Stress Disorder	0.7
Other Anxiety Disorder	0.2

Source: McManus S, Bebbington P, Jenkins R, Brugha T. (eds.) (2016) *Mental health and wellbeing in England: Adult Psychiatric Morbidity Survey 2014*. Leeds: NHS Digital.

Prevalence
How common something is.

Challenge

Look at this definition of mental health:

'Mental health is defined as a state of well-being in which every individual realises his or her own potential, can cope with the normal stresses of life, can work productively and fruitfully, and is able to make a contribution to her or his community.' (Source: World Health Organization, 2014)

Use this definition of mental health to write a description of someone who would be suffering from mental health problems.

Time for some maths

1. Each year, what **percentage** of British children have a clinically diagnosed mental health disorder?
2. Use **standard form** to express the number of people that the WHO estimates to suffer mental health problems across the world.
3. What is the modal value in the data from the 2016 APMS?
4. According to the APMS data, what percentage of the population were diagnosed with panic attacks? Give your answer to the nearest whole number.
5. An English town has an adult population of approximately 30,000. Estimate how many adults would be diagnosed with an obsessive compulsive disorder over the next year.

Chapter 3 Psychological problems

▲ If you are on a busy street in the UK, you can assume that for every four people that pass you, one is likely to have been diagnosed with a mental health problem in the past year.

The APMS also looks at the prevalence of mental health problems by factors such as age and sex, as shown in the graphs below.

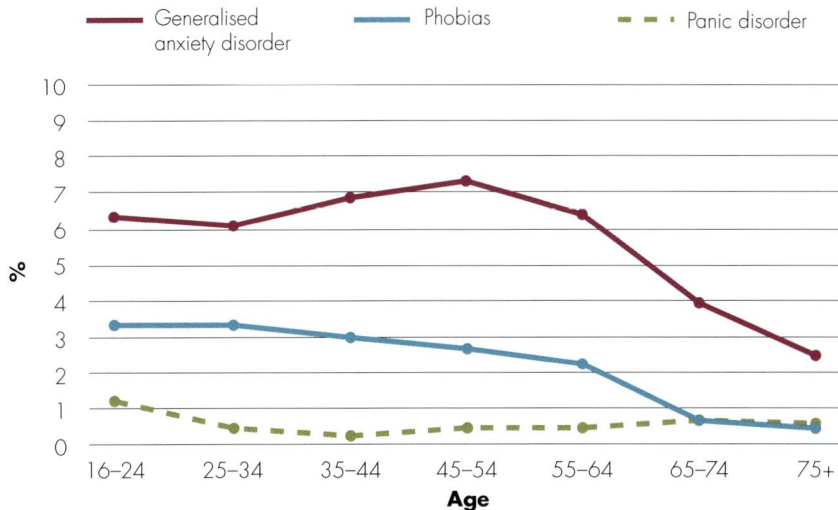

A line graph to show the prevalence of mental health problems by age.

Time for some maths
Using the graph to answer the following questions:
1 Which disorder was the least commonly experienced by people aged 16–24?
2 Which disorder was the least commonly experienced by people aged 75 or over?
3 At what age were people most likely to experience a mental health problem in general?
4 What is the pattern for people's experience of depression over time?

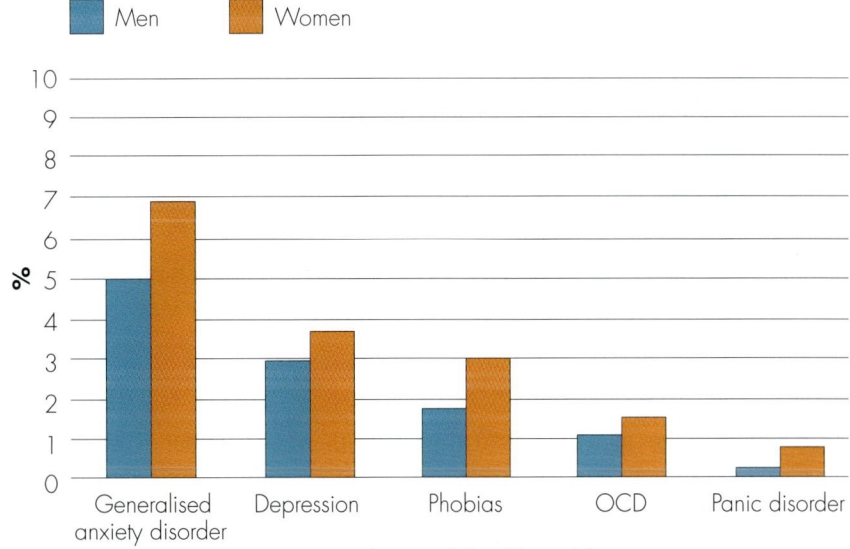

A bar graph to show the prevalence of mental health problems by sex.

Time for some maths
Use the graph to answer the following questions:
1 Which sex is more likely to experience mental health problems?
2 Which is the most common disorder for both women and men?
3 Which disorder shows the largest difference between women and men?
4 Which disorder shows the smallest difference between women and men?

Evidence suggests that people who identify as lesbian, gay, bisexual or transgender (LGBT) are particularly at risk of experiencing mental health problems. This higher prevalence may be related to a wide range of factors, including stigmatisation, discrimination and homophobia. In 2011, a British survey of nearly 7,000 respondents found that one in ten gay or bisexual men aged 16–19 had tried to take their own life in the year prior to the survey.

The survey also found that one in seven bisexual or gay men were experiencing moderate to severe levels of mixed depression and anxiety. A UK study found that bisexual women have poorer mental health than lesbian women, with higher rates of marijuana use, eating disorders, self-harming, anxiety and depression. In Scotland, one in five LGBT young people consider themselves to have a mental health condition, with the highest levels of poor mental health reported by transgender individuals and bisexual women.

The incidence of significant mental health problems over time

Incidence measures the number of new cases of mental health problems occurring in a time period, for example a year. It is actually quite difficult to track the incidence of mental health problems over time for a number of reasons:
- Not all mental health problems are diagnosed and recorded.
- The symptoms used to diagnose mental health problems change over time following new research and discoveries, so someone diagnosed with a particular disorder 30 years ago may not be nowadays.
- Many trends rely on **self-report** surveys, which may not be accurate due to relying on people's accuracy, honesty and memory.

Despite these issues, there seems to be a general agreement that the incidence of mental health problems is on the rise in the United Kingdom, with an increase in cases every year. This is particularly true of mood disorders (including depression) and anxiety disorders. In a fact sheet published by the NHS in 2016, it was reported that the proportion of the English population aged between 16 and 64 meeting the criteria for one common mental disorder increased from 15.5 per cent in 1993 to 17.6 per cent in 2007. The fact sheet went on to quote that by 2030, it is estimated that there will be approximately two million more adults in the UK with mental health problems than there were in 2013.

(*Key fact and trends in mental health: 2016 update*, NHS Confederation, March 2016)

> **Something to think about**
> Why do you think mental health problems are on the increase? Are we getting worse at treating mental health problems or are there other explanations?
> Think about factors such as people's awareness of mental health problems, how and when diagnosis takes place, and the causes of mental health problems.

Changing classification

We can see changes in **attitudes** to mental health in the way that psychiatrists have changed how psychological disorders are diagnosed. The International Classification of Diseases (ICD), which is used to diagnose disorders, is on its eleventh edition. Changes might include what counts as a symptom, how long it has to be present for, or whether it has to be present at all.

Similarities and differences

More significantly, some disorders have been added and others have been taken away. For example, anorexia nervosa is now accepted as a significant health problem, but did not appear in the ICD until its ninth edition in the middle of the 1970s. Meanwhile, homosexuality was classed as a mental disorder until the early 1990s, when it was eventually taken out of the ICD in its tenth edition.

> **Challenge**
> There are now many more statistics out there on mental health problems amongst young people. Use the internet to find out more.

> **STUDY HINT**
> Don't get too bogged down by learning statistics for the prevalence of mental health problems. It is more important that you know and understand the patterns and trends in terms of prevalence.

> **Extension**
> There are now many more statistics out there on mental health problems among young people. Use the internet to find out more.

Attitudes
Feelings of like or dislike towards something.

It is worth noting that not everything changes when it comes to mental health problems. For example, Kirkbride *et al.* (2012) published a study of diagnosis of schizophrenia and other psychotic disorders in England between 1950 and 2009, which found no significant difference in rates of diagnosis. The seventh edition of the ICD, published in 1955, listed many disorders that we still recognise today, including bipolar disorder (then called manic depression reaction), depression (then called neurotic-depressive reaction), phobias and obsessive compulsive disorders.

Changes in attitudes towards mental health

How attitudes have changed towards mental health in the UK since the Mental Health Act (1959)

The term 'mental health' became popular in the early 1900s, when certain professionals wanted to reduce the **stigma** surrounding mental illness and show that it is not abnormal. They felt that the word 'illness' reinforced prejudices because it implied that those with psychological problems were somehow 'sick'. By focusing on 'health' instead, they began to challenge the idea that only a small number of people are prone to psychological disorders.

Nowadays, we try to avoid outdated and stigmatised words such as 'insanity', 'lunacy' and 'madness' because they suggest that people with psychological health problems are out of control and beyond help.

The **Mental Health Act (1959)** was significant in changing attitudes towards mental health problems. It was the first time the term 'mental disorder' was used officially. The Act also had two important aims. One aim was to ensure that people with psychiatric illnesses were treated in similar ways to people with physical illnesses, for example by **consenting** to treatment where possible. The other was to make local councils responsible for the social care of people with mental health problems who did not need in-patient medical treatment. This was the beginning of the idea of care in the community.

In the 1960s, the media began to break the 'taboo of silence' around mental health problems by running programmes and writing articles on various conditions. Along with this new openness about mental health problems came more debates. Szasz (1961) published his 'Myth of Mental Illness', arguing that mental illness was not a real illness, and that patients should be held responsible for their actions.

In the 1970s, the charity Mind campaigned vigorously for the rights of people with mental health problems, arguing that, too often, they were detained and treated against their will. Mind's preferred term of 'mental distress' rather than 'mental disorder' was less stigmatising and intended as a mark of respect to show that patients were people first and foremost and had rights. This was also a time when the first Mental Patients Union (MPU) was set up in England to represent the views of survivors of what was seen as an oppressive psychiatric system.

The 1980s saw a rise in community care for those with mental health problems. Unfortunately, it was not well funded, which led to cases where people who were not receiving the right care and treatment ended up committing violent acts. Although rare, these cases received a lot of coverage in the media and fuelled negative attitudes towards people with mental health problems.

Stigma
A strong sense of disapproval for something.

Mental Health Act (1959)
A set of laws and declarations to address issues around mental health.

Challenge

Carry out some of your own research on changes in attitudes towards mental health over time. Add what you find out to the information from this book by creating a timeline to show how things have changed since the early 1900s or even earlier.

Through the 1980s and 1990s many organisations and events were set up to promote a more positive image of people with mental health problems. For example, World Mental Health Day was launched in 1992 and the Royal College of Psychiatrists launched their 'Changing Minds' campaign in 1998. Popular TV series were encouraged to run storylines that dealt sensitively with issues of mental health. The National Attitudes to Mental Illness survey was first conducted in 1993, and additional analysis by the Institute of Psychiatry, King's College London has been carried out to measure overall levels of change each year since 2003.

The most recent data shows that since the beginning of the current Time to Change programme (2011), an estimated two million people have improved their attitudes towards people with a mental illness. It also shows that there was a 2.8 per cent improvement in attitudes between 2012 and 2013 – the biggest annual shift for a decade.

As part of the survey, a number of statements were tested to measure the general public's attitudes to mental health problems. Key results included the following:

- a 6 per cent rise in willingness to 'continue a relationship with a friend with a mental health problem' (82 per cent to 88 per cent)
- a 7 per cent rise in willingness to 'work with someone with a mental health problem' (69 per cent to 76 per cent)
- a 5 per cent rise in willingness to 'live nearby to someone with a mental health problem' (72 per cent to 77 per cent)
- a 5 per cent rise in willingness to 'live with someone with a mental health problem' (57 per cent to 62 per cent)
- 79 per cent of people acknowledged that 'people with a mental illness have for too long been the subject of ridicule' (compared with 75 per cent in 2008)
- 83 per cent of people agreed with the statement 'no one has the right to exclude people with a mental illness from their neighbourhood' (compared with 74 per cent in 2008).

▲ Thirty years ago, a person's sexual orientation may have been diagnosed as a mental health problem.

Check your understanding

1. What is meant by the mental health continuum?
2. How has the incidence of significant mental health problems changed over time?

Time to Change

'We're supporting Time to Change – let's end mental health discrimination.' Time to Change was formed in 2009 by mental health charities Mind and Rethink Mental Illness, aiming to reduce mental health-related stigma and discrimination.

The effects of significant mental health problems on the individual and society

Significant mental health problems describe those disorders, such as schizophrenia and severe depression, which are often long lasting and sometimes permanent. They tend to seriously impact on the individual suffering from them, as well as raising issues for society in general in terms of how we deal with these problems when they arise.

The effects of stigma on individuals before and after diagnosis

We have already considered the stigma attached to mental health problems in the past but stigmatisation can still happen today. This is despite the fact that we better understand the causes of mental health problems, and people are generally better informed.

Stigma relates to how we think about certain things; things that make us feel uneasy or distressed. This is how some people perceive mental health problems. This means there is a strong **cognitive** element to stigma.

Cognitive factors – like stigma – are difficult to investigate because we cannot observe the mind. However, psychologists can measure attitudes using self-report methods. These give us some idea of how people think and feel.

DIY

Your task is to investigate the stigma associated with the label of a 'mental health problem'. You will need a scenario that describes a person, like the one below:

'Julie has recently been diagnosed with a mental health problem. She has been told to take some time off work, but still decides to go in. Her colleagues are uncomfortable about her being there and put pressure on her to stay home. At home, Julie is very short tempered with her children, who do not really understand how much strain her illness is putting on her. Julie tries to cope by going out for long walks but often finds herself just sitting down and bursting into tears. The doctors have said she will get better but it might take a while for any treatment to work.'

You can use this passage as it is, modify it, or write one of your own – but it must refer to a character who has a 'mental health problem'.

You will need to select some participants to read the passage, and then ask them a series of questions about Julie to see what kind of attitudes they have towards her. This is just one condition of your **experiment**.

For the second condition, you are going to change the passage so that it now reads that Julie has recently been diagnosed with a *physical* health problem. Everything else stays the same, so the **independent variable** is whether you use the word 'mental' or the word 'physical'. You now find another set of participants to avoid any **demand characteristics**. They will read this new passage and then answer the same set of questions.

It makes sense to use **closed questions** so that you can easily compare the answers from both conditions. Participants' attitudes to Julie will be your **dependent variable**.

For example, you could ask something like:

On a scale of 1 to 6, how selfish do you think Julie is?

Not selfish at all   1   2   3   4   5   6   **Very selfish**

When you have the two sets of responses, decide if there are any differences. Is there evidence of stigma when participants are told that Julie has a mental health problem as opposed to a physical one?

If there is evidence of stigma then how do you explain it? Why does it occur?

| For more information on experiments see page 181. |
| For more information on independent and dependent variables see page 172. |
| For more information on demand characteristics see page 202. |
| For more information on closed questions see page 184. |

Before diagnosis

The stigma attached to mental health problems is essentially a negative stereotype that can be triggered when someone sees or hears behaviour which they consider abnormal. An individual with a developing mental health problem may be perceived in negative ways and labelled as 'weird', 'crazy' or similar.

After diagnosis

For some people, particular disorders are also associated with their own negative stereotypes. For example, a person with schizophrenia may be stereotyped as 'violent and dangerous', or a person with depression may be stereotyped as 'suicidal'. Individuals who are constantly labelled in these ways are being subjected to stigma and may be at risk of becoming a **self-fulfilling prophecy**.

The effects of discrimination on individuals before and after diagnosis

The stigma attached to mental health problems is more of an issue when people decide to act on their thoughts. This is no longer a cognitive issue but becomes a behavioural issue – especially if it leads to **discrimination**.

Before diagnosis

Imagine a teenager, Poppy, who has started to experience symptoms of depression. She has not yet realised how low she is and so has not sought out help. However, Poppy has become very withdrawn and does not have the energy to do much outside of school. She has less time for her friends and they have noticed that when she is in school, she appears quite scruffy and does not seem to be keeping herself very clean. Poppy's friends decide they want less to do with her. They decide that she is not much fun anymore and, because of her appearance, they don't want to associate with her. When Poppy's friends reject her, this is an example of discrimination.

Imagine a woman, Dawn, who is shopping in town and quite suddenly hears a voice in her head that she does not recognise. It is a nasty voice that is being critical of her and makes her feel scared. She begins to panic, drops to the floor, and shouts out that someone is talking to her and that she is afraid this person in her head is 'out to get her'. There are lots of other shoppers around her – some stare but most ignore her. Every single one passes her by, with some rushing by very quickly. Coincidentally, just around the corner, a woman about the same age as Dawn is having a seizure. Now, a number of these pedestrians slow down and stop to see if they can help. When people come to the aid of certain individuals and not others, it is an example of discrimination.

After diagnosis

Imagine a man, Scott, who has just been diagnosed with schizophrenia. Scott has always been popular with his two young nephews and visits them often. However, since his diagnosis, his sister and brother-in-law have decided that their sons should not see him for the time being. They are worried that Scott might do or say something to scare the boys. The boys ask after their uncle and are told that he is too sick to want to see them. When Scott's family exclude him in this way, it is an example of discrimination.

Self-fulfilling prophecy
When an individual behaves in the way an assumption about them expects them to.

Discrimination
To treat people differently (normally less favourably) based on a perceived issue or problem.

> **Extension**
>
> There are laws in place to stop discrimination happening. Look at the four examples of discrimination again. Which of these could be against the law and where would it be more difficult to challenge the discrimination on legal grounds. Explain your decisions.

> **STUDY HINT**
>
> Note that there is a distinction between stigma and discrimination before and after diagnosis of a mental health problem. Check carefully to see if this distinction is being made in the exam.

> **Challenge**
>
> Work in a group if you can, and look at each of the examples above – Poppy, Dawn, Scott and Faruk. For each one, write down some of the possible effects of the discrimination that they experience. How would it make them feel? What might it make them think? Could it affect how they behave in the future?

> **Challenge**
>
> Search the internet for the Time to Change TV adverts. Watch the TV adverts and analyse each one to explain how it is trying to challenge stigma and discrimination.

Care in the community
Administering health and social care outside of hospitals and instead treating people in their homes and living in their normal communities.

> **Extension**
>
> Write an article to detail the arguments for and against the use of care in the community to treat mental health problems.

▲ 'Not in my back yard'. Members of the public may or may not be supportive of care in the community.

> **Challenge**
>
> Do some research using the website for Time to Change (www.time-to-change.org.uk). What are the main messages that you take from this website?

Imagine a call centre operator, Faruk, who has recently been diagnosed with depression. He was off work for a couple of weeks waiting for his anti-depressant drugs to work. He is now coping well enough to be back at work. There is an opportunity for a promotion, but Faruk's supervisor recommends that he does not go for it. She says he will only be disappointed when he does not get an interview. She has heard that the bosses are looking for someone with some 'get up and go' and so she has encouraged a number of Faruk's peers to apply as they don't have any psychological issues. When the supervisor treats his colleagues differently like this, it is an example of discrimination.

The effects of significant mental health problems on the wider society

When individuals experience mental health problems, this doesn't just affect them, it also affects others around them – from family members to members of the wider society.

Effects on public services

If the prevalence of mental health problems is on the increase, this obviously puts more demand on the health and social care services which are there to support individuals with these problems. For example, this means that the taxpayer may need to contribute more to finance more or better services. Or it might mean that existing funds need to be shared out between more different types of services, meaning all are stretched.

Historically, mental health care has not been well funded so if more people need help it may mean the quality of care goes down as services are more and more stretched. One way of dealing with the increase in people with mental health problems is to make greater use of '**care in the community**'. Up until about 30 years ago, people with mental disorders were kept in psychiatric institutions or on psychiatric wards, but increasingly, this is seen as a temporary solution. The policy is to use these places if sufferers need to be monitored closely, if they need intensive treatment, or where they need protection from potential harm. If patients get better while they are hospitalised, then they will be discharged back into the community. They still receive treatment, including taking medication, but this happens in the home.

Critics of community care say that this is just a money-saving exercise which puts pressure on families and communities who do not have the time, expertise or resources to care for these people. They argue this is why some sufferers end up going in and out of hospital, or even drop out of society altogether and end up living on the streets.

Supporters of community care say that people are more likely to get better in their usual surroundings, such as where they have grown up, where they know and where they can still go to work. They suggest this is more beneficial than professionals trying to isolate them and treat them in a controlled setting.

Effects on the law

Because of the issues around discrimination, society has had to pass laws to protect people with disabilities, including those with a mental illness. The Equality Act 2010 protects disabled people from unfair treatment. For example, people with mental health problems have the right to get their employer to make reasonable adjustments to enable them to still do their job. It also protects against discrimination in areas such as housing and **education**.

Effects on society's attitude

The rise in the number of people diagnosed with mental health problems and a greater use of care in the community may mean that people are more likely to interact with individuals with psychological problems. This interaction can break down prejudices. Of course, the opposite may happen. Communities may be anxious or resentful about having direct contact with more people with mental health problems and this can lead to more **conflict**. Because of the widespread stigmatisation of mental health problems, society has responded by campaigning to raise awareness of mental health problems. This is often done through charities such as Mind and Time to Change.

> For more information on how attitudes can be changed to reduce stigmatisation and discrimination, see the applications of research into social influence on page 114.

Schizophrenia

Schizophrenia is one of the most significant mental health disorders that a person can be diagnosed with as it is very severe and can last a lifetime. Schizophrenia comes from Latin and can be literally interpreted as a 'split mind'. In broad terms, it is a disorder where individuals lose touch with reality.

The clinical characteristics of schizophrenia

The **International Classification of Diseases** (ICD) uses the following criteria for diagnosing schizophrenia.

Check your understanding

1. How have attitudes to mental health problems changed over time?
2. What is the difference between stigma and discrimination in relation to mental health problems?
3. In what ways might a person with mental health problems be discriminated against?

Conflict
A serious disagreement.

Schizophrenia
A psychotic disorder where people lose their sense of self and reality.

International Classification of Diseases
A manual listing hundreds of mental disorders with their associated symptoms used by medical professionals to diagnose mental health problems.

▼ Table 3.2: The criteria for diagnosing schizophrenia (ICD tenth edition)

At least one of the symptoms below	OR at least two of the symptoms below
○ Thought echo, thought insertion or withdrawal, or thought broadcasting.	○ Persistent hallucinations in any modality, when occurring every day for at least one month, when accompanied by delusions (which may be fleeting or half-formed) without clear affective content, or when accompanied by persistent over-valued ideas.
○ Delusions of control, influence, or passivity, clearly referred to body or limb movements or specific thoughts, actions, or sensations; delusional perception.	○ Neologisms, breaks or interpolations in the train of thought, resulting in incoherence or irrelevant speech.
○ Hallucinatory voices giving a running commentary on the patient's behaviour, discussing him between themselves, or other types of hallucinatory voices coming from some part of the body.	○ Catatonic behaviour, such as excitement, posturing or waxy flexibility, negativism, mutism and stupor.
○ Persistent delusions of other kinds that are culturally inappropriate and completely impossible (e.g. being able to control the weather, or being in communication with aliens from another world).	○ 'Negative' symptoms such as marked apathy, paucity of speech, and blunting or incongruity of emotional responses.

Source: 'The ICD-10 Classification of Mental and Behavioural Disorders', *World Health Organization*, 1992, p. 87–88

Symptoms should be present for most of the time during an episode of psychotic illness lasting for at least one month.

Chapter 3 Psychological problems

Clinical characteristics
Symptoms or features of a disorder.

> **STUDY HINT**
> It is not necessary to remember all of the technical terms and detailed symptoms used by the ICD to diagnose schizophrenia. It is enough to recall the broad categories of **clinical characteristics**:
> - thought disturbances
> - **delusions**
> - hallucinations
> - disorganised speech
> - catatonic behaviours
> - negative symptoms.

> **Challenge**
>
> There are some tricky technical terms in the table on the previous page. If there are any you are not sure about, use the internet to look them up.

> **Challenge**
>
> Read the case of Peter, a man diagnosed with schizophrenia.
>
> Peter was diagnosed with schizophrenia at the age of 23. He claimed to hear the voices of secret agents who were plotting to kidnap him. He strongly believed that the agents were able to read his mind and that they were intercepting his thoughts as they left his head. He was convinced that he was in real danger and as a consequence locked himself in his flat for days on end. On one occasion, when his brother broke in and found him, Peter was sitting on a chair but in a contorted, uncomfortable way. His brother described Peter as being a statue-like and completely unresponsive. Peter has spent time on a psychiatric ward. On the ward, Peter became very agitated and spoke almost constantly – although there was little substance or meaning to anything that he said. His symptoms subsided after a while and, following drug treatment, he was allowed to go back to his family home. Since being with his parents again, Peter has become very withdrawn and seems to lack any motivation.
>
> Can you identify the examples of the following symptoms of schizophrenia?
> - thought disturbances
> - delusions
> - hallucinations
> - disorganised speech
> - catatonic behaviour
> - negative symptoms.

Ethnicity
Reference to a group of people with a common culture or nationality.

Recovery rate
The number of people that get better after suffering a disorder.

Key statistics of schizophrenia

The diagram below shows the key statistics surrounding schizophrenia.

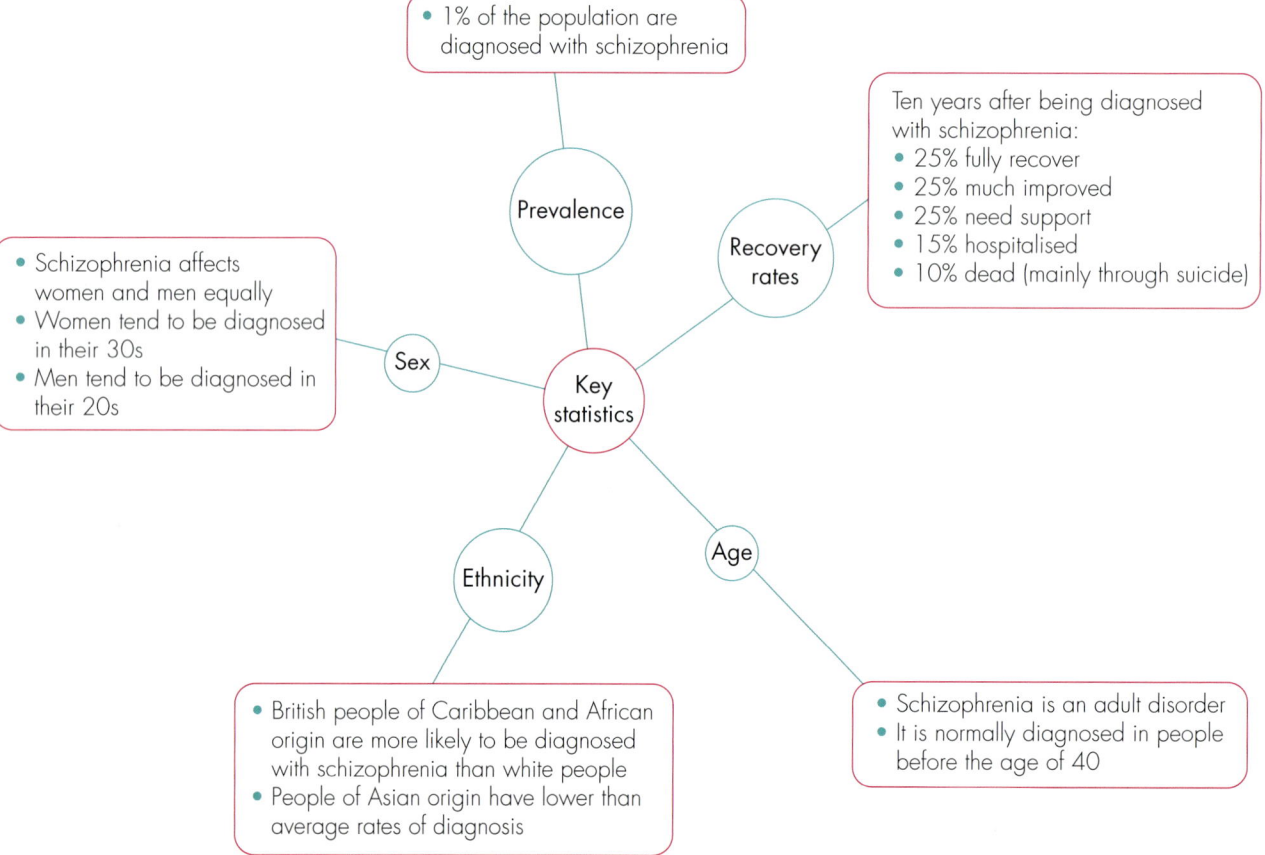

Check your understanding

1. What are the main clinical characteristics (symptoms) of schizophrenia?
2. What is the prevalence of schizophrenia in the population?
3. Which sex is more likely to be diagnosed with schizophrenia?
4. Which ethnic groups have low rates of diagnosis for schizophrenia?
5. What percentage of people with schizophrenia have fully recovered within ten years?

Theories of schizophrenia

If psychologists and other professionals are able to explain why people suffer from schizophrenia, this then gives ideas on how best to treat, or even prevent the problem. At this point in time, researchers cannot agree on the causes of schizophrenia. Some prefer to look at **biological** factors as the cause, while others focus more on psychological explanations.

The psychological theory – the social drift theory of schizophrenia

Social drift theory is a psychological theory of schizophrenia which tries to explain why there is a relationship between social class and this particular mental health problem. Schizophrenia is one of the disorders most strongly

▲ Estimates suggest that about one third of homeless people suffer from a serious mental health problem, including schizophrenia. But does being homeless cause this? Or do people end up homeless because of their mental health problem?

Social drift theory

The idea that individuals drift to the bottom of society when they have a mental health problem, as it takes away any status they may have.

linked to class, with working class people being about five times more likely to be diagnosed with schizophrenia than higher social groups. Many people belonging to the middle and upper classes who develop schizophrenia do not stay in the social class they were born into. By the time they have contact with psychiatric services, patients have often moved into a lower social class.

Social drift theory has a very straightforward explanation for the above results. When people begin to develop schizophrenia, and lose touch with reality, they begin to opt out of society because it does not necessarily make sense to them in the same way that it does to other people. This means that they are not interested in 'normal' activities such as getting a decent education, being promoted or even holding down a job. They may not be motivated by the things that an income is needed for – paying a mortgage or renting a home, having holidays, buying gadgets, clothes and other possessions, or doing leisure activities. Even if people with schizophrenia do want to remain a part of normal society, this may be difficult due to their diagnosis. For example, they may find it hard to keep their job if they are frequently off ill or they may leave their job because they are not able to cope with the demands. With a diagnosis of schizophrenia and the chance that they might not recover, people with schizophrenia may find it difficult to find new employment. Add to that the fact that people with the label of schizophrenia may experience stigma and discrimination in general, we can see how they may find it hard to feel part of their communities.

The theory is that the people with schizophrenia get caught in a cycle, which leads to a downward spiral into poverty and loss of status. The cycle involves the **disengagement of individuals** who do not feel part of society, possibly because of the symptoms they are suffering. As individuals begin to 'drop out' and stop following social norms, they then experience **rejection by society**. Rejection leads to further disengagement, which results in further rejection and so on. It is very difficult for anyone to recover from being at the bottom of society. When this also involves having schizophrenia, it is then very hard for that person to 'get better'.

Criticisms of social drift theory

- **There are problems with establishing cause and effect in social drift theory.** Rather than schizophrenia driving people into the lower social classes, an alternative theory (Social Causation) is that being in the lower social classes drives people to develop schizophrenia. In other words, factors associated with being at the bottom of society – poverty, living in a deprived area, being more likely to be a victim of crime, more discrimination, feeling excluded – lead to stressors that trigger schizophrenia.
- **Physical factors associated with low social classes may be the cause of schizophrenia.** Factors such as complications in pregnancy and childbirth can increase a child's chances of developing schizophrenia. So can poor diet and nutrition as a child grows up. These are more likely to be issues for lower class families, which may explain why many people with schizophrenia are found in this class – especially as most people end up in the same position in society as their parents.
- **There may be a bias in diagnosis.** Rather than more people with schizophrenia ending up in the lower social classes, it may be that psychiatrists and other professionals are more likely to diagnose this group of people with the disorder. For example, they may assume that people from lower classes are more likely to be suffering from schizophrenia because of

Challenge

Revisit the symptoms of schizophrenia. Draw up a table with these symptoms and for each one, decide how they could lead to individuals disengaging (in one column) and to rejection by society (in another column).

Disengagement of individuals
When people withdraw from groups and activities.

Rejection by society
When the majority does not accept and actively excludes certain individuals.

everyday stress, whereas a person from the higher classes may just be seen as 'eccentric' if their behaviour is bizarre or unusual. It does not help that psychologists often belong to the higher classes and so may not relate to working class people enough to understand their problems properly.

- **There is too much focus on the role of society.** Critics say that rather than just looking at wider social factors, theories should focus 'closer to home' to look at the family as a cause of schizophrenia. There is evidence that family conflict, domineering parents, or families that express high levels of emotion could contribute to the disorder.
- **Focusing on the interaction between the sufferer and society tends to ignore biological factors involved in schizophrenia.** Even if society makes matters worse by rejecting people with schizophrenia, the fact is that the disorder still needs to start somewhere and there is a lot of evidence that it starts with genes that affect the way the brain works.

STUDY HINT
The problem of cause and effect is something you may have to specifically refer to when evaluating. Remember that it is important to find out what actually causes something to happen so that it can be controlled. In this case, we are trying to control schizophrenia – either by treating it or stopping it from happening in the first place.

Check your understanding

1. How does the idea of 'disengagement of the individual' relate to social drift theory?
2. How does the idea of 'rejection by society' relate to social drift theory?
3. In what ways is social drift theory not an effective explanation of schizophrenia?

The biological theory of schizophrenia

The biological theory aims to explain schizophrenia by looking at the biological factors behind it. Many biological psychologists agree that there is a genetic basis to this particular mental health problem. If there is a gene for schizophrenia, then it is possible that it goes on to affect the brains of people who are diagnosed with it.

So what is different about the brains of people with schizophrenia? One idea is that there is too much of a **neurotransmitter** called **dopamine** in their brains. All humans produce dopamine and it is linked to behaviours such as movement, perception, **attention** and mood. However, when there is too much dopamine movements may become erratic, and people may experience hallucinations and delusions. Research shows that the messages from **dopaminergic neurons** that transmit dopamine fire too easily or too often, which can lead to many of the symptoms of schizophrenia. People with schizophrenia seem to have unusually high numbers of dopamine (D2) **receptors** on certain neurons, resulting in more dopamine binding and therefore more neurons firing across **synapses**. This could explain why people with schizophrenia may believe, hear or see something that does not exist.

Neurotransmitter
A chemical that passes messages around the brain from neuron to neuron.

Dopamine
A neurotransmitter.

Chapter 3 Psychological problems

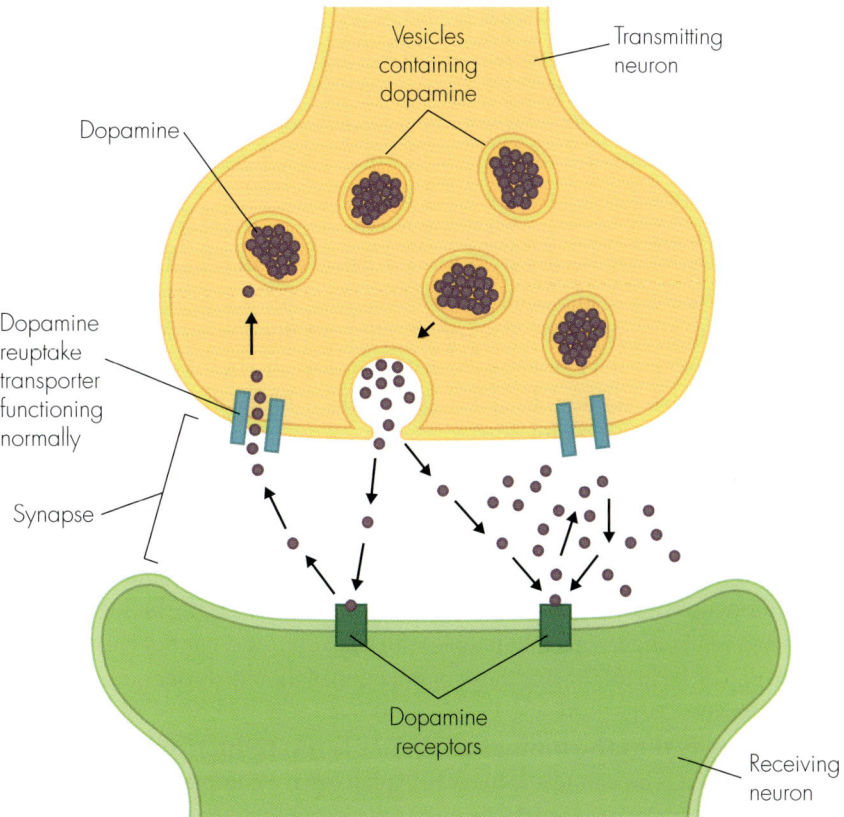

▲ We all rely on dopamine to send messages through the network of the brain. Neurons communicate with each other by sending chemical messages across a synapse. However, if too much dopamine is received because there are too many receptors, this leads to the brain having to cope with too many messages being fired around.

Neuropsychology now
The biological of theory of schizophrenia allows you to demonstrate your knowledge of how the brain works, including referring to neurons and synapses.

Challenge
Look at the functions of the different parts of the brain referred to above. How many of these functions can you link to the symptoms seen in people with schizophrenia?

Temporal lobe
Corresponding parts of the brain that are responsible for functions such as sensing information, understanding speech and generating language.

Hippocampus
The part of the brain responsible for making new memories. It is important for forming semantic and autobiographical memories.

Dopamine affects the way the brain functions. However, there is evidence that differences in the **brain activity** of people with schizophrenia is also down to **brain structure**. When scanned, a person with schizophrenia's brain will look different from a person without schizophrenia.

- Tests have shown that in people with schizophrenia, blood flow is lower in the frontal cortex region of the brain, and this area is less frequently activated when certain tasks are carried out. There is also some evidence that this part of the brain is smaller in volume. The **prefrontal cortex**, which acts like a 'control centre for the brain', appears to be defective. This may explain why people with schizophrenia lose control over their psychological functioning, such as planning ahead, being organised and making judgements. The **temporal lobes** are also lower in volume in people with schizophrenia. This is mainly due to a lack of grey matter in this part of the brain.
- The **hippocampus**, which has a role in formation of memories and the emotions that go with them, is smaller in volume in people with schizophrenia. Research shows that in general the more severe the disorder is, the more deflated this part of the brain is.

Researchers have argued that, even though the effects may not be seen until many years later, some of this neurological damage in people with schizophrenia may occur before they are born, when their brain is exposed to an infection whilst still developing in the womb.

Criticisms of biological theory

- **By only focusing on nature, the theory ignores the effect of nurture on the development of schizophrenia.** Even if evidence shows that the brains of people with schizophrenia look and work differently, this is not enough to cause the disorder by itself. The brain still needs to interact with what is happening in the environment to be able to produce symptoms like hallucinations, delusions and disorganised speech.
- **It is possible that brain dysfunction is an effect of schizophrenia, not its cause.** Because a lot of evidence comes from investigating the brain using post mortems or scans after the diagnosis is made, researchers cannot be sure what came first. Brain function and brain structure may change after something else has triggered the disorder. In other words, brain dysfunction is like a symptom.
- **Critics say that the biological theory is too deterministic.** Schizophrenia may not be completely controlled by what is happening in the brain. People may choose to let their symptoms take over rather than trying to mentally control them. Critics say that it is pessimistic to see people with schizophrenia as having no free will. Is the biological theory really suggesting that people with schizophrenia cannot control their disorder at all? Saying they cannot control their disorder is quite pessimistic.
- **Critics say that the biological theory is too reductionist.** They argue that it is too simplistic to try to explain such a complex disorder by just looking at a part of the brain or one neurochemical. A number of different psychological factors may be working together to cause schizophrenia to occur rather than reducing it to one biological cause.
- **For some psychologists, 'schizophrenia' is too broad a label that covers a diversity of symptoms.** If this is true, it may not be realistic to look for a biological cause for something that may be partially constructed by society.

Brain dysfunction
When the brain is not working as normal.

Brain function
The role or activity of the brain.

STUDY HINT
If you can remember each of the opening statements for this evaluation, your discussion will have breadth. The more that you can develop and explain each of these points, the more depth there is to your discussion.

Check your understanding

1. What is the neurotransmitter associated with schizophrenia, according to biological theory and why?
2. What parts of the brain are associated with schizophrenia and how?
3. What are main limitations of social drift theory and biological theory as explanations of schizophrenia?

Schizophrenia Research Study: Daniel, Weinberger, Jones et al. (1991) – a study into the effect of amphetamine on regional cerebral blood flow during cognitive activation in schizophrenia.

Background
Several studies had shown low levels of activity in the prefrontal cortexes of people with schizophrenia. This had been linked to the activity of dopamine in the brain. Studies had suggested that dopamine is important in suppressing random brain activity and helping to focus on specific stimuli in the environment.

Hypothesis
The researchers hypothesised that if dysfunction in the prefrontal cortex was related to problems in dopamine-controlled **synaptic transmission**, then a substance that stimulated dopamine activity (known as an agonist) should increase activity in that area during a cognitive task. The agonist the researchers chose was amphetamine, a chemical that increases alertness and energy, and improves mood. The researchers used **Single-Photon Emission-Computed Tomography** (SPECT) to scan the participants' brain activity during the task.

Single-Photon Emission-Computed Tomography
A type of nuclear imaging test that uses gamma rays to show how blood flows to tissues and organs.

> **Challenge**
> Use the internet to find the Wisconsin Card Sorting Test and try it for yourself.

Method
Design
In this experiment, the independent variable was whether participants had been given amphetamine or not. The dependent variable was performance on the Wisconsin Card Sorting Test.

Sample
The participants were ten in-patients from the National Institute of Mental Health research wards in Washington, USA. The study had the approval of the institutional review board and radiation safety committee, and the participants all gave informed consent to take part in it. The details of the **sample** are shown in the table below.

▼ Table 3.3

Participant	Age	Sex	Race	Years of education	Years since first hospitalisation
1	22	F	Black	12	6
2	45	M	White	16	23
3	29	M	White	9.5	11
4	20	F	White	12	2
5	33	F	White	12	14
6	40	M	White	15	15
7	34	F	White	12.5	11
8	37	M	White	12.5	18
9	21	M	Black	8.5	5
10	35	M	White	13.5	5

Source: Daniel et al (1991): 'The effect of amphetamine on regional cerebral blood flow during cognitive activation in schizophrenia' in *The journal of neuroscience: the official journal of the Society for Neuroscience*, 1991, p. 1909.

Each patient met criteria for chronic schizophrenia. Before receiving the amphetamine, the participants had been stabilised for at least six weeks on a fixed dose of an anti-psychotic drug (haloperidol).

Although the participants were too ill to live independently in the community, they were clinically stable at the time of the study and able to cooperate with the SPECT and testing procedures. They were free of any illnesses that could have affected blood flow in the brain, and free of alcohol or drug abuse.

> **Time for some maths**
> Look at Table 3.3 and answer the following questions:
> 1. What was the **mean** age of the participants?
> 2. What percentage of participants were female?
> 3. What **fraction** of participants were black?
> 4. What was the modal number of years the participants had spent in education?
> 5. What was the **median** number of years since the participants were first hospitalised?

Materials and Apparatus

Images of brain activity were recorded using SPECT technology, which was capable of collecting a full set of 80 projections in five seconds. Each participant underwent two scans two to four days apart. During scanning, the participant was seated in a semi-reclined position in a comfortable chair, with their head positioned in the scanner. The head was kept still using foam-rubber inserts.

Each scan involved:

- a mock test to get the participant used to the set-up
- a test of simple **sensori-motor** control, where the participants match bars on screen based on their orientation (the BAR task)
- the prefrontal activation test (the WCST).

Procedure

Five participants did the BAR task first, and five did the WCST first – this is known as **counterbalancing**. On the two test days, each participant received either a dose of amphetamine or a **placebo**, again in an order that was counterbalanced between participants. Both tasks were carried out on computer and required similar motor responses.

Results

The main results were:

- Amphetamine had a minimal effect on regional **cerebral blood flow** when participants completed both the BAR task and the WCST.
- There was no significant differences in the effects of amphetamine and the placebo on brain activity when completing the BAR task. However, there were some significant differences in blood flow in particular regions of the brain when completing the WCST. The left dorsolateral prefrontal cortex, the occipital and anterior cingulate **cortices** were all affected.
- Amphetamine had a small but significant positive effect on two performance measures of the WCST, including the number of correct responses. There was no such effect when the placebo was used.
- Behaviour changes caused by the amphetamine were highly variable and generally mild, ranging from increased cooperation, optimism, and improved mood to irritability and dysphoria. Three patients showed clinically significant improvement, whereas one patient significantly deteriorated.

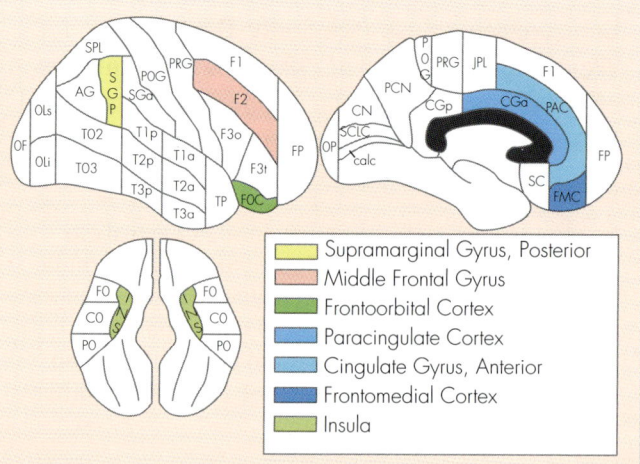

Placebo

A fake drug designed to have no effect (so it can be tested against a real drug).

Cerebral blood flow

Supply of blood to the brain at any one given time.

> **Challenge**
>
> What type of **experimental design** was used in this study? Justify your answer. What were the advantages of using this type of design in this study?

Conclusion

Amphetamine significantly increased prefrontal cortex activity during performance of a cognitive task, despite it reducing blood flow in the brain. The results were in line with animal studies that had suggested the role of dopamine and other similar neurochemicals in modulating and enhancing cortical activity. This implies that some of the problems associated with schizophrenia and prefrontal cortex dysfunction are, in part, reversible through drug treatment.

Overall, the study showed a link between brain function and key symptoms of schizophrenia in support of the biological theory.

Criticisms

- **The sample size was too small to draw reliable conclusions**. It is difficult to generalise the results to other people with schizophrenia, as the sample may not have been **representative** and the participants were all volunteers.

- **The sample was potentially culturally biased.** The sample was drawn from a small area of the USA and consisted mainly of white people. Because there is evidence of different rates of schizophrenia between different ethnic groups and different countries, we should be cautious about making generalisations about the relationship between the brain and schizophrenia.
- **The study may lack temporal validity.** The results may become outdated over time because the study used a different system for diagnosing schizophrenia than the one that is used today.
- Some psychologists would be concerned about the **ethics** of using scans when we are unclear on their long term **consequences**. This is especially an issue because the participants were scanned just for the sake of research and sometimes after only being administered a placebo.
- **The difference in brain activity may have been affected by the haloperidol given to the participants before the other drugs.** Although haloperidol was necessary for stabilising the patients, it becomes an **extraneous variable** that makes it harder to establish cause and effect.

Challenge

Which of these criticisms of the study do you think are the most valid, and why? Which criticisms are you less persuaded by, and why?

Neuropsychology now

Although this study is included to support the biological theory of schizophrenia, it also represents neuropsychology – especially as it was published in the Journal of Neuroscience.

Check your understanding

1. What scanning technique was used by Daniel *et al.*?
2. Why were the same participants used in both conditions?
3. Which other **controls** were used in the study?
4. According to the results, when did amphetamine have an effect?
5. What are some of the criticisms of Daniel *et al.*'s study?

Clinical depression

Most people feel a little down from time to time. We might argue with our friends or fail on a test and that might make us feel sad for a few days. However, if these feelings persist for weeks or even months and get more severe, then a doctor would diagnose clinical **depression**. Clinical depression is not the same as the depression caused by the death of a loved one or by a physical condition such as a thyroid disorder. Depression can affect anyone, including children. There are different therapies available to help improve the symptoms of depression.

The clinical characteristics of clinical depression

According to the ICD, there are three main grades of depression: mild, moderate and severe.

The ICD defines someone suffering from a depressed mood as having 'loss of interest and enjoyment, and reduced energy leading to increased fatigability and diminished activity. Marked tiredness after only slight effort is common'. Two of these symptoms, as well as two from the list below, should generally be present for a diagnosis.

▲ Clinical depression can affect anyone, regardless of their age, culture or social status. Cricketer Andrew 'Freddie' Flintoff has talked openly about suffering from depression.

Depression

A loss of interest and enjoyment in everyday life, with increased tiredness and reduced activity.

The patient suffers from:
- lowered mood
- reduction in energy, and decrease in activity
- reduction in capacity for enjoyment, interest, and concentration
- marked tiredness after even minimum effort
- disturbed sleep
- diminished appetite
- reduced self-esteem and self-confidence (even in the mild form some ideas of guilt or worthlessness are often present)
- loss of interest and pleasurable feelings
- waking in the morning several hours before the usual time
- marked psychomotor retardation and agitation
- weight loss
- loss of libido.

Depending upon the number and severity of the symptoms, a depressive episode may be specified as mild, moderate or severe.

Diagnosis

For all three grades (mild, moderate or severe), diagnosis is usually given if symptoms persist for more than two weeks for most of every day, but may be less if the symptoms come on very suddenly and are severe.

Challenge

Read the case of Ellie, a woman diagnosed with clinical depression.

Ellie was diagnosed with depression aged 20. She was at university but had stopped going to her classes. Whenever she saw her roommates she snapped at them and started staying mainly in her own bedroom and sleeping. She didn't really feel like eating much and found that her clothes were getting too loose for her. She was offered a job at the university working as a research assistant for one of her lecturers but she turned it down because she didn't think she would be any good at it. She normally spent at least a couple of hours a day updating her social media pages and posting photos but she stopped doing this and when her friends messaged her to check on her she just ignored them. She tried to continue with her university work but found that she just couldn't be bothered to read the research papers and it was too much effort to focus on it.

See if you can identify the symptoms of depression that Ellie is showing. Make sure you use the correct terminology from the ICD.

Key statistics of clinical depression

According to the Mental Health Foundation (www.mentalhealth.org.uk):

- Between four and ten per cent of people in England will experience depression at some point in their lives.
- A combination of anxiety and depression has been estimated to account for one fifth of work days lost within the UK.
- People from disadvantaged backgrounds are disproportionally more likely to experience depression and other mental health issues than those people from more advantaged backgrounds.
- Major depression is thought to be the second leading cause of disability worldwide.

Time to Change also report on the Mental Health Survey of Ethnic Minorities (2013):

- A survey of 740 Black and Minority Ethnic (BME) people experiencing mental health difficulties was conducted in 2013.
- 49 per cent of participants had been diagnosed with depression.
- Asian participants were more likely to experience depression than Black participants.
- The highest rates of depression were reported by Indian respondents (61 per cent).
- 93.2 per cent reported that they had experienced some form of discrimination as a result of their mental ill health.

Mental Health Network (www.nhsconfed.org) report:

- 33 per cent of females report having been diagnosed with a mental health problem compared to 19 per cent of males
- 19 per cent of adults report having been diagnosed with depression at some point in their lives
- 27 per cent of men and 42 per cent of women who have the lowest income reported having been diagnosed with a mental health problem, compared with 15 per cent of men and 25 per cent of women who have the highest income.

According to the Office for National Statistics (2004):

- 0.9 per cent or nearly 80,000 children and young people suffer from severe depression in the UK
- 0.2 per cent or about 8700 five-to-ten year-olds are seriously depressed.
- 1.4 per cent or about 62,000 eleven-to-sixteen year-olds are seriously depressed
- more than half of all adults with mental health problems were diagnosed in **childhood**. Less than half were treated appropriately at the time
- the number of young people aged fifteen to sixteen with depression nearly doubled between the 1980s and the 2000s.

Source: ONS, *Mental health of children and young people in Great Britain, 2004*

According to Nursing in Practice (2011):

- 42 per cent of those who completed an NHS psychological treatment programme during 2011 were 'no longer showing measurable symptoms of depression or anxiety disorders' by the time they reached their last therapy session.

> **Challenge**
>
> Why do you think the number of young people with depression has nearly doubled between the 1980s and 2000s?

- The rates of recovery using NHS psychological treatments vary widely between **Primary Care Trusts** between 7 per cent and 63 per cent (Nursing in Practice is an evidence-based website designed for health professionals).

STUDY HINT
You will need to know some statistics for the prevalence, age, sex, ethnicity and recovery rates for depression, as these are named in the specification.

Challenge
Create a spray diagram on an A3 sheet of paper, like the one on page 66 for schizophrenia, to illustrate the key statistics for the prevalence, age, sex, ethnicity and recovery rates that are described above. Where is the best place in your house to put up the poster to help you with your revision?

Check your understanding
1 What are the main characteristics of clinical depression?
2 Which minority ethnic group reports the highest levels of depression in the UK?
3 Where is someone with severe depression likely to be cared for?
4 Approximately how many children and young people suffer from depression in the UK?

Primary Care Trust (PCT)
A part of the National Health Service in England covering different parts of the country.

Evolutionary psychology
A branch of psychology that theorises that our behaviour has adapted over thousands of years to help us survive.

Something to think about
Why do you think the rates of recovery vary so widely between the different primary care trusts?

Theories of clinical depression

The theories of clinical depression help us understand how and why we get depression. **Evolutionary psychologists** think that thousands of years ago depression was a survival strategy that helped maintain the society so that if we were defeated, the depression would stop us fighting to regain what we lost and allow social change to occur without too much conflict.

The cognitive approach assumes that depression comes from us having an irrational perspective of the world around and how events affect us.

A psychological theory – the ABC Model of clinical depression

Rational versus irrational beliefs

Ellis (1962) proposed that depression occurs as a result of irrational thinking. How we perceive events can make the difference between us being happy or depressed. He put forward a three-stage model to explain this. Ellis theorised that 'disturbed' individuals usually have at least one but sometimes two or three 'core' irrational beliefs to which other irrational beliefs are related. These beliefs can be related to themselves, such as how they need to succeed to be worthwhile, or to circumstances, such as having to have good surroundings and conditions in order to be happy. Ellis also suggests that individuals are not consciously aware of these core beliefs.

Ellis states that it is not the actual event itself that causes the individual to experience negative thoughts and emotions but the individual themselves and how they interpret the events in an irrational way. Ellis believes that if an individual spends a lot of time thinking irrationally then it becomes a habit that is hard to break and leads to depression.

ABC Model (including activating events, beliefs and consequences)
A theory that view depression as being the result of irrational thinking.

Chapter 3 Psychological problems

STUDY HINT
You can be asked to describe a whole theory, or you can expect more specific questions on features of the theory. Like the ABC model, you may just get asked about rational and irrational beliefs or about the role of activating events, beliefs and consequences.

Challenge
Create your own scenario to explain how the ABC model works. Explain how someone could view a situation from both a rational and irrational point of view. Read out your scenario to the rest of the class and give the irrational view of the situation. Give the other students, in pairs, two minutes to come up with as many positive explanations for your scenario as they can. Get everyone to share their positive perspectives. Get other students to share their scenarios and negative perspectives and see how many positive explanations the class can think of.

Ellis suggests that rational thinking results in good mental health. A therapy based on this model called Rational Emotive Behavioural Therapy (REBT) was developed to help clients identify what their negative or irrational beliefs are and help challenge them. REBT is a type of cognitive behavioural therapy as it challenges how people both think and behave.

▲ Having irrational thoughts can make you think people are talking about you when they aren't.

Extension
Using the internet, find out more about how Rational Emotive Behavioural Therapy works. What conditions is REBT most helpful for?

The ABC Model

This theory explains depression by focusing on the roles of activating events, beliefs and consequences. If an event occurs, a person may interpret it irrationally. This belief can lead to negative consequences which can either worsen or lead to depression.

The roles of activating events, beliefs and consequences

The ABC model is explained as follows:

A = Activating event

An activating event is a situation which triggers the individual to potentially have an irrational thought. For example, you see your best friend in town and call out to them but they completely ignore you.

B = Beliefs

This is how the event is interpreted by the individual.

If it is interpreted *irrationally* you might assume that you have done something wrong, and that they are no longer speaking to you because you have upset them.

If it is interpreted *rationally* you might assume that that perhaps they were listening to music with their earphones and they didn't hear you.

C = Consequences

The consequences of the beliefs can be what you do or how you feel or any other thoughts you may have about the situation. Ellis suggested that the beliefs and the consequences are actually quite similar.

According to Ellis, if you have interpreted the event in an *irrational* way you might feel:
- upset and worried that they will no longer want to be your friend
- that you will be lonely
- that they might tell other people that you have done something wrong
- that other people then won't like you either
- therefore you should avoid them.

All of these feelings could result in depression.

On the other hand, if you have interpreted the situation *rationally*, you might call your friend later and make a bit of a joke about the fact that they ignored you, and perhaps find out that they were actually listening to music and hadn't heard you.

The free will/determinism debate

One of the great debates within psychology is whether humans have free will and are able to make choices about how they think and act or whether their behaviour is determined by factors that are outside of the control of the individual.

Free will

Humanist psychologists such as Abraham Maslow and Carl Rogers believed that behaviour is not determined and we have the choice and freedom to choose who we want to be and how we want to behave. This view is important when considering how many therapies work, such as cognitive behavioural therapy, where the individual makes a conscious decision to change how they think about their life and problems and how they will behave in the future.

One of the key issues with the concept of free will is that it does not support the view of psychology as a science. Being able to test and predict behaviour is one of the important aspects of being viewed as a science. However, the concept of free will suggests that behaviour is not predictable because everyone makes their own choices.

The reality is that our thoughts and behaviour are likely to be partly determined by external or internal factors but that we also have the ability to change these.

Determinism

Behavioural psychologists like John Watson, believe that all babies are born a 'blank slate' and that their behaviour can be conditioned (determined) from birth so that the individual's choices and behaviour have actually been determined by external factors such as their upbringing or how they were punished or rewarded at school. For example, a child that is always polite will not be doing so from free will but because they have been taught to by their parents and been rewarded when they have been polite and punished if they have been rude. Equally, a child who has been brought up in a violent household is more likely to be violent themselves as this is the behaviour that they have observed and copied.

Biological psychologists also believe that behaviour is determined internally by our genes and brain chemistry (a determinist view). For example, some biological psychologists believe that schizophrenia is caused by a problem with the levels of dopamine in the brain. This suggests that the individual has no control at all over their illness. The determinist view also has implications for psychological treatment because, if as it suggests we have no free will or choice over our behaviour, then potentially we would not be able to change it.

STUDY HINT
You need to know how the free will/determinism debate is related to this model of depression, as it is named in the specification. However, in the application question, you may also have to apply it to another topic.

Free will
The idea that we have control over our own destiny and can change our behaviour and ways of thinking.

Determinism
The idea that how we think and behaviour is determined by outside forces such as genetics or environmental influences such as our upbringing.

Check your understanding

1. Name the three parts of the ABC model.
2. Explain how an irrational belief could lead to depression.
3. What is the name of the therapy that was based on Ellis' model?

▲ Anthony Stevens and John Price suggest that depression has evolved to help us deal with losing.

Social Rank Theory

This theory suggests that depression is an evolutionary adaptation that reduces conflict by stopping the loser in a contest from trying to compete again. This allows society to maintain a stable balance without too much conflict.

Challenge

Can you describe the social rank theory in no more than 60 words? Did you manage to include all the key points? Compare your 60 words with the rest of the class. Who gave the best description?

STUDY HINT

You need to know about how the **reductionism** and **holism** debate is related to the social rank theory of depression as it is named in the specification.

Criticisms of the ABC model

- **The model assumes that the individual becomes depressed due to an irrational evaluation of a situation; however, the evaluation may actually be considered rational.** For example, loss of a job which results in a loss of income and possibly the family home would not necessarily involve an irrational assessment of the situation. This might be especially so in some circumstances, such as if finding alternative work is not easy due to lack of employment in the area they are living.
- **The model is too reductionist.** It focuses on faulty cognitive processes, assuming that depression is simply the result of irrationally evaluating a situation. However, it fails to take into account biological factors such as the role of neurotransmitters in depression and how these may influence how we perceive situations and events.
- **Depression that comes from nowhere may be better explained by innate, biological processes.**
- **It is hard to conclude cause and effect using this model.** The ABC model suggests that the individual makes irrational or 'faulty' conclusions about events but it is unclear whether these irrational thoughts cause the depression or occur as a result of the depression.
- **By supporting the idea of free will, Ellis' model assumes that the individual is responsible for their illness.** If the individual thinks that they are responsible for their illness, then if the therapy does not work, it might actually make them more depressed as they could feel that it is their fault. Alternative theories, such as a biological explanation might suggest that depression is determined by irrational thoughts due to brain differences or neurotransmitters which are not functioning correctly. This would suggest that although the irrational thought comes from the individual, they actually have little control over it. Therefore, if therapy doesn't work, they will feel less of a failure if they think the cause of their depression is beyond their control. For example, if they can change how they perceive situations and events through therapy, then this suggests that the individual has freewill but also suggests that they have some choice over how they perceive the events in the first place.

A biological theory – the social rank theory of clinical depression

The evolutionary function of depression

Evolutionary psychologists Anthony Stevens and John Price (2001) suggest that depression has evolved to have a specific purpose that helped us adapt and survive.

If we lose at something, depression is a natural reaction which allows us to come to terms with the fact that we have lost and the consequences of this. It also prevents us from aspiring to achieve a higher status than we currently have and to stop competing.

For example, if we applied for a more senior position at work and the position goes to a colleague instead, **social rank theory** suggests that the depression as a result of this failure serves to allow us to come to terms with the fact that we will not have a position of seniority, nor will we have the financial rewards that would have accompanied the job. It prevents us from arguing that we should have had the position ourselves and helps maintain the 'status quo' in the office. We have evolved to accept a subordinate role. The function is to prevent the loser from suffering defeat. Therefore they reduce efforts and ambitions which leads to depression.

The role of a lower rank in reducing conflict

In evolutionary terms, by accepting a position of lower rank in society, this prevents the person who has won from 'inflicting further injury' on the loser and ensures the loser will not try again to gain a higher rank in society. This means that social change can happen relatively quickly without too much on-going conflict.

By yielding to the winner, it allows the loser to maintain a place in society, which millennia ago, would have allowed the loser to have continued protection of the group, which was essential for survival. Although being unpopular and losing rank is not a pleasant experience, it is preferable to being ejected from the group entirely.

For more information on the reductionism and holism debate see page 34.

Criticisms of the theory

- **The social rank theory of depression can be considered reductionist as it only views depression as a process of evolution.** It suggests that it is an instinctive reaction to a situation where you have been a 'loser'. However, it ignores **individual differences**, for example where one person could react with depression if they lose out on a job opportunity, someone else might view it as a challenge and work harder to ensure that they get the next promotion.
- **The theory suggests that depression is limited to 'losers' and people of low social rank, but the evidence does not support this.** Although the statistics suggest that depression is more common in people who are poorer and therefore more likely to be of lower social rank, there is still a significant proportion of people of high social rank who experience depression including actors, musicians and politicians.
- **The theory also ignores instances of depression that can be triggered by life events other than social rank conflicts such as the stress of being a carer.** Being a carer for a sick relative, such as a partner with Alzheimer's disease, can result in depression as coping with the symptoms which only get progressively worse can be hard to manage, especially if the carer has little social support. This is not explained by the social rank theory.
- **The social rank theory is also reductionist within the biological approach as it fails to take into account other biological explanations for depression.** Evolutionary psychology is biological and suggests that we inherit psychological traits and have evolved so that we adapt and are more able to survive. However, there are other biological theories. One suggestion is that depression might be caused by an imbalance of chemicals in the brain called neurotransmitters, such as dopamine and serotonin. Therefore, the evolutionary view of depression is too narrow (reductionist) even within the biological approach to psychology.

Check your understanding

1. What is evolutionary psychology?
2. According to the social rank theory of depression, why is depression viewed as beneficial for society?
3. Why would depression have been beneficial to the individual millennia ago?

Chapter 3 Psychological problems

Clinical Depression Research Study: Tandoc, Ferrucci, Duffy (2015) – a study into Facebook use, envy, and depression among college students: Is Facebooking depressing?

▲ Does spending too much time on social media make you depressed?

Background

The transition between school and university is a difficult time for young adults, according to Wright *et al.* (2012). They propose that many of the factors involved in this transition can lead to depression. These can include: leaving home for the first time; making new friends, both platonic and romantic; learning to be more independent and increased pressures on studying.

A study by the Centre for Disease Control and Prevention (2011) found that young people aged between 18 and 24 years were most likely to suffer from depressive disorder symptoms.

Another study (AP, 2010) found that five times as many high school and college students are experiencing symptoms of anxiety and other mental health issues compared to young people of the same age who were studied during the Great Depression in America.

The Great Depression took place between 1929 –1939 and was a time of a great and long-lasting recession that had a huge economic impact worldwide with high levels of unemployment and many people suffering financially. These factors were likely to contribute to people becoming depressed.

Tandoc *et al.* suggest that there are many factors that may have contributed to the significant increase in incidents of depression among young people in more recent times. These include:

- better diagnostics (doctors finding it easier to diagnose depression)
- attention paid by those working in higher education to student well-being
- heavy use of social media such as Facebook and other mobile technologies.

Facebook allows its users to express themselves, but also to observe other people such as friends, family and acquaintances (Ellison *et al.* 2007). Facebook can promote happiness (Kim and Lee, 2011), however, some studies have questioned whether or not it can lead to depression. Jelenchick *et al.* (2013) found no **correlation** at all between Facebook use and depression. On the other hand, Wright *et al.* (2012) found a significant **positive correlation** between the number of hours spent on Facebook and depression.

The social rank theory of depression suggests that when humans compete for the same resources, those who are unsuccessful can feel 'subordinated'. Tandoc *et al.* suggest that feelings of subordination are similar to feelings of envy and can make people more vulnerable to depression.

> For more information on the social rank theory of depression see page 79.

Aim

Tandoc *et al.* aimed to see whether depression (using the social rank theory) could be predicted by Facebook usage. They also aimed to see if using Facebook can lead to subordination (feelings of envy), which in turn can lead to depression.

Hypotheses

1. Heavy Facebook users would report feeling higher levels of envy than light Facebook users.
2. Users with a large network of friends would also report feeling higher levels of Facebook envy than users with a small network.
3. Those who report feeling higher levels of Facebook envy would also report more symptoms of depression than those who felt lower levels of Facebook envy.

Method

Research method/design

The method was self-report using an online survey. The online survey collected participants' responses to questions and coded them into numerical form so that the researchers could statistically analyse them.

Sample

854 students from a large Midwestern university in the USA were invited to participate in the research. 736 chose to participate. 68 per cent of the participants were female. The average age of the participants was nineteen.

> **Time for some maths**
> Work out how many participants were male and how many were female.

Materials

The online questionnaire asked participants about a number of different variables.

Facebook

Participants were asked to:

- report the average hours per day they spent on Facebook
- rate using a five-point scale (1 = never, 5 = very frequently) how often they: write a status; post photos; comment on a friend's post; read the 'newsfeed'; read a friend's status update; view a friend's photo; and browse a friend's timeline (Tandoc et al. called the last four items 'Facebook surveillance' because the users were looking at friends' statuses but not commenting or posting their own information).

Envy

Participants were asked to rate the following eight different items relating to envy using a five-point Likert scale (where participants had to rate how much they agreed with each statement):

1. I generally feel inferior to others.
2. It is so frustrating to see people always having a good time.
3. It somehow doesn't seem fair that some people seem to have all the fun.
4. I wish I could travel as much as some of my friends do.
5. Many of my friends have a better life than me.
6. Many of my friends are happier than me.
7. My life is more fun than those of my friends.
8. Life is fair.

Depression

Participants completed the Centre for Epidemiology Studies Depression Scale (CES-D) which consists of twenty items asking participants to respond about symptoms associated with depression, such as the quality of their sleep, appetite and their feelings.

Procedure

Participants completed and then submitted the online survey/questionnaires.

Results

- Hypothesis 1 was supported. Results showed that heavy Facebook users did show stronger feelings of envy.
- Hypothesis 2 was not supported. The size of the network of Facebook friends was not related to envy.
- Hypothesis 3 was supported. Facebook envy was a significant positive predictor of depression among college students.
- No direct significant relationship was found between frequency of Facebook use and depression among the college students.
- Facebook surveillance is not a predictor of depression.
- Surveillance does however have an indirect effect on depression as it can lead to envy which leads to depression.

Conclusions

- The use of Facebook does not directly lead to depression.
- Facebook envy can lead to depression.
- Surveillance on Facebook can lessen feelings of depression if it does not lead to envy.
- Social rank theory offers a useful basis on which to understand how depression can occur in college-aged students.

Criticisms

- **The study had cultural bias.** The sample was only based on students from one university in the USA. It might be that these students all come from a similar background or upbringing which affects that way they interact with Facebook. Therefore the results may not be generalisable to other universities in the USA or in other countries. Also, the samples of journalism students are likely to have an interest in Facebook.
- **The study had age bias.** The sample consists of only college-aged students. Therefore the results may not represent how Facebook use and depression correlates in people of a different age.
- **Participants might have given socially desirable answers which would have affected the reliability of the study.** The study used self-report measures. People do not always respond honestly when answering surveys – even when they are conducted online. They may have not been honest about how envious they felt of their peers on Facebook and may have given socially desirable answers instead, i.e. those that made them look good. This could have biased the results.
- **The results lack construct validity as complex phenomena was measured using simple number scales.** Scores do not necessarily give the full picture of participants' depression or envy.

Time for some maths

Sketch out a scattergram which demonstrates a positive correlation between number of hours spent on Facebook and depression. Don't forget to give it a title and label your axes. Use the data below. Is there any data that does not fit with the theory? (NB: this data is not from the Tandoc study)

Number of hours spent on Facebook	Depression (1 = not at all depressed, 7 = extremely depressed)
15	4
25	7
19	6
7	2
8	7
19	7
5	1
22	6
26	7
10	2

DIY

Facebook is obviously only one of the many social media tools. Carry out a questionnaire of your fellow students to see if certain social media networks lead to more **envy** than others. It's up to you whether you ask one question or a number to measure envy. However, make sure you ask the same question for each site or app (e.g. WhatsApp, Snapchat, Twitter, Instagram etc) to find out if there are any patterns. If some social media networks do cause more envy, have you got any theories as to why?

Envy
A negative emotion created by seeing other people having things that you don't have but wish to have.

Application: the development of treatments

By learning about how depression works and what causes it, we are able to create therapies and medications to treat it. Sometimes, treatments are discovered by accident, such as anti-psychotic medication. These were used at first as an anti-histamine, which decreased the body's response to things that can cause an allergic reaction, and by accident they were found to reduce the symptoms of psychosis. Other treatments are psychologically based and involve the client changing their perspective on their illness and how they react, such as with cognitive behavioural therapy for treating depression.

The use of anti-psychotics to treat schizophrenia and how they improve mental health

Anti-psychotic drugs are a type of medication that is available on prescription and is used to treat mental illnesses such as schizophrenia and severe depression. Anti-psychotics can be taken in different ways such as in liquid or tablet form. They are also sometimes given as a long-acting injection.

According to mental health charity Mind, there are a number of theories as to how anti-psychotics work.

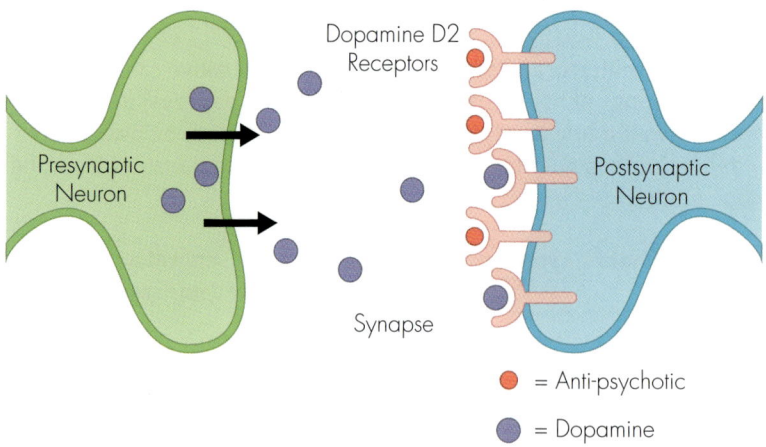

▲ How anti-psychotic drugs block the dopamine receptors.

> **Neuropsychology now**
>
> **Blocking the action of dopamine within the brain.**
>
> One theory is that some symptoms of psychosis are caused by an over-production of the neurotransmitter dopamine within the brain. By blocking some of the dopamine receptors in the brain, it reduces the number of messages that are passed around the brain. In schizophrenia, it is thought that too many messages are transmitted during a psychotic episode. By blocking the receptors using anti-psychotic medication, the reduced transmission helps stop or reduce the psychotic episode by reducing the number of neurotransmitters that are able to bond with the postsynaptic neuron, therefore reducing the amount of messages that are able to be sent around the brain.

Types of anti-psychotics

There are two types of **anti-psychotics**: conventional and atypical.

Conventional anti-psychotics were first licensed for use in the 1950s. Among the side effects are: tiredness, Tardive Dyskinesia (involuntary jerky movements of the face or body), seizures and heart problems, neuro-muscular problems (resembling symptoms of Parkinson's disease including loss of movement and trembling). Not everyone will experience side effects and some people will only experience some of the side effects.

Atypical anti-psychotics were licensed for use in the 1990s. People who take the atypical anti-psychotics are less likely to experience neuro-muscular side effects but are more likely to experience rapid weight gain.

Although there are a number of side effects of anti-psychotics which can have a significant impact on the individual, they can reduce the severity of the psychotic episode so that the individual is able to function within society.

Anti-psychotic drugs act by blocking some of the dopamine receptors, which stops some of the chemical messages passing through the brain. By reducing the number of messages, it is thought that this helps reduce the effects of the psychotic episode.

Which symptoms of schizophrenia can they help with?

According to Mind, all anti-psychotic drugs can help with the **positive symptoms of schizophrenia**. However, only the atypical anti-psychotics can also help with the **negative symptoms of schizophrenia**.

> **Check your understanding**
>
> 1 What emotion is subordination most like according to Tandoc *et al.*?
> 2 How does social rank theory relate to the Tandoc *et al.* study?
> 3 How many people actually participated in Tandoc *et al.*'s research?
> 4 Which different questionnaires were used in the survey?
> 5 What were the main results of the study?

> **Challenge**
>
> Look at the image of the neuron on the previous page, showing how the anti-psychotic drug blocks the dopamine receptors for two minutes, then close your book and try to draw and label it. How much did you get correct?

Anti-psychotics

Medication designed to help people who are experiencing psychotic episodes such as with illnesses like schizophrenia.

Positive symptoms of schizophrenia

Thoughts and feelings that the individual does not normally have when they are well, such as delusions and hallucinations.

Negative symptoms of schizophrenia

Thoughts or behaviours that the individual had before being ill and either no longer has or has to a lesser extent, such as feeling lethargic or social withdrawal.

Chapter 3 Psychological problems

> **Extension**
>
> Visit the Mind website and watch the videos about people who have been prescribed anti-psychotics and are speaking about their experience taking them. It is really important, where possible, that each individual has a say in what medication they are given and to give informed consent, so that they understand both the risks and benefits of what they have been prescribed. Sometimes someone will be too unwell to be able to make that decision themselves and the doctor will prescribe which medication they think is most suitable at the time. However, once that person is well enough to be able to understand what the treatment options are, then it is important that they are given the choice. Especially if they become ill again in the future and are unable at that time to make their wishes known, a record of what treatment they think will work best for them can be kept on file.

Anti-depressants

Medication that is used to help people who are depressed.

The use of anti-depressants to treat depression

According to NHS Choices, **anti-depressants** work by increasing the number of neurotransmitters in the brain such as serotonin or noradrenaline, which can help people feel less depressed. Anti-depressant medications such as SRRIs work by preventing the serotonin being reabsorbed into the pre-synaptic neuron (this is where the serotonin is normally recycled to be used again). This leads to a build-up of neurotransmitters in the synapse. It is thought that the excess serotonin in the synapse helps the neurons communicate better, which in turn helps people feel less depressed.

The use of psychotherapy for treating clinical depression and schizophrenia and how it improves mental health

▲ A CBT session

Psychotherapy

'Talking' therapy designed to help people with their problems using psychology rather than medicine.

> **Challenge**
>
> Investigate how psychoanalysis or counselling has been used on depression and schizophrenia.

Psychotherapy is known as a 'talking therapy' and was first introduced by Sigmund Freud at the end of the 19th century. More recently, talking therapies have been combined with the behaviourist approach, such as cognitive behavioural therapy (CBT). CBT is used to treat a wide range of mental health problems, including depression and schizophrenia. CBT originates from Ellis' ABC model. It is the idea that if someone perceives something in a negative and irrational way it can affect how we think, feel and act. After a while, this type of thinking becomes routine for the person and may affect their lives.

For example, if a child struggles to make friends at a new school, they may think that there is something wrong with them and that no one wants to be their friend, instead of understanding that other children might be feeling the same way and just being too shy to talk to them. This might make them feel sad and as a result they stop trying to make new friends and just withdraw into themselves. This might result in the child feeling isolated and depressed.

Ellis added D and E to the model. This D stands for 'disputing' or questioning the person's irrational beliefs. This is a role the therapist takes.

For example, if the client is experiencing a **delusion** that the chairs in the therapist's office are fitted with microphones so that the government can spy on the client, the therapist could invite the client to fully inspect the chairs to see if any microphones are present. They could also discuss with the client why these beliefs may not be true.

The E stands for the 'effect' of changing the person's interpretation of an event. If therapy is effective then the person will be able to view events in a less irrational way. This helps improve the person's mental health.

Cognitive behavioural therapy combines both the cognitive and the behaviourist approaches to create a therapy which aims to change how the individual both thinks and behaves and to confront the negative and irrational thoughts and how they impact on the individual.

Rather than focusing on issues from the person's past, it focuses on the current issues that the individual is experiencing and aims to deal with problems in a more positive way. It is used to help people with a variety of conditions as well as clinical depression, such as schizophrenia and phobias.

How the therapy works

CBT is generally a short-term treatment that can last between five and twenty sessions. Sometimes the client will be seen on a one-to-one basis with the therapist. The therapy can also take place in group sessions. CBT can now also be delivered to the client online. This means that the client can access the treatment programme from home and avoid having to make the effort to attend appointments, which can be difficult for people experiencing depression or schizophrenia.

In a one-to-one session, the client will meet with their therapist every week or fortnight for one-to-one sessions. A client who has depression will be asked to identify what the problems are and break these down into thoughts, feelings and actions. The therapist then analyses the client's responses and works out whether they are irrational and what effect they are having on the client. The client then works with the therapist to overcome the problems that have been identified. This may be achieved by completing worksheets or diagrams.

For example, they might record their thoughts and feelings about what makes them depressed and then the therapist will support them in re-evaluating their negative thoughts and attitudes and how to view them from a different, more positive perspective. The client may be given exercises to complete in between

Challenge

Go to the Mind website and search 'cognitive behavioural therapy'. Go to the CBT page and watch the video 'What is CBT?, Making Sense of Cognitive Behavioural Therapy'. According to the clip, what are two reasons why CBT might not be suitable for everyone?

Check your understanding

1. Who first introduced psychotherapy?
2. Which neurotransmitters do anti-depressant medications work on?
3. How does CBT help people with schizophrenia?

Chapter 3 Psychological problems

sessions to further explore how they are feeling and reacting to situations that would normally make them feel depressed, such as keeping a diary of their thoughts and feelings. At the end of the therapy, the client should have learnt how to challenge irrational or negative thoughts and be able to think of more positive ways of approaching their depression.

CBT and depression

CBT has been found to be effective at treating people with both moderate and severe depression. The therapist and client will focus on what negative thoughts and emotions the client is experiencing that are making them feel depressed. By helping them to re-evaluate their negative thoughts and behaviour, the therapist aims to reduce the symptoms of depression.

CBT and schizophrenia

The use of CBT to treat people with schizophrenia was first reported by Beck in 1952, who wrote a paper about how he had successfully treated a patient who was experiencing a delusional belief, using CBT. CBT can help people with schizophrenia by supporting them in a non-judgmental way to re-evaluate what their voices are saying, for example, and providing ways of coping with them. CBT can also help people overcome the negative symptoms of schizophrenia.

For more information on the Wisconsin Card Sorting Test see p71

The development of neuropsychology for studying schizophrenia and depression.

Neuropsychological tests

Neuropsychological tests are designed to help doctors understand the cognitive and behavioural problems that the patients is experiencing. The tests are standardised. This means that they have been used on many people and have been shown to be a reliable measure. The patient's scores on the tests will be compared against normal samples to give the doctor or clinical psychologist a clear picture of what the exact problems are. They are used for people with depression and schizophrenia. For example, performance on the Wisconsin Card Sorting Test for people with schizophrenia. The Wisconsin Card sorting test checks the function of the frontal lobe of the brain. The client is given a set of cards and told to match them but not given any criteria for how to do this. They are also not told if their matchings are correct or not. One neuropsychological test used for people experiencing depression is the Beck Depression Inventory (BDI) which measures the severity of the depression. It is a multiple choice, self-report test which looks at different aspects of depression such as feelings of irritability and hopelessness and symptoms such as tiredness and weight loss.

Neuropsychological tests
These are tests designed by psychologists to measure how well the brain is functioning. They are often used with people who have experienced some form of brain injury to allow the psychologists to understand what damage has occurred to the patient's cognitive function, i.e. how their thinking/memory has been affected.

Brain imaging techniques

Neuropsychologists use **brain imaging** techniques to look at differences in brain structure and activity in people with depression and schizophrenia, to help them better understand the conditions. Techniques such as the Positron Emission Tomography (PET) scan allow neuropsychologists to see brain activity by using a radio active tracer which is injected into the patient and travels up to the brain and can show the effect of medicine on the neurotransmitters. This can help neuropsychologists understand why the medication works for some patients and not for others and work towards creating more effective treatments in the future.

Brain imaging
Machinery that allows us to scan people's brain to see what activity is occurring or see differences in structure.

> **SUMMARY**
> This chapter has shown that, first, psychologists need to be able to decide on what counts as a mental health problem, how we categorise different problems and how to reliably diagnose these. We also need to be aware that, after diagnosis, people with mental health problems may experience stigma and discrimination. This is something else that needs to be tackled. Two significant disorders are schizophrenia and clinical depression. Some psychologists look more towards the environment to explain such disorders; the social drift theory of schizophrenia shows this. Others look more at what is happening in the mind, like the ABC cognitive model of clinical depression. Some psychologists are more interested in the role of nature – such as the biological explanation of schizophrenia which looks at the brain and neurochemicals, and the social rank theory of clinical depression which looks at the process of evolution. Studies like Daniel *et al.*'s and Tandoc *et al.*'s focus on the role of nature in mental health problems.
> Psychologists have developed different ways of treating mental health problems depending on the explanation they believe in. For example, those who support the biological explanation would recommend the use of drugs, such as anti-psychotics for schizophrenia or anti-depressants for depression. Those who support the cognitive model would recommend more psychological treatments, such as cognitive behavioural therapy for clinical depression and schizophrenia.
> Neuropsychological tests are also used to identify specific problems that people may be experiencing and brain imaging techniques can help us understand how anti-psychotic medication actually affects the brain.
> To summarise, there are a range of different mental health problems and it may be that if they have different causes then they may require different forms of treatment.
> Neuropsychological tests and brain imaging have also helped to better understand what is happening in the brains of people with mental health problems and the degree to which they can be treated.

Practice questions

The questions in this textbook have been written by the authors, Mark Billingham and Helen Kitching. They have not been produced or endorsed by OCR.

1. Identify **two** characteristics of schizophrenia. [2 marks]

   Two characteristics: hearing voices and hallucinations.

There is overlap here as hearing voices is an example of a hallucination. Since these two characteristics are not distinct enough, the answer earns just one of the two marks.

2. Outline one conclusion of Daniel *et al.*'s (1991) study into regional cerebral blood flow in schizophrenia. [2 marks]

   Amphetamine increased activity in the prefrontal cortex area of the brain during performance on a cognitive task.

One mark for the reference to amphetamine increasing activity in the prefrontal cortex and an additional mark for reference to the fact that a cognitive task was taking place at the same time.

3. **a** Identify one part of the brain associated with schizophrenia. [1 mark]

   The prefrontal cortex.

This is a relevant part of the brain so is worth one mark.

   b Explain how this part of the brain plays a part in schizophrenia. [2 marks]

   It is the control centre so it explains why people with schizophrenia have less control.

One mark earned here. The answer needs to be elaborated on to show what the prefrontal cortex is responsible for and how this relates to schizophrenia.

4. Outline the relationship between clinical depression and ethnicity using key statistics. [3 marks]

   Time to Change charity did some research with black and ethnic minority participants and found that 49 per cent had been diagnosed with depression. The highest rate of depression (61 per cent) was reported by the Indian participants. 93 per cent of participants who had depression had experienced discrimination because of their mental health problem.

This is a three mark response – essentially it is easy to 'score' by giving a mark for each statistic. It is impressive that the candidate has quoted accurate statistics although this is not a requirement. However, candidates should be able to speak about broad patterns (supported by statistics) to secure high marks.

5. Evaluate the biological theory of schizophrenia. [4 marks]

The biological theory only looks at nature and ignores the effect of nurture on schizophrenia. Although researchers have found brain differences in people with schizophrenia, it is not easy to establish cause and effect. The theory also has the problem of being too deterministic and too reductionist.

Although four relevant points are made about the theory, they generally lack depth and explanation – especially the last two. However, the response is credited for its range and earns three out of the four marks.

6. Outline two criticisms of the results of Tandoc *et al.*'s (2015) study into Facebook envy. [4 marks]

1. *The study had cultural bias so it is not generalisable.*
2. *The participants might have given socially desirable answers.*

Both limitations are relevant and creditworthy but they are quite brief and, more importantly, not in context. The candidate needs to develop them by relating them more explicitly to the study so that they are less generic. A mark for each limitation, giving two in total.

7

> **The case of Rhianna**
>
> Rhianna is suffering from depression. She was diagnosed not long after her long-term girlfriend left her to move in with a man that they both used to know. The man was somebody that Rhianna used to look up to.

Using the source, describe how social rank theory could be used to explain Rhianna's depression. [5 marks]

The social rank theory says that depression is an evolutionary adaptation which helps avoid conflict when someone loses. Becoming depressed stops the person from trying to fight for what they have lost because they lack things like energy and motivation. This also helps them to accept the situation. In the case of Rhianna, she has lost her girlfriend to someone who she saw as being of higher status. Social rank theory would say that her depression stops her from trying to win her girlfriend back from this man and helps Rhianna accept that her girlfriend has moved on.

This answer earns all five marks. It starts with an accurate and reasonably detailed account of social rank theory which demonstrates the candidate's understanding. The response finishes by referring to the source and, in so doing, shows good application skills.

Chapter 3 Psychological problems

8. Describe how anti-psychotics and anti-depressants are used to treat mental health problems. Refer to neurons and synapses in your answer. **[6 marks]**

Anti-psychotics work by blocking some of the dopamine receptors in the post-synaptic neuron. This helps reduce the number of messages that are passed around the brain. It is thought that during a psychotic episode too many messages are sent around the brain — leading to symptoms like hallucinations and delusions - so by blocking them it can stop the episode from happening.

Anti-depressants such as SRRIs work in the opposite way by preventing serotonin being reabsorbed by the pre-synaptic neuron. Neurotransmitters then build-up in the synapse. Psychologists think that the extra serotonin in the synapse helps the neurons communicate better, which in turn helps people have better control over their mood.

The candidate has sensibly dealt with the two types of drugs separately and earns three marks for the two parts of the response. In both cases, synapses and neurons are referenced as required by the question. More importantly, the candidate demonstrates sound technical knowledge and understanding and clearly relates the effects of the drugs to the mental health problems under consideration.

4 Social influence

Social psychology is an area that looks at how other people influence our behaviour, thoughts and feelings. In this chapter, we will look at what influences people to conform and obey and how we behave in crowds. We will look at situational factors, which consider how external influences affect our behaviour, and dispositional factors, which consider how our personality and individual differences influence whether we conform or obey. We will also consider the stigma of mental health discrimination and how it can be reduced by minority and majority influence.

This chapter should enable you to:
- develop an awareness of conformity and obedience
- develop an awareness of collective and crowd behaviour, including pro-social and anti-social behaviour
- explain and evaluate the theories of situational factors with reference to the effect of majority influence on conformity, crowd behaviour including deindividuation, culture on pro-social and anti-social behaviour, authority figures on obedience and the free will/determination debate
- describe and evaluate Bickman's (1974) study of obedience and the power of a uniform
- explain and evaluate theories on dispositional factors, with reference to the effect of self-esteem on conformity, locus of control in crowd behaviour, morality or pro-social and anti-social behaviour, authoritarian personality on obedience, and issues of generalisability, as well as the effect of morality on pro-social and anti-social behaviour
- understand the influence of the brain in dispositional factors, including hippocampal volume in self-esteem, and regions of the prefrontal cortex in morality
- describe and evaluate the NatCen study into the 2011 riots in Tottenham, London
- explain how minority and majority influence affects social change in relation to changing attitudes and behaviour towards, increasing awareness of, and reducing mental health stigma and discrimination.

Hippocampal volume
Volume of the hippocampus part of the brain.

Key concepts of social influence

The first part of the chapter will focus on **majority influence** and how other people around us and other external factors, such as the environment we find ourselves in, can affect whether or not we conform and obey.

Conformity including majority influence

Crutchfield (1955) defined **conformity** as 'yielding to group pressures'. This involves changing how you think and behave in order to fit in with a group. People conform in many different situations. For example, students conform in order to fit in with their classmates, so that they do not feel isolated or different.

Majority influence
When the majority of a group tries to influence others in the group to conform to their beliefs.

Conformity
Yielding to group pressure.

Chapter 4 Social influence

STUDY HINT
Make sure you understand these key terms on a number of levels. Consider the difference between being asked to state what is meant by obdience as opposed to being asked to describe or explain it.

▲ Vaping just to be like the others in a group is conformity.

Crowd and collective behaviour
The actions of people who have gathered together for a particular purpose. The behaviour of crowds can often be spontaneous and unplanned. For example, people might find themselves acting in a way that they wouldn't normally do.

Obedience
Following orders from someone we perceive as having more authority than us.

The pressures they may feel could be related to being bullied or teased for not conforming, or being criticised.

Conformity may be pretending to like the same music as the other people in a group, taking up smoking or vaping to fit in or joining in with bullying other children to avoid being bullied themselves.

Collective and crowd behaviour

Collective behaviour
According to Smelser (1962), **collective behaviour** refers to 'the behaviour of two or more individuals who are acting together or collectively'.

Blumer (1939) contrasts small group behaviour with collective behaviour. He states that in a small group, the individual has a sense of personal control. In contrast, collective behaviour suggests that the individual has lost this sense of personal control and is now part of a greater power that has the ability to influence individuals within the collective.

Crowd behaviour
Crowd behaviour refers to a group of people who have come together for a common purpose. This might be to protest against government policy or to watch a football match. However, it is important to remember that a crowded place will not always exhibit a crowd mentality. For example, in a busy shopping centre everyone is there for a similar purpose, but each shopper has their own individual tasks.

Anti-social and pro-social behaviour
Anti-social behaviour can be defined as actions that go against society and harms it in some way. **Pro-social behaviour** is the opposite and benefits society and its members.

For example, the 2011 London riots can be seen as anti-social behaviour. The 2014 ALS Ice Bucket Challenge can be seen as pro-social behaviour.

Obedience

Obedience differs from conformity because it usually involves following a direct order from an individual who has superior authority. Conformity rarely involves a direct instruction to do something.

▲ Taking the ice bucket challenge was a demonstration of pro-social behaviour as it also involved donating and raising awareness of ALS (a motor neurone disease).

We obey in many different situations in our everyday life, such as doing what our parents tell us and following school rules. Obedience is important in society because without it there would be chaos. However, blind obedience to authority, where people do not question the morality of what they are being told to do, can result in harmful behaviour. An example of this is the Second World War Nazi officers who obeyed Hitler without question, resulting in the deaths of millions of innocent victims.

> **Challenge**
>
> Summarise conformity, obedience and collective and crowd behaviour each in a maximum of 50 words. Make sure you have only the key information. Can you now reduce each paragraph to one sentence? Compare your sentences with the other students. Who has written the most effective sentence for each key point? Use these as memory triggers during your revision.

> **Check your understanding**
>
> 1 Why is it important that people obey?
> 2 What is the difference between small crowd and collective behaviour?
> 3 What is the definition of conformity?
> 4 What is the difference between conformity and obedience?

Situational factors
How external influences affect our behaviour.

Normative conformity
Where people yield to group pressure because they want to fit in and are concerned about being rejected by the others in the group.

Group norm
Specific ideas or assumptions held by a particular group about what is considered acceptable behaviour within that group.

Theories and explanations of social influence

The effect of situational factors on behaviours

Situational factors, such as the influence of other people, are external factors that influence the way we behave and how likely we are to obey or conform.

Majority influence on conformity

There are different ways that the majority can influence people to conform. In some cases, people will outwardly change their behaviour or views to fit in with the group, but will retain their personal opinion. In other cases, they will actually change their personal views as well.

Normative conformity

People may only comply with **normative conformity**. This means that although they go along with the **group norm**, internally, they still keep their own opinions. For example, if the group say they like horror films, the student will agree that they like them to fit in, even though privately they don't like the genre at all and actually prefer comedies. Other norms in society can be seen more broadly, such as everyone driving on the left, because it would be chaos if a few of us decided to drive on the right! This sort of conformity ensures that society generally functions successfully.

In a famous **experiment**, Solomon Asch (1956) investigated whether participants would conform in a situation where the majority were clearly wrong.

▲ A group norm for someone in a Steampunk group would be to go out wearing Victorian-style costume.

Confederate
Someone who appears to be a participant in an experiment but is actually working for the researcher to manipulate the experiment.

STUDY HINT
You do not have to know about studies like Asch's for the exam but they may help you to explain the effects of different situational factors.

Something to think about
Do you think there were any ethical issues with Asch's research?

Informational conformity
People conform because they want to be perceived as correct and so follow the lead of others.

Something to think about
It is important for psychologists to learn about crowd behaviour in situations like this, because they can use their knowledge to inform people of what to do if they are caught up in similar situations. They just may save their lives!

Challenge
Think of as many different situations in everyday life as you can where people might experience informational conformity. Share your ideas with the class.

Participants were put in a group and shown a series of three lines on a card. One line was on another card and participants were asked to say which of the three lines it matched. The answer was clear. However, all of the participants were **confederates** apart from one real participant. Out of 18 trials, the confederates gave the wrong answer 12 times. In this study, a third of real participants gave the wrong answer, yielding to group pressure. It is likely that these participants still thought the answer was wrong but they didn't want to go against the group norm as it could have been embarrassing.

In the Asch experiment, the confederates were verbally influencing the participants to conform to their group norm of giving the wrong answer.

Asch did some later variations of his line experiment and found that only three confederates were needed to make participants comply. In fact, increasing the number of confederates who gave the wrong answer did not increase the amount of conformity. However, having one confederate who did not agree with the group was enough to hugely reduce the rates of conformity – even if the 'dissenter' gave another wrong answer, just as long as it was different to the majority.

Check your understanding
1. How many people do you need in a group in order to make people comply?
2. According to Asch, what reduces the rate of conformity?
3. Why did the participants comply in Asch's study?

Informational conformity
With **informational conformity**, people yield to group pressure because they are unsure of the answer themselves or if the situation they are in is unclear. Normally, when people conform in this situation, they internalise their response, so not only do they agree publicly with the other members of the group, they also change their personal opinions. For example, if a teacher asks the class a difficult question and gives two possible answers, a student who does not know the answer might go with whichever answer the majority of the class has gone for, simply because they think that the other students must be correct.

Collective and crowd behaviour
In his 1896 book, *The Crowd*, Gustave Le Bon explained that when people are in a crowd, they lose their sense of self, responsibility and morality – the crowd works together with a group mentality. He suggests that the behaviour is unconscious and driven by instinct so there are no conscious cognitive processes, meaning people are not thinking about their behaviour; they are simply acting on instinct. This can lead to violence and people acting in ways that they would never normally contemplate if they were on their own.

Reicher (1984) suggests a different view on how crowds work. He proposes that crowds act under a common social identity. This means that members of the crowd all share a similar background, **culture**, interests or come from a similar area. He researched the St Paul's riots, which took place in 1980, and found that although rioters attacked police cars, they left other cars alone and actually helped the traffic pass unharmed. They also did not damage property around them. He suggested that this was because the rioters shared a common social identity: they were all from the same area in Bristol and were protesting for the same reasons. Therefore, they did not attack traffic or passers-by who they saw as sharing their social identity and being part of their 'in-group', but did attack the police who they viewed as being part of an 'out-group'.

Reicher (1996) suggests that another explanation for why crowds can turn violent is when the police use heavy-handed methods to control the crowd, viewing the whole crowd as dangerous rather than the few trouble-makers. Members of that crowd who might otherwise have protested peacefully feel angry that the police are trying to stop them doing something that they see as valid. They now become part of an in-group with a common experience (heavy-handed treatment by the police), and whereas before they might not have been willing to act against the police, they now feel empowered to do so by a common group goal.

Deindividuation

Social psychologists are interested in why people sometimes behave differently when they are in a crowd to when they are on their own. One explanation for this is **deindividuation**.

Deindividuation can happen in different situations. For example, people can feel a sense of deindividuation when at a music festival, football match or a protest march. They lose their sense of individuality and become part of the crowd mentality. According to psychologists, this could result in the crowd becoming violent and acting instinctively. Deindividuation can lead people to act in ways that they would not normally do, committing anti-social acts and following a 'mob mentality'. Prentice-Dunn and Rogers (1989) suggested that in a crowd, people not only lose their sense of self and their personal sense of morality but also feel less accountable for their actions in general due to a sense of lacking public self-awareness. Any violent behaviour that follows becoming deindividuated comes from the assumption that there will be no negative **consequences** for their behaviour. For example, football hooliganism, where fans become violent after a match, could be explained by deindividuation. Similarly, the crowd behaviour at the 2011 London riots could also be explained by the individuals becoming deindividuated.

Leon Mann (1981) investigated 21 cases where crowds were present while someone was threatening to jump from a building, bridge or tower. He found that baiting or jeering occurred in ten of the cases. Mann suggested that this might be due to deindividuation as they occurred at night time and with a large crowd who were a distance away from the person who was threatening to jump. Each of these factors are associated with anonymity, which can lead to deindividuation.

In-group
Someone who is part of your group. This could be someone who lives in the same area as you, shares the same interests or is in the same class or team.

Out-group
Someone who is not in your group. It could be that they support a different football team to you or are in a different class.

Deindividuation
When people are in a crowd and they lose their sense of individuality and feel more anonymous. This can also happen if someone is wearing a uniform or costume.

Check your understanding
1. What is the difference between in-group and anti-group?
2. Why might a crowd turn violent?
3. What is meant by deindividuation?
4. How could someone become deindividuated?

Challenge
Research a riot that has happened recently (not the Tottenham riots as you will be looking at these in more detail later). It doesn't have to be in the UK. What sparked the riot? How did the crowd behave? Do any of the theories above explain the behaviour of the crowd? If not, why not? Create a poster to demonstrate how psychology explains, or doesn't explain, the behaviour of the crowd.

Culture on pro-social and anti-social behaviour

Pro-social behaviour

When considering cultural differences, psychologists often look at the difference between **collectivist** and **individualist cultures**.

Children who are raised in a collectivist culture are often expected to help out with the family chores, whether this is helping around the house or helping to gather food. They are also more likely to help care for younger siblings.

Children raised in individualist cultures are raised by their parents to be competitive and to work hard at school to ensure that they succeed. If they are given housework to do, it is often for a reward such as pocket money.

Researchers tend to measure pro-social behaviour in children by looking at how they help with the family chores and look after other members of the family. As such, children in collectivist cultures tend to be viewed as demonstrating more pro-social behaviour.

Researchers Whiting and Whiting (1975) conducted a **naturalistic observation** of children aged three to eleven years in six different countries. They found that children from Mexico and the Philippines generally acted in a more pro-social way than those from Japan, India and the USA. The most pro-social children were from Kenya; 100 per cent of Kenyan children, compared to eight per cent of American children, demonstrated **altruism**. One major difference between the children was how much they helped with household chores and looked after their younger siblings.

Other studies have compared children raised on a Kibbutz, a collectivist culture where resources and domestic tasks are shared among the community. Moghaddam (1993) compared children raised on a Kibbutz to children raised in Europe and the USA, finding that the children raised on the Kibbutz were more likely to show altruistic, helping behaviour than those children in Europe and the USA, who were raised in individualist cultures. In a similar study, Nadler (1986) found that children brought up on a Kibbutz were much more likely to give help to others and ask for it in return compared to children brought up in a city environment.

Tower (1997) investigated sharing behaviour in children from the UK and Russia. He found that children from Russia were more likely to choose resources that benefited others, whereas the children from the UK were more likely to choose resources that benefited themselves.

This research shows that culture and upbringing can have an impact on children's pro-social behaviour. In societies where children are expected to help their families from an early age, either around the house, with siblings or by working or gathering resources, they are more likely to demonstrate altruistic behaviour.

Collectivist culture
The needs of the group are seen as more important than the needs of the individual, and the individuals in the society view themselves as interdependent or connected to other people.

Individualist culture
The needs of the individual are seen as more important than the needs of the group, and the individuals in the society view themselves as independent.

Altruism
Helping or showing concern for others without expecting any reward. It is an unselfish act which could end up disadvantaging the person who is offering the help.

> **Extension**
>
> Research has looked at 'the culture of honour' and how this can influence aggressive behaviour in groups. Carry out your own research on this to give another example of the link between culture and anti-social behaviour.

▲ Children raised on a Kibbutz tend to show more helping behaviour.

Check your understanding

1 Children in which cultures are more likely to demonstrate pro-social behaviour?
2 Children in which cultures are less likely to demonstrate pro-social behaviour?

Anti-social behaviour

The 2010 Gallup World Poll found that countries such as Mexico, which had the highest level of income inequality (this means countries who had a few people who are very rich but also many people who are very poor), also reported the highest levels of anti-social behaviour. In contrast, countries with a higher level of income tended to report higher levels of pro-social behaviour. The report showed a **correlation** between income inequality and anti-social behaviour.

Piotrowska *et al.* (2015) found similar results when they reviewed research that had been conducted in many countries across the world and found there is a correlation between anti-social behaviour and social economic status; more reports of anti-social behaviour were associated with people who have a lower income. Behaviours included fighting, bullying, lying, stealing and vandalism.

Research has shown that a key cultural influence on anti-social behaviour tends to be the economic status of the country. Being able to see injustice, for example, where a chosen few live in great wealth and most of the rest of the population live in poverty, can act as a trigger for anti-social behaviour such as vandalism, theft and aggressive acts.

Authority figures on obedience

Psychologists are interested in what makes us obey rules and what makes us break them.

During the Second World War many people lost their lives in concentration camps. Psychologists wanted to understand how the Nazis could commit such acts of atrocity. At his trial, one of these Nazis, Adolf Eichmann, who was responsible for much of the organisation of the concentration camps, expressed surprise that he had been taken to trial. In his eyes, he had only been 'following orders' and had therefore done nothing wrong.

▲ Adolf Eichmann on trial for war crimes committed during World War II.

Chapter 4 Social influence

Stanley Milgram, a famous psychologist, investigated the effects of situational factors on obedience. He was interested to see whether there was something different about the Nazis that caused them to commit such terrible crimes against humanity, or if anyone, given the right circumstances, would act in the same way. During the 1960s, he conducted many variations of a **controlled observation** into obedience called 'The Electric Shock' study. The research involved participants teaching a word list to a learner and administering an electric shock if the learner got a series of word pairs incorrect. A 'researcher' wearing a lab coat sat in the room with the participants and prompted the participants to continue giving shocks, even when they heard the 'learner' calling out and saying that he did not want to continue. When the participants asked the researcher who was responsible if something happened to the 'learner', the researcher would respond that the responsibility was his and not the participant's. What the participants didn't know was that the learner was actually a confederate who did not actually receive any shocks. Milgram found that 65 per cent of participants were willing to obey the researcher and go all the way to 450 volts on the shock generator. This led Milgram to believe that the Nazis were no different to other people and given the right situation, anyone would obey orders, even if it goes against their moral conscience. Milgram believed there were a number of situational factors that influenced participants to obey in his research including:

- the presence of a legitimate **authority figure**: the researcher wearing a lab coat
- the location of the research: it was held in a well-respected university
- the fact that the learner was in the other room and the participant couldn't actually see him
- the researcher had said he would take responsibility if anything happened to the 'learner'. This is called agency theory, where the legitimate authority figure says that they will take responsibility for any consequences.

Authority figure
Someone we perceive as having more power than ourselves.

Agency theory

Milgram proposed a theory that people obey orders that they know to be ethically wrong because they have moved from being in an **autonomous state**, where they have power over their own actions, to being in an **agentic state**, where they are acting as 'agents' of the authority figure and are therefore not responsible for their actions. In Milgram's experiment, the participants were acting as agents of the experimenter and understood that it was the experimenter's responsibility if anything happened to the learner.

Autonomous state
Where the individual feels responsible for their own actions.

Agentic state
An individual does not feel responsible for their actions as they are acting under orders from an authority figure.

Hofling (1966) conducted a field study into obedience. He had a confederate pose as a doctor in a hospital and give instructions to a nurse over the phone. They were told to give a patient some medicine, the dose of which was too high. In reality, it was not a real drug and could not have caused the patients any harm if it had been given to them. Hofling found that 21 out of 22 nurses obeyed the doctor's orders, despite the high dose and the fact that it was forbidden for them to take orders to give medication over the phone. When questioned afterwards, the nurses stated that in a busy hospital nurses are expected to follow doctor's orders, who might have disapproved if they had not obeyed. When Hofling asked a different set of nurses what they would do if they were in the same situation, almost all of them stated that they would not have followed the doctor's orders. This shows that what we say we will do and what we will actually do can be two very different things. Milgram found the same results with his electric shock experiment. When he questioned a wide range of people before he started his research, they all answered that they thought no one would obey the orders and shock the learner with the maximum strength of the shock generator.

> **STUDY HINT**
> Milgram's electric shock experiment is a really interesting study that many students are good at remembering the details of. However, don't forget you won't be asked specifically about this study in the exam. It is more important that you understand what it shows us about the effect of authority upon obedience.

> **Something to think about**
> Think about the one nurse in the Hofling experiment who did not obey the doctor's orders. With a partner make a list of as many reasons as you can as to why you think that one nurse did not obey.

For more information on field studies see page 182.

Charismatic leaders

Another theory as to why people obey authority figures is down to the leader themselves. House *et al.* (1991) suggest that it is the charismatic personality of the leaders that enables them to create a special bond with their followers and allows them to exert power. House *et al.* suggest that the charisma actually refers to the special relationship between leader and follower. The leader is seen as almost being superhuman and is idolised by his followers.

> **Something to think about**
> Can you think of any leaders who have charismatic personalities? Think about recent global political events. What was it about them that made people want to follow them? How did they create the relationship between themselves and their followers?

> **Extension**
> Search online for original footage of Milgram's 1963 experiment. What do you think of the **ethics** of Milgram's research?

Criticisms of the effect of situational factors

- **Themes focusing on situational factors suggest our behaviours are simply determined by what is happening around us and that we do not resist this.** It does not take into account our capacity to think and use our **free will** to make a conscious decision as to whether we will conform, follow the crowd, act pro or anti-socially or obey.
- **Deindividuation does not always lead to violence.** Research has shown that crowds do not necessarily become mindless and violent and actually deindividuation can be a positive experience. People can feel themselves as part of the crowd, losing their sense of individual self but in a good way as they are simply enjoying the atmosphere, such as at a music festival. It can also lead to pro-social behaviour.

STUDY HINT
Among the criticisms, you are expected to know the free will/**determinism** debate and how it related to the situational factors.

- **Not everyone conforms in the same way.** Psychologists often generalise their results to all cultures. However, some psychologists have found that people in individualist cultures are less likely to conform than those people in collectivist cultures.
- **If research only focuses on one area, then it may not give a valid representation of people's behaviour.** People may conform in some situations and not in others. This makes it hard to predict how they will behave. For example, students may conform at a new school to fit in but may not conform at a drama group that they have attended for several years, as they feel more confident expressing their own opinion.
- **The theories are reductionist in that they fail to take into account individual differences.** For example, people may be more willing to obey because they have a particular type of personality, rather than simply the situation that they find themselves in.
- **Milgram's results on obedience can be viewed as deterministic.** He assumed that people obeyed in his research study because of the situation that they found themselves in and had little free will over their behaviour. However, not everyone obeyed in his study and it could be argued that these people exercised their free will not to obey and perhaps it was something to do with their personality that enabled them to disobey the experimenter.
- **Many people have a problem with Milgram's theory because it would suggest the people who commit atrocious acts are not responsible for their actions and therefore should not be held accountable for them.** This is because Milgram's theory suggests that people are not responsible for what they do when acting on orders of a higher authority.
- **Too much of the research into cultural differences in pro-social behaviour is conducted on children.** However, as adults they may act in a very different way and it could just be that children's pro-social behaviour develops at different times in different cultures.
- **The situational theories do not explain why some people do not obey.** The situational argument is determinist because it assumes that anyone, given the right situation, would obey. However, it fails to explain why some people in the Milgram electric shock experiment refused to obey the orders of the experimenter.

For more information on the free will/determinism debate see page 78.

Check your understanding

1. According to Milgram, why do people obey authority figures?
2. What have researchers found is correlated with anti-social behaviour?
3. Explain what is meant by being in an agentic state.

OCR GCSE Psychology

Situational Factors Research Study: Bickman, (1974) – a study into the social power of a uniform.

Background

According to Leonard Bickman, obedience to authority is based on a number of different factors.

The clothing people wear often highlights them as someone in a position of authority, like a police officer in uniform. In the Milgram study, the researcher's lab coat showed the participants that he was an authority figure and it was this presence of authority which encouraged them to obey.

Research by Joseph and Alex (1972) has also shown you can determine someone's status, group membership and legitimacy from what they are wearing.

Challenge

Use the library or go online and find examples of clothes that demonstrate that someone is a figure of authority. What is it about those clothes that make people obey?

DIY

Write four different scenarios about obedience, making sure they are ethical, i.e. not asking someone to break the law. Use images of both males and females in authority, wearing the same uniform. Ask different people about the four scenarios and how likely they would be to obey in the different situations and whether they would react differently to the male and female figures. Scale the answers from 1–5 (extremely unlikely to obey - extremely likely to obey).

Is there a gender difference in the responses to the male or female in uniform?

Work out the **mean, median, mode** and **range** for male participants, where the figure in the image is female, and then where the figure in the image is male. Do the same for the female participants. Is there a gender difference in responses from your participants?

- How would you ensure that you conduct your research ethically?
- How would you ensure that answers were anonymous?
- What would you need to do to try and ensure your participants did not give socially desirable answers?
- Are there any other reasons, apart from gender difference, that could explain your results?

▲ A uniform can give the impression of authority.

Aim

The aim of this study was to investigate the degree of social power the uniform has on other people.

Hypothesis

A uniformed guard has more ability to influence individuals than the same person in a low-authority uniform, such as a milkman's, or someone wearing non-authoritative clothes.

Experiment 1

Method

Field experiment which took place on a street in Brooklyn, New York.

Design

It was an **independent measures design** as participants saw only one of three levels of authority: civilian, milkman and guard.

Materials

The three 'uniforms'.

Sample

153 adult pedestrians aged between 18 and 61 who happened to be on the street. The age of the participants was estimated by the experimenters. It was an **opportunity sample**.

Procedure

There were four white male experimenters aged eighteen to twenty. They were all of similar build and so all fitted into the same size suit.

They were not told the purpose of the experiment and were told to act in exactly the same way, regardless of the uniform they were wearing.

All of the experimenters completed about the same number of experimental sessions using the three different situations (Table 4.1) and three different uniforms (Table 4.2).

▼ Table 4.1 The three situations used by the experimenters

Situation	Description
Picking up a bag	E stopped the chosen participant and pointed to a small paper bag on the ground and said 'pick up this bag for me'. If the participant did not comply immediately, the E also said 'I have a bad back'.
Dime and meter	E stopped the chosen participant and pointed to a confederate standing beside a car parked next to a parking meter and said 'This fellow doesn't have any change. Give him a dime!' If the participant did not comply immediately, the E added that he did not have any change either.
Bus stop - no standing	E chose the participant if they were standing alone at the bus stop. The E approached them and said 'Don't you know you have to stand on the other side of this pole? The sign says 'No standing' (the no standing actually referred to the fact that it is illegal for a car to be parked/waiting in a bus stop). If the participant did not comply immediately, the E added 'Then the bus won't stop here, it's a new law'.

The experiment was conducted on week days with the majority of the data collected in the afternoons.

In addition to the variation in uniforms, the experimenters (E) also presented three different situations to examine whether the relationship between the uniform and social power generalised across different scenarios.

▼ Table 4.2 Uniforms worn by experimenters and their corresponding level of authority

Type of uniform	Description	Level of authority
Civilian	Sports jacket and tie	Lowest
Milkman	Dressed in white, carrying milkman's basket with empty milk bottles	Slightly higher
Guard	Similar to policeman, but with a different badge and insignia; no gun was carried	Highest

In all three situations, the participant was considered to have obeyed if he followed the experimenter's instructions. If the participant did not obey after the explanation was given, the experimenter left.

Results

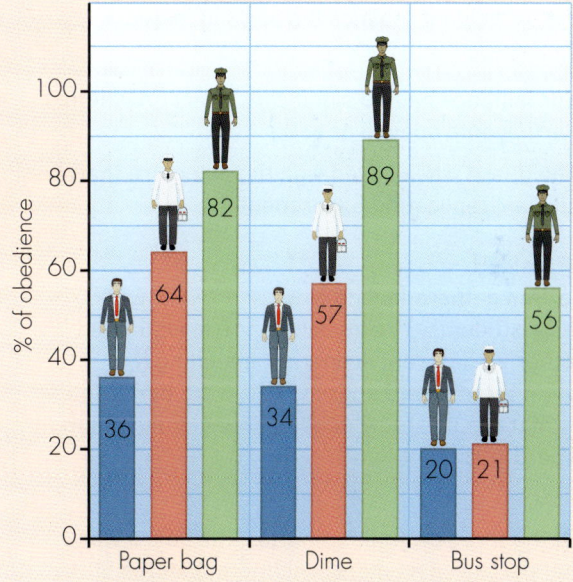

▲ Graph showing the percentages of participants who obeyed in the different conditions

Challenge

Look at the results in the graph above. How many different things can you say about the data? Why do you think there was a difference in levels of obedience between the paper bag and the dime and meter scenarios, compared to the bus stop?

The results showed that there was no significant difference in obedience between the civilian and the milkman uniforms across all three scenarios.

The guard was obeyed significantly more than the civilian.

Experiment 2

Experiment 2 is also a field experiment, which took place in another part of Brooklyn, New York. The participants were 48 adult pedestrians of an estimated average age of 46 years old. The dime and meter scenario was used, as in Experiment 1.

There were two independent variables.

- Two levels of authority were used: guard and civilian.
- Surveillance and non-surveillance: in the surveillance condition, the experimenter stood with the participant next to the parking meter while the confederate stood nearby the car. In the non-surveillance condition, the experimenter approached the participant in the street, asked them to give the dime, then walked away and was out of sight before the participant reached the parking meter.

Results

- Surveillance had no significant effect on whether participants obeyed or not.
- The guard was obeyed significantly more than the civilian, replicating Experiment 1.

Experiment 3A

Data was gathered using a questionnaire with 141 college students. The questionnaire investigated whether 29 different scenarios, including the original three from Experiment 1, were perceived as legitimate requests by either a young man, milkman or guard.

Results

- Of the three original scenarios, the guard was not perceived as more legitimate than the other uniforms when giving the order. This suggests that participants did not think the experimenter's uniform made their request any more legitimate.
- Some of the new scenarios were seen as more legitimate than others.

Experiment 3B

This experiment used 189 students from Smith College, who had not completed the previous questionnaire. Participants were asked to predict what they and people in general would do in one of the scenarios from Experiment 1.

Results

Results showed that participants did not think the guard would have more social power in these situations, compared to the milkman or the civilian.

Conclusions

- Wearing a uniform gives people more power and influence over others' behaviour than people not in uniform.
- The higher status the uniform is perceived to have, the more power it provides.
- How people *think* they would behave in a situation is not a good predictor of actual behaviour in that situation.
- Situational factors (type of uniform) have an influence on obedience in a real life setting with the higher the perceived status of the uniform resulting in increased obedience.

Criticisms

- **The participants were selected by opportunity sampling.** As the participants were selected opportunistically on the street, unknown factors could affect their behaviour. For example, if someone is rushing to get to a job interview, then they may be less likely to stop and pick up a piece of litter, regardless of who is giving the order.
- **The research is culturally biased.** The research only took place in a street in one city in America. Other cultures might react very differently in the same situation. Results could also differ within different areas of America.
- **The study was unethical as participants did not know they were being studied.** As it was a field experiment, participants did not know that they were taking part in a research study, therefore they did not give their consent to take part and were deceived. They might also have felt embarrassment at being asked to pick up litter or give someone a dime. Also, they were not debriefed after the experiment.
- **There was gender bias.** All of the confederates were male. If the person wearing a uniform had been female then the results might have been very different.
- **As it was a field experiment, there was little control over extraneous variables.** For example, researchers were unable to control the weather. If it was raining, it might have affected obedience levels as participants might have wanted to quickly get out of the rain.

> **Something to think about**
>
> Can you think of any other variables that the researchers might have been unable to control for? How might they have affected the results?

> **Extension**
>
> Think back to the original footage of the Milgram electric shock experiment that you watched. Think about the different reasons why the participants in the study obeyed. Can you make any comparisons with the Bickman study?

> **Check your understanding**
>
> 1. What was the **sampling method** used by Bickman *et al.*?
> 2. Where did the study take place?
> 3. Which 'uniform' were the participants most likely to obey?
> 4. Which 'uniform' were the participants least likely to obey?
> 5. What were the three situations in Experiment 1?
> 6. How did the results of Experiment 3A differ from Experiment 1?

Dispositional
How our own personality can affect whether or not we will obey or conform.

The effect of dispositional factors on behaviours

We will now focus on the effect of individual differences and personality (**disposition**) on conformity and obedience and crowd behaviour.

Self-esteem on conformity

Self-esteem is how we perceive ourselves. Someone with low self-esteem will generally have a low opinion of themselves and what they do. Someone with a high self-esteem will feel confident in who they are and how they behave.

Someone with a low self-esteem is more likely to conform, due to a lack of belief in their own ability, whereas someone with a high self-esteem is more likely to have confidence in their views and beliefs and is more likely to maintain their independent views. However, some degree of conformity is important for society to function effectively. We need to fit in with others ideas and plans to some degree even if we have high self-esteem, otherwise we would be continuously thinking of our own needs over others.

Kurosawa (1993) performed a recreation of Asch's line experiment in Japan. The researcher found that under high pressure, the participants with low self-esteem were more likely to conform. In another study in Japan, Tainaka *et al.* (2014) found that female participants who were all students at a university were more likely to agree with a co-witness to a crime and conform to their viewpoint if they had low self-esteem, even though unknown to them both, they actually saw different clips of the crime. Tainaka managed to get each pair to see the different clip, even though they were together when they saw it, by wearing special polarised glasses, which meant they were only able to see one of the two films which were projected on the screen.

Only female students were used in this research and Tainaka acknowledges that male participants might have behaved differently.

> **Something to think about**
>
> What do you think someone could do to have higher self-esteem? Have a discussion in class and write as many ideas as you can on the board. Use the internet to find more ideas and create a poster giving advice to someone suffering from low self-esteem. How good were the ideas you came up with in class? Were they the same as the ideas you found online? Do you think it would help someone avoid conforming?

For more information on the Asch line experiment see page 94.

Informational conformity can be explained by low self-esteem. People who are unsure of their ability to respond and behave in a 'correct' manner tend to look to others in the group for guidance and imitate their behaviour. This is because they assume the majority are correct and they do not have the self-belief to give a different answer or behave differently.

Locus of control in crowds

Julian Rotter first developed the idea of **locus of control** in 1954. He suggested that there were two types of locus of control: internal and external.

Internal locus of control

People who have an internal locus of control believe that they have the ability to control their decisions about their own lives and any success or failure is due to the choices that they have made. They tend to be more confident and more motivated than people with an external locus of control. However, if they do experience failure, they will blame themselves. People with an internal locus of control tend to be middle aged.

External locus of control

People with an external locus of control believe they have very little or no control over their own lives and how other people act around them. They may also believe that other people have control and they consequently have no option but to obey them. They tend to be passive and accepting of what fate has in store for them. People with an external locus of control tend to be young or elderly. Bradley and Webb, 1964, found that adults over 60 scored higher on a locus of control scale than those participants aged 35–50. Staats, 1974, looked at three age ranges: 5–15, 16–25 and 46–60. She found that internal locus of control increased with age.

Some people can have a mixture of both an internal and external locus of control, often depending on the situation. For example, a young person may have an internal locus of control at home, where they may feel that they have more control over the choices they make, and an external locus of control at school, where they believe their fate is in the hands of teachers.

In crowd situations, people with an internal locus of control are less likely to be influenced by how the crowd is behaving, not only because they believe they are in control of their own behaviour but also because they tend to be more confident. According to the University of West Virginia, people with an internal locus of control are more likely to take part in protests and they feel they can have an influence over changes in society. However, taking part in protests does not necessarily mean that their behaviour will become violent.

Ransford (1968) investigated violent behaviour in crowds. He questioned men immediately after a large-scale riot had taken place in America in 1965 and found that males with an external locus of control, and a feeling that they were not in control of the situation, reported to be more prepared to resort to violence to achieve their aims than those with an internal locus of control. After the 2011 London riots, of those who were brought before the courts, around half were aged under 21 and only 5 per cent were over the age of 40. If internal locus of control increases with age, then this would explain why only 5 per cent of the rioters who were charged were over the age of 40.

The effect of morality on pro-social and anti-social behaviour

Psychologist Lawrence Kohlberg (1968) conducted a **longitudinal study** into **morality**. He followed the same group of boys over a period of 12 years to see how their moral thinking changed and developed over time. As a result of this research, Kohlberg proposed his stage theory of moral development.

The theory has three levels and six stages:

Locus of control
How much control a person feels they have over their own life, with reference to external and internal factors.

> **Challenge**
>
> You can find out your own locus of control online. Search 'Locus of control questionnaire' online and take the questionnaire.
>
> Do you think your locus of control changes depending on the situation that you are in? Can you think of any examples where your locus of control might change?

Morality
Understanding what is right and wrong in how we think and behave. It includes being honest, truthful and responsible for your own actions.

Pre-conventional

Stage 1: This stage is all about **punishment**. At this stage, children are focused on the consequences of any action rather than whether the action has a value.

Stage 2: Action is based on what is most beneficial for the individual and sometimes for others – but generally only if there is an assumption that the other person will return the favour at some point.

Conventional

Stage 3: At this stage, action is about pleasing and getting approval from other people – being seen as 'good'. Behaviour is judged on what the intention was rather than just the action.

Stage 4: Behaviour in this stage is based around obeying authority and maintaining social order.

Post-conventional

Stage 5: Moral behaviour is defined by what has been agreed upon by society as a whole. The key aspect of this stage is what is considered 'lawful'.

Stage 6: In the final stage of moral development, behaviour is based on more abstract ideas of justice and what is ethical. Human rights and the respect for other human beings is seen as the most important element.

▲ Imitating pro-social behaviour

Challenge

Consider the following scenarios and decide at which level of moral development the children are in.
1. Georgia's friends try to persuade her to skip school and go into town with them but she refuses as she is worried that she will get in a lot of trouble.
2. Charlie meets a child refugee when returning from a holiday in France. He knows that it is against the law to bring the child into the country but the child is living in a very dangerous environment, with no one to protect him but he has family in the UK. Charlie decides that helping the child is more important than obeying the law.
3. Mohammed is asked by Thomas, another boy in his class, to tell the teacher that he was with him at lunchtime, to give Thomas an alibi because he was actually spraying graffiti in the boys' toilets at the time. Mohammed agrees because he is often in trouble himself and hopes that Thomas will do the same for him sometime.

Langdon *et al.* (2011) suggest that, according to Kohlberg's theory, anti-social behaviour is most common in the second stage of moral development, where morality is egocentric. This means that the focus is on what is right for the individual, rather than what is right for society. That doesn't mean that everyone who is in the second stage of moral development will automatically be anti-social. When people pass on to the next stage of moral development, where the focus is on getting approval from others, levels of anti-social behaviour drop and people begin to act in a more pro-social manner. Chen and Howitt (2007) found that young offenders who were in prison for crimes such as violent behaviour or theft were at a lower level of moral reasoning compared to a **control group**. Janssens and Dekovic (1997) found that children who grow up in an environment where their parents are supportive but also set rules for their children, are more likely to behave in a pro-social way and show higher levels of moral reasoning. This suggests that our family background is very important to how we think morally and whether or not we will behave in a pro-social or anti-social way.

Eisenberg (1987) suggested that those people who have a higher level of moral reasoning are less likely to act in an anti-social way because they hold themselves as responsible for the way in which they act.

The influence of the brain in dispositional factors

Researchers have found evidence that suggests that brain differences can have an effect on personality. For example, Argoskin *et al.* (2014) found a **positive correlation** between self-esteem and grey matter. People with low self-esteem tend to have reduced amounts of grey matter in the **hippocampus**. This area of the brain is associated with emotion and the ability to control stress levels. Therefore, there may be a **biological** element to conformity, as research has found that people with low self-esteem tend to be more conforming.

Research has also indicated an association between damage in the **prefrontal cortex** and faulty moral reasoning. Anderson *et al.* (1999) found that two individuals who had suffered brain damage to the prefrontal cortex as babies, were unable to understand the difference between right and wrong behaviour and showed personality traits similar to that of **psychopaths**.

Effect of the authoritarian personality on obedience

▲ Children who had very strict parents are more likely to grow up to obey those in authority.

Theodor Adorno (1950) wanted to explain how the Nazis were able to gain such a following in Germany during the Second World War. He suggested that rather than it being due to situational factors, such as becoming deindividuated by wearing a uniform, or the charismatic leadership of Hitler, it was something to do with the personality types of the individuals.

He proposed that a certain personality type, which he called the **authoritarian personality**, was more likely to obey those in authority and discriminate against those that they saw as inferior.

Adorno tested his theory by developing a questionnaire which he called the F-scale (F standing for Fascism). He found that people who had an authoritarian personality:
- see the world in 'black and white', meaning that rules were absolute and if someone breaks the law, regardless of the reason, they should be punished
- offer blind obedience to those they see as being of a higher authority to themselves

---

Something to think about
Kohlberg didn't think that many people would reach the final stage of development. Why do you think this is?

For more information on the hippocampus see page 122.

Neuropsychology now
Brain differences may affect people's personality. For example, having less grey matter in the hippocampus is correlated with low self-esteem.

Psychopath
Someone who has a mental illness which is defined by having a lack of empathy for other people and a tendency to act immorally.

Authoritarian personality
A personality type that is very obedient to authority.

STUDY HINT
If you get asked to outline the effect of <u>one</u> dispositional factor you can choose from self-esteem, locus of control, morality and the authoritarian personality. All are relevant and credit worthy.

- are contemptuous and prejudiced against those they see as being inferior to themselves
- are very conformist.

Adorno found that people who scored highly on the F-scale had often been subjected to a very strict and rigid upbringing, particularly by their fathers, of whom they were consequently afraid. He suggested that as they saw their father as a figure of authority, they were unable to express their negative feelings directly towards him. Instead they displace these feelings onto someone weaker.

Milgram and Elms (1966) retested participants from his electric shock experiment. Half of the participants had defied orders to administer the full 450 volt electric shock and the other half had obeyed. Participants were asked to take part in further research in which they were given Adorno's F-scale. Milgram and Elms found that significantly more of the obedient participants scored highly on the F-scale, compared to those who had been defiant.

This study offers more evidence to support Adorno's theory that those with an authoritarian personality would be more likely to obey an authority figure.

> **For more information on Milgram's electric shock experiment see page 99.**

Criticisms

- **Dispositional explanations focus too much on the individual, making generalisations difficult.** To tackle issues like disobedience and anti-social behaviour, we need to be able to identify situations where we can predict anti-social behaviour and create interventions that can address this and encourage pro-social behaviour instead.
- **Dispositional explanations of conformity and obedience are reductionist.** They ignore the evidence that suggests that we are also influenced by those around. Therefore it does not give us a complete picture of why people conform and obey.
- **Kohlberg's research is not generalisable.** It is biased to Western cultures and does not take into account other cultures' perspectives on morality. This means that it may not give a valid idea of the levels of morality in other cultures.
- **Locus of control may not be a good explanation for crowd behaviour as people can have a different locus of control depending on the situation that they are in.** Therefore, this may make behaviour harder to predict and may not offer a useful explanation for how people behave in crowd situations.
- **Authoritarian personality does not explain why people who have not experienced harsh parenting are obedient.** The theory is limited in that it only really explains one aspect of why people obey. It cannot be generalised to people who have not experienced harsh parenting.
- **Kohlberg's research is gender biased.** Kohlberg's research on moral development only used a male **sample**. The results from this research were used to create the stages of his theory. Gilligan, another psychologist, found that females generally score lower on the scale than males, leading Gilligan to suggest that females may view morality in a different way to males – that males are more focused on justice, while females focus more on caring. This means that Kohlberg's theory may not offer a good view of why females behave in pro or anti-social ways.

Check your understanding

1. According to Adorno, why are people with an authoritarian personality more likely to obey?
2. Why is having a low self-esteem going to make you more likely to conform?
3. What is the difference between an internal and external locus of control?
4. How are people with an internal locus of control more likely to behave in a crowd situation?
5. What is the link between morality and pro-social behaviour?

Dispositional Factors Research Study: NatCen Morrell, Scott, McNeish, Webster, (2011) – a study into the August riots in England.

Background

Rioting took place in London from 6 August to 11 August 2011. It started during a peaceful protest in response to the fatal shooting of Mark Duggan by the police.

> **STUDY HINT**
> Although this study looks at different areas in London where rioting took place, you only need to be familiar with the events that took place in Tottenham.

Background to the Tottenham riot

Tottenham has a history of rioting. In 1985, a protest started outside a police station following the death of a local woman who collapsed during a raid on her home. This became violent and that evening a police officer was killed during intense rioting on the Broadwater Farm estate. Although there has been some improvement, those interviewed for the study reported a deeply ingrained mistrust of the police.

Tottenham is an area of high unemployment, due to a declining local industry, and 48 per cent of children who live there are classified as living in poverty.

Interviewees viewed the future as hopeless for young people due to very few opportunities.

However, Tottenham was still viewed as a good place to live where openness and tolerance were valued, and there was a sense of belonging among the various different communities.

Community stakeholders suggested that the recent investments in local secondary schools were starting to pay off with increased educational achievement, but it was acknowledged that this had come too late for those who had left **education**.

Aim

The aim of the study/report was to investigate what had triggered the August 2011 riots and the extent and nature of the youth involvement.

Hypothesis

Morrell *et al.* wanted to know why young people got involved in the riots.

They did not have specific hypotheses but the report was broken down into the following sections:

- What occurred in Tottenham based on police, media and eyewitness reports.
- Who was involved.
- Why and how young people were involved.

Method

Research method/design

This report was prepared for the Cabinet Office by Morrell *et al.* on behalf of the National Centre for Social Research (NatCen).

Sample

In Tottenham, 36 participants were interviewed.

The sample comprised an even split between over and under eighteen year olds and a diversity of gender, **ethnicity** and work status, although the vast majority were still in education.

Procedure

Data was gathered only five weeks after the riots had taken place.

The researchers were careful to gain fully informed consent from their participants. Participants were assured that the research was both confidential and anonymous. However, while the researchers agreed not to report any criminal activity that took place before the research, they explained that they would have to report any details of potential future criminal activity, such as if a participant disclosed any plans to commit a crime in the future or to harm others.

Participants were interviewed individually or in groups of two or four; some participants felt more comfortable in a group situation.

Community stakeholders and participants from the areas unaffected by the riots were interviewed in focus groups.

What happened in Tottenham?

There was an alleged incident between the police and a girl. This incident was described as the trigger for the peaceful protest becoming violent by participants.

6 August 2011

16.00	Family and friends of Mark Duggan gather outside Tottenham police station. The protest is peaceful and around 300 people join the demonstration.
19.20	Bottles are thrown at police cars near the police station and one of the vehicles is set alight.
20.20	Riot officers and police on horseback arrive to disperse the crowds but are attacked by protesters using bottles, fireworks and other missiles.
20.45	The London Fire Brigade receives its first call to attend.
22.45	Shops are set alight.

The rioting continued until 06:15am on 7 August and by 12.00pm the fire brigade had the fires under control.

Results

Who was involved?

The **interview** data proposed that a wide range of different people were involved, including a mixture of age groups, ethnicities and people who were employed, unemployed or still in education or training.

The researchers used the data to create different categories of involvement in the riots, as shown in Table 4.3. Some young people were involved in more than one activity. For example, some were both rioters and looters.

▼ Table 4.3 Categories of involvement in the riots:

Watchers: young people who were present during the incidents and observed what happened but did not personally become involved in the criminal activity	1. Bystanders: young people who happened to be there - either because they lived locally or were passing through at the time of the rioting. 2. The curious: young people who deliberately chose to be there so they could see what was going on.
Rioters: young people who were actually involved in violent disturbances and vandalism	1. Protesters: young people who were acting out because they were upset about the death of Mark Duggan. 2. Retaliators: young people who acted to get their own back on the 'system' or the police. 3. Thrill-seekers: young people who got involved because they enjoyed the excitement or 'buzz'.
Looters: young people involved in breaking into shops, stealing from broken-into shops or stealing goods that had been left on the street	1. Opportunists: young people who saw the chance to steal things for themselves or their family, or to sell. 2. Sellers: young people who planned their involvement to maximise their 'profits'.
Non-involved: young people who did not take part	1. Stay-aways: young people who chose not to get involved or observe. 2. Wannabes: young people who weren't there but would have liked to have been.

Source: Gareth Morrell et al., The August riots in England: Understanding the involvement of young people, *NatCen*, 2011, p25

Why did people get involved (or not)?

Key motivations for getting involved in the rioting and looting were found to be: benefiting from an exciting experience; having the opportunity to acquire items without paying, either to keep or to sell on for profit; and getting back at the police.

The young people identified different factors that influenced their involvement in the riots:

Nudge factors: these were things that *encouraged* them to get involved.

Tug factors: these were things that *discouraged* them from getting involved.

In both nudge and tug factor, there were a range of situational (social) and dispositional (individual) factors involved.

The factors are summarised in the tables below.

▼ Table 4.4 Dispositional/individual factors affecting decision-making in young people.

	Nudge factors	Tug factors
Previous criminal activity	Easy to get involved: 'this is what they do around here'.	Been caught once, know the risks.
Attitude towards authority	Cynicism towards politicians, authority figures. Negative experience with the police.	No negative experience with the police.
Prospects	Poor job prospects, low income, limited hope for the future: 'nothing to lose'.	In work or having expectations of future work, aspirations for the future: 'a lot to lose'.

Source: Gareth Morrell et al., The August riots in England: Understanding the involvement of young people, *NatCen*, 2011, p34

▼ Table 4.5 Other factors affecting the decision-making in young people.

	Nudge factors	Tug factors
Family attitudes	Relatives not disapproving.	Relatives not approving: 'not brought up like that'.
Community	Attachment to a community with a culture of low-level criminal activity.	Attachment to a community with pro-social values (including religious communities).
Belonging	Little sense of ownership or stake in society.	Sense of ownership or stake in society.
Poverty and materialism	Desire for material goods but no means to pay for them.	Adequate resources to purchase the desired goods.

Source: Gareth Morrell et al., The August riots in England: Understanding the involvement of young people, *NatCen*, 2011, p34

Challenge

Make a matching game using the different nudge and tug factors. Write the nudge and tug factors and the situational and dispositional factors onto separate pieces of card. Spread them out on a table face down and match them up. Did you get them in the right group? Were you correct?

Summary of results

- It was a day like no other for the young people involved. Normal rules did not seem to apply, leading to atypical behaviour.
- Decisions about whether to get involved were based on what the young people thought was right or wrong and whether they thought the benefits outweighed the risks.

Conclusions

Anti-social criminal behaviour is influenced by:

- collective behaviour/group processes
- dispositional/individual factors
- what young people believe is right and wrong
- an individual's assessment of the risks and benefits of involvement.

Criticisms

- **People's memory of events is not always reliable.** The participants were interviewed five weeks after the event. The study used retrospective data. After this time, their memories of the event might have faded or been distorted by talking to others about the event or by seeing media coverage of the riots.

- **A distrust of authority may have affected participants' honesty.** Many of the young people involved in the riots had an intense distrust of those they see as authority figures. As the data relied on **self-report**, they might not have been honest about their involvement or the reasons behind their involvement.

- **Participants might have been affected by social desirability when responding to the interviewers.** They might have given the answers they thought made them sound good. This could have worked both ways, either a person with a criminal background exaggerating their involvement or the reasons behind it to make themselves sound tougher, or someone who did not get involved citing reasons such as believing it was wrong when the real motivation might have been a lack of opportunity.

- **The researchers had difficulty recruiting participants, making it hard to generalise the results.** As they wanted to get the data as soon as possible after the event, so that the memory was as fresh as possible, they did not have time to build relationships and trust with the communities. Many of the young people did not want to disclose their involvement in the riots, meaning the researchers had to then recruit participants from those who had been sent to **prison** for their involvement. However, this sample of prisoners may not have represented all of the people who took part in the riots – for example, they might have been arrested as they had been in trouble before and were therefore known to the police. Their reasons for taking part in the riot might have been very different from someone who had never been in trouble before.

DIY

Carry out an **observation** in school or a similar setting, on different occasions: one where there is more of a crowd, and one where there are fewer people around. Decide how long each observation should last – keep it the same for both. During the observation focus on a particular number of people (e.g. for five mins at a time) and keep a record of their behaviour to see if they do anything they should not be doing. When are people more likely to break rules or norms: in crowds or not?

You do not need people's consent to carry out this observation. Can you suggest why not? You may also find it useful to carry out the observation with a second researcher. Can you explain why? Are you going to collect **quantitative** or **qualitative data** or both? Justify your decision.

Extension

Go to the original report and read about what happened in the other towns. How did the other riots differ to Tottenham's? How were they similar? (Go to www.gov.uk and search for the 'August Riots in England' and it will give you access to the PDF document.)

Check your understanding

1. What was the specific incident that was thought to have sparked the riots in Tottenham?
2. How long did the riot in Tottenham last?
3. Who were the main people involved in the rioting?
4. Which dispositional factors explain why people got involved in the riots?
5. Which dispositional factors explain why people did not get involved in the riots?

Application: changing attitudes
How minority influence affects social change in relation to mental health stigma and discrimination

It might seem common sense that majority influence is more powerful than **minority influence**, as there are many more voices. However, evidence has shown that minorities can be extremely powerful at changing public opinion and behaviour. For example, in the late 1800s and early 1900s, women in the suffragette movement fought for the right to vote. As a minority group, they were prepared to sacrifice their personal well-being and safety in order to ensure equality for women. Additionally, in the American civil rights movement, when Rosa Parks refused to give up her bus seat for a white person simply because she was black, this act of defiance was enough to spark social change.

Moscovici (1985) had a theory of why and how minorities are able to influence the majority. He proposed the following three key elements:
1. The message that the minority put forward must be consistent. They must not change the message as it will not be as effective.
2. The minority must show how committed it is to the cause.
3. The argument must be persuasive. For example, having a charismatic representative giving a speech or being used for an advertising campaign will make the majority more likely to change their view to that of the minority. It is important that the majority change their view both internally and externally.

Charities and government organisations, such as Mind, Time to Change and Young Minds, all campaign to increase awareness of mental health problems and how people who are experiencing issues with their mental health can seek support and help. At the same time, they are campaigning to reduce the **stigma** and **discrimination** associated with mental health.

In 2016, members of the Royal Family spearheaded a campaign called Heads Together, which was designed to reduce the stigma of mental health. Prince Harry has talked about his regret at not speaking out more about his grief and **depression** when his mother, Princess Diana, died. Prince William, Prince Harry and Catherine, Duchess of Cambridge, are all persuasive, charismatic voices and by encouraging people to talk about mental illness, they help reduce the stigma. The prominence of this family has resulted in the campaign being publicised in the national press, which has widened the number of people who have heard about the campaign.

Time to Change go into schools to discuss issues around stigma and mental health and train young people to become leaders, who will teach and challenge other students about mental health stigma. These young people have often experienced mental health problems and the effect of mental health discrimination first-hand. By hearing this persuasive account by one of their peers, the students are more likely to be persuaded to change their views and behaviour towards students experiencing mental health problems, and in turn act as **role models** for other children in challenging discrimination.

Minority influence
The idea that small groups of people can change the opinion and beliefs of larger groups of people.

For more information on stigma and discrimination see page 59.

STUDY HINT
The examination will focus on what are called 'synoptic' elements. This is where you have to make links between different topic areas. Here is a good example of when you could make a link between Psychological Problems and Social Influence.

Challenge
See if you can apply Moscovici's theory of minority influence to the Heads Together campaign. Google the campaign first, to find out more about how the campaign works and what different things the Royal Family has been involved in to promote the campaign.

▲ Members of the Royal Family have spearheaded a campaign to reduce the stigma of mental health.

STUDY HINT
Take care with questions about 'minority influence' and 'majority influence'. It would be easy to mix up the words 'minority' and 'majority' in the pressure of an exam.

Another way that minorities are able to influence majorities is through the snowball effect (Van Avermaet, 1996). Members of the minority slowly change the opinion of the majority and as more people adopt the minority view, it could eventually become the majority view. By changing one person's opinion of mental health, that person could speak with their family and friends and they too will change their opinion, triggering a snowball effect.

How majority influence affects social change in relation to mental health stigma and discrimination

Major mental health charities often aim to reduce the stigma of mental illness through the use of nationwide campaigns that seek to explain and normalise mental health. We have seen that majority influence is where the majority of the group try to influence others to conform to their beliefs. Therefore, the majority could help change the minority's discriminatory view by trying to get them to conform to the group norm and internalise the beliefs and behaviour, rather than just complying.

In 2014, Time to Change launched a national campaign called 'Time to Talk' to get people talking about mental health to try and reduce the stigma surrounding it. It is an annual event that takes place every February. Time to Change encourage school and workplaces to sign up and spend the day having conversations about mental health. People can then log their conversations on the Time to Change website. In 2017, over 29,000 conversations were logged, showing that the campaign was having a significant impact. Schools can sign up to receive emails from Time to Change giving details of the next 'Time to Talk' day, so that they can get involved.

The National Attitudes to Mental Illness survey, which was first conducted in 1993, also shows the impact of Time to Change's national campaigning about mental health. According to the Time to Change website, since the campaign began in 2011, around two million people in the UK have shown an improvement in their **attitudes** towards people with mental illness. This demonstrates that majority influence can have a significant impact on people's attitudes.

Attitudes
Feelings of like or dislike towards something.

At school if you were trying to reduce stigma surrounding mental health, the majority of the class could avoid using stigmatising vocabulary. If the majority of the class stopped using it, then the minority who still used such language might feel compelled to stop so that they are still part of the 'in-group'.

Challenge

As a class, design a campaign to reduce the stigma of mental health for your own school. Have a look at the Time to Change website for ideas and materials. Think about the psychology we have covered in this chapter and Chapter 3. What information could you use to help your campaign?

Additionally, mental health stigma could be reduced if we discussed it in the same way as a physical health problem. Not being able to see the medical ailment does not mean it isn't there. If someone is off school with a mental health issue, the majority group should welcome them back when they return and include them in activities, as though they had been away with a broken arm. Through seeing this, those in the minority who perhaps do not understand mental health and so stigmatise it, may feel more able to follow the lead of the majority and help include the person back into the school. This could help change their attitude towards mental illness.

SUMMARY

In this chapter, we have learnt that other people can influence our behaviour in a variety of ways. For example, when we are in a group environment, we often conform because we want to fit in, or we follow and imitate those we assume know better than us. We obey because we assume that the person in authority holds responsibility in case the order has negative consequences.

The Bickman study has shown that we will also obey those who have the appearance of authority, even if that authority is not legitimate, for example, if someone is wearing an authoritarian uniform, but actually have no authority at all.

In crowds, some psychologists believe we behave out of character because we have lost our sense of individuality and taken on the crowd mentality; we have become deindividuated. Other psychologists believe that we act with the crowd because we share a common social identity, whether it be living in the same area or supporting the same cause. Additionally, the Morrell *et al.* research has found that young people join in rioting behaviour for a number of complex reasons. Some people do it for personal gain, such as looting, while others feel swept along by events or see it as an excuse to 'get back' at those in authority.

By learning about how social influence works, psychologists can use this knowledge to help make positive changes to society, such as finding the most effective ways to reduce prejudice and discrimination towards people experiencing mental health problems.

Chapter 4 Social influence

Practice questions

The questions in this textbook have been written by the authors, Mark Billingham and Helen Kitching. They have not been produced or endorsed by OCR.

1 Explain the difference between pro-social behaviour and anti-social behaviour. **[3 marks]**

Pro-social behaviour is behaviour that benefits society. Anti-social behaviour is behaviour that is likely to cause harm or distress to an individual or individuals who are not from the same household. Pro-social behaviour tends to result in positive outcomes for the person who displays it, whereas anti-social behaviour has the potential to have negative consequences for the person that displays it.

One mark is awarded for an accurate statement showing what pro-social behaviour is. Another is awarded for an accurate a statement showing what anti-social behaviour is. A third mark is awarded for a distinction that draws out another feature of these two behaviours.

2

> **Family Influence**
>
> Bindiya's family expect to have a say in who she marries. She would rather be able to make the decision independently, but instead goes along with her family's decisions.

Using your knowledge of situational factors, explain why Bindiya allows her family to influence who she marries. **[4 marks]**

Bindiya respects her parents and therefore will listen to their views on whom she should marry. They know her well and want her to be happy, so she needs to trust that they will choose well for her. If she went against their wishes, she might disappoint them and she doesn't want to do that.

One mark for a response that reads like a common sense answer. Although the family situation can count as a relevant factor, it does not allow the candidate to demonstrate what they know about situational factors from studying psychology. A stronger response might focus on the majority influence of the family and how this makes Bindiya conform. Alternatively, it could also look at obedience to authority or the effects of culture on pro-social behaviour.

3 Describe the brain's influence on dispositional factors related to social influence. **[4 marks]**

Dispositional factors refer to our personality. Researchers have found evidence that brain differences can affect our personality. For example, researchers found a positive correlation between self-esteem and grey matter. Those people with high self-esteem tend to have more grey matter in the hippocampus, the area of the brain linked to emotion and the control of stress. Also, people who have damage in the prefrontal cortex tend to have problems understanding the difference between what is right and wrong, which makes them have a similar personality to a psychopath.

Relevant parts of the brain have been identified and accurately related to key dispositional factors. The level of detail demonstrates understanding of the links. This is a good enough response to earn all four marks.

4 Describe and evaluate the effect of **two** dispositional factors on social behaviour. [8 marks]

One factor is authoritarian personality. Adorno thought that some people were obedient because they had an authoritarian personality. He suggested that as children these people had very strict upbringings, especially by their fathers. They saw their father as an authority figure and could not express their negative feelings towards him. Instead, they displaced those feelings towards people they saw as weaker than them. This caused them to act in a prejudiced way towards those they saw as inferior, but very obediently towards those they saw as being in authority.

One problem with this theory is it doesn't explain why people who have not had a very strict upbringing are obedient.

Another factor is locus of control. People who have an internal locus of control believe that they are able to control what happens in their lives. They tend to be quite confident and motivated. However, if things go wrong, they tend to blame themselves. These people are less likely to obey or be open to social influence in general. People with an external locus of control don't think they have much control over their lives or how people act around them. They tend to be passive and accepting of what happens to them. They would also be more likely obey without question, or to be influenced in general.

A criticism of locus of control is that people might have a different locus if control depending on the situation, making behaviour hard to predict.

The candidate has selected two relevant dispositional factors and then described them with clarity and related them appropriately to social influence. This part of the answer is strong and earns all four AO1 marks. The evaluation is weak in comparison and relies on two brief points – one criticism for each factor. This earns just two of the AO3 marks on offer. In total, the answer gets six marks.

5 Use your knowledge and understanding from across the psychology course to explain how far you agree with the following viewpoint:

'It is more valid to study behaviour using natural situations rather than situations which have been set up.'

In your answer you should refer to the NatCen (2011) study into the August riots in England, and **at least one** other study from psychology. **[13 marks]**

> Psychologists often use laboratory settings to conduct their research because it allows them to have much more control and can make the results reliable when establishing cause and effect. However, a laboratory setting can sometimes affect the ecological validity of the study because it is too different from real life situations.
>
> Researchers looking at the effects of conformity in emergency situations used a controlled setting for their research, but set it up to look like a normal room where participants were filling in a questionnaire. This allowed them to create an event that looked like an emergency but was actually controlled. They caused smoke to blow into the room to see whether participants would report it if the other people in the room (confederates) ignored it. If the participants were in a room with a real fire, the study would have been really unethical, and people could have got hurt. However, the participants did not know the smoke wasn't real, so it was a valid way to study the behaviour.
>
> Zimbardo's prison experiment was carried out in a controlled setting as well, but set up to look and feel like a real prison. Arguably, the study had ecological validity and gave a good idea of why people behave in different ways when they are in that type of situation.
>
> The NatCen study looked at a real life event — the Tottenham riots. The data was gathered about five weeks after the event. It's good that the data was gathered quite soon after, as people should still have been able to remember what happened quite clearly. However, other things could have happened to interfere with people's memory of the events, making the data less valid.

By interviewing the young people who were directly involved with the riots, researchers should have been able to gather valid data about a real life event. However, an issue with studying real life events such as the Tottenham riots is that the participants may not have been honest about what they did and why they did it. They might have been afraid of getting into trouble, even though the researchers said that they would not report any past criminal activity. If the young people were not honest about their involvement or motivations, this would have affected the validity of the results.

It is possible to set up controlled research so that it is like a real life situation, but still be able to control variables. This means that research done under controlled situations can be valid and give us an idea of how people would behave in real life. It is useful to be able to research real life events as well, but there are issues with this too. It is much harder to control for extraneous variables that could affect the results.

This response demonstrates strong analytical skills and presents a well-balanced argument about the strengths and weaknesses of both setting up situations and of studying those which are naturally occurring. The points are well developed and easy to follow, securing all seven AO3 marks.

The candidate refers to the NatCen study as required, as well as bringing in other relevant studies. However, their coverage of the NatCen study is quite brief and describes it implicitly rather than explicitly. The student clearly understands the study, but can only earn three AO1 marks. In total, the response is worth ten marks.

5 Memory

Brain structure

This refers to the different parts of the brain.

Semantic memory

Memory of facts, names or general knowledge, for example knowing who the Prime Minister is. You don't have to have to know the time and place to be able to answer.

Autobiographical memory

Memories that we collect during our lifetime, of things we have done and places we have been.

Auditory cortex

The part of the brain that processes information it receives from the ears.

Information processing

Taking sensory information and changing it, like a computer to produce an output.

This chapter looks at some of the theories of memory put forward by cognitive psychologists. They are interested in how our memory works and why we sometimes cannot recall things. They are also interested in which parts of the brain are involved in memory and what happens if we damage these parts of the brain. Neuropsychology has allowed us to actually look at those parts of the brain, and different types of brain imaging scans let us see what activity is taking place while we recall or learn different things. It also allows us to see which parts of the brain have been damaged if someone has an injury. Cognitive psychologists are also interested in how accurate memory is and how easy it is to manipulate someone's memory.

This chapter should enable you to:

- develop awareness of how our thought processes can be compared to a computer, how and why we forget, and the different parts of the brain involved in memory
- be able to explain and criticise the structure and process of the multi-store model of memory including sensory store, short-term memory, long-term memory, and the differences between the stores in terms of duration, capacity and encoding, and rehearsal versus meaning
- develop an understanding of different types of forgetting including decay, displacement, and retrieval failure
- describe and criticise the Wilson *et al.* (2008) Clive Wearing study
- explain and criticise the structure and process of the theory of reconstructive memory, with reference to schemas, the role of experience and expectation on memory, the effect of leading questions, confabulation, distortion, and the reductionism/holism debate
- describe and criticise the Braun *et al.* (2002) study into how advertising can change our memories of the past
- demonstrate an understanding of memory research into techniques used for recall, including measuring different memory functions.

Key concepts of memory

Cognitive psychologists are interested in 'internal mental processes', or in other words, how we think and perceive the world and how our memories are formed. **Cognitive** psychologists test their ideas scientifically and a lot of research in this area takes place in a laboratory under controlled conditions. This means that psychologists can measure the effects of the **independent variables** on the **dependent variable** and minimise any **extraneous variables** which could affect the dependent variable. For example, psychologists could test whether learning words that have been put in categories are easier to recall than words that are just presented in a random order. By doing the **experiment** under laboratory conditions, psychologists can control extraneous variables such as noise, which could affect the participants' ability to concentrate on what they are learning.

Information processing

Cognitive psychologists look at how the brain works compared to a computer. They believe there are five main stages of **information processing**. In the first stage, the information is **input** into the brain through the body's senses, such as sight and sound.

These are registered by the eyes and the ears which send the information through to the brain. The information is then **encoded**. That means that it is changed from one format, like sound waves such as music or words that enter the ear, to nerve impulses which travel up to the **auditory cortex** in the brain. Here, they are decoded and converted into what we perceive as sounds.

The information is then held there so that it can be retrieved at a later date. This is called **storage**. The information can then be recalled from memory, which is a process known as **retrieval**.

The final stage is **output**, where the information that you have retrieved from memory is used in some way. This could be by saying someone's name that you have recalled or just having a thought that you have recalled from an earlier time.

Input
Where information enters the body through the senses.

Encoding
Information is transformed into a format that we can understand. For example, sounds waves being transformed into music

Storage
Where information is kept within the brain.

	Input	Encoding	Storage	Retrieval	Output
Computer	Downloading a song.	The computer turns it into computer code, such as binary.	You save the song on the hard drive in a folder.	You go into the folder and find the song you have saved.	You play the song on your computer.
Human	Perceiving sensory information from the environment, such as hearing a song on the radio.	The information is converted into nerve impulses, where it is recognised by the brain.	Information is stored in the brain.	You search the memory store for the information (song) you want to recall.	You sing the song you have just recalled.

▲ Table 5.1 How a computer compares to a human brain.

Structure and functions of the brain

> ### Neuropsychology now
> The role of the **hippocampus** in memory
>
> The hippocampus is a horseshoe-shaped part of the brain that is involved in making new memories. It forms part of the **limbic system**. Psychologists think that new memories must pass through the hippocampus before entering long-term storage. The hippocampus is thought to be particularly important for creating **semantic** memories of facts and **autobiographical memories**. However, research has shown that people with damage to the hippocampus can still form memories for new skills. After information from the different sensory information has been decoded in the sensory areas of the brain, it is combined by the hippocampus into one single experience.
>
> Autobiographical memory contains both semantic and episodic memories. For example, we know when and where we were born but will not have memories of these actual events, so these are semantic memories. However, they are also part of our personal history, so form part of autobiographical memory.

Retrieval
Recalling information from where it is stored in memory.

Output
Using the information that you have retrieved.

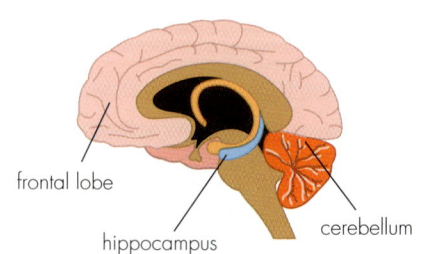

Episodic memory

Memories of places, events and people.

> Actual memories of past events, such as our birthday parties, are **episodic memories** but also part of our past history, so are also autobiographical. (remember, an autobiography is a book people write about themselves and what they have done, experienced and achieved during their life).

> **Something to think about**
>
> Maguire *et al.* (2000) studied London Black Cab taxi drivers. They found that the hippocampus in the taxi drivers was significantly greater in volume than that of a control group. They concluded that either the difference found was because the taxi drivers were born with this difference and that predisposed them to take a job as a taxi driver or that learning and retaining a huge amount of information about London roads had actually caused a change in the volume of the hippocampus.
>
> If we are able to change the volume of parts of our brain with practice, what do you think this might mean for people who have had brain injuries?

Anterograde amnesia and retrograde amnesia

Amnesia is a condition which can significantly affect a person's ability to recall stored memories or to form new memories. A number of different things can cause amnesia, such as a brain injury, illness or psychological reasons like post-traumatic stress disorder. Certain drugs also cause amnesia such as some of those prescribed to treat Parkinson's disease. Illegal drugs can also cause memory loss.

There are different types of amnesia.

The role of the hippocampus in anterograde memory

People who have **anterograde amnesia** are unable to form, or have problems forming, new memories because the information is unable to pass from short-term to long-term memory. This is because there is usually damage to the hippocampus, a vital element in the formation of new memories. Information from short-term memory is not able to pass through the hippocampus to be turned into long-term memory. People with damage to the hippocampus can usually hold conversations with people as the information stays in their short-term memory. However, they will be unlikely to remember the conversation later.

> **STUDY HINT**
>
> If you are trying to remember the difference between anterograde and retrograde amnesia, think about what 'retro' means – things from the past. Therefore, people with retrograde amnesia have trouble recalling things from their past.

The role of the frontal lobe in retrograde amnesia

Retrograde amnesia is where people cannot recall existing memories from their long-term memory. This could be anything from not being able to recall what happened just before an accident, to being completely unable to remember their past. Having this type of amnesia is much more severe than simply forgetting something. People with Alzheimer's disease also experience retrograde amnesia. Damage to the **frontal lobe** – the part of the brain located behind your forehead – can result in retrograde amnesia. Research has suggested that there is a relationship between frontal lobe damage and retrograde amnesia in Alzheimer's patients. **Remote memory tests** were performed on participants with frontal lobe damage and the results were significant; retrograde amnesia was positively correlated with having frontal lobe damage (Mayes, 1986).

People can experience *both* anterograde and retrograde amnesia.

Anterograde amnesia

The inability to form new memories after damage.

Retrograde amnesia

The inability to recall memories from the past, after damage.

Frontal lobe

A part of the brain that is its 'control centre' and is responsible for functions such as planning, organisation and making judgements.

Remote memory test

This test looks at how accurate someone's memory is of their distant past.

Procedural memory

It is responsible for 'motor' skills. These are things like walking and being able to feed ourselves.

The role of the cerebellum in procedural memory

Procedural memory is sometimes also called our motor skills. It is our memory for how to do things and is stored in our long-term memory. For example, one of the first things we learn to do using procedural memory is feed ourselves. Other types of procedural memory might be our ability to remember how to ride a bike or play the piano. Research has shown the damage to the **cerebellum** can affect our procedural memory and stop us learning new skills or improving on old ones. The cerebellum is not the only part of the brain involved in procedural memory but it is the part that helps to time and co-ordinate complex movements. This is why damage to this part of the brain would make it difficult to learn to knit, for example.

Cerebellum
This part of the brain can be found at the back of the skull. It is responsible for the ability to learn sequences of movements and our motor control. It is important for procedural and semantic memory.

Sensory store
Where information goes first and is held there very briefly.

Attention
This allows us to select information, which is then encoded.

> **Something to think about**
>
> If you want to find out more about cases of amnesia, you can find lots of cases online.
>
> Follow the website link to read the **case study** of a man who has anterograde amnesia. What things does he use to help him overcome his memory difficulties? Can you think of any other ways he could cope with his memory problems?
>
> www.memorylossonline.com/pastissues/winter2000/patient.html

Check your understanding

1. What is encoding?
2. How is a human brain similar to a computer?
3. What is the difference between anterograde and retrograde amnesia?
4. Why is the hippocampus important for memory?
5. Why might someone forget?
6. What is procedural memory?

Theories and explanations of memory

The Multi-store Model of memory

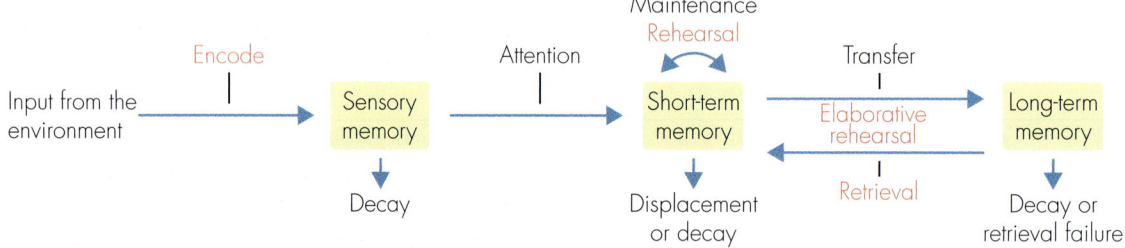

▲ The Multi-store Model of memory

Psychologists Richard Atkinson and Richard Shiffrin (1972) proposed a theory that views the human memory system as being made up of three separate stores.

Sensory store

Stimuli from the environment around us, such as sights, smells and sounds, enter the **sensory store** whether or not the person is paying **attention** to the source. If we do not pay attention to the information, then it **decays**.

The sensory store can hold a lot of information, but only for a very brief time: approximately two seconds. We do not pay attention to the majority of information that enter the sensory store. Information is encoded by the separate senses.

Multi-store Model
A theory which separates memory into three distinct stores: sensory, short-term and long-term.

Decay
The fading of information that is not paid attention to until it is forgotten.

Short-term memory

Short-term memory

This store has limited capacity and duration and is where information goes from the sensory store if attention is paid to it.

Capacity

The amount of space available to store information.

Maintenance rehearsal

This process refers to repeating information so that it stays in storage.

Long-term memory

This has unlimited capacity and duration is potentially forever, and is where information goes from STM to be permanently stored.

Auditory

What we hear.

Duration

How long information can be stored for.

Visual

What we see.

> **Challenge**
>
> Think about the sensory store, short-term memory and long-term memory. How could you ensure that the information you have learnt about the encoding, capacity and duration for each store has passed from your short-term to your long-term memory?

Experimental group

A group of participants for whom the independent variable is manipulated.

Control group

A group of participants for whom the independent variable has not been manipulated. Psychologists use control groups to compare against the experimental group.

Short-term memory

Information that is paid attention to in the sensory store then moves to the **short-term memory** store (STM). Short-term memory has a limited **capacity**. It can only hold an average of seven items, plus or minus two, depending how large the item is. This is known as Miller's Magic Number Seven, after the cognitive psychologist who first proposed the capacity of short-term memory. If STM reaches its capacity and more information enters, then the information that is already in the store becomes displaced.

The theory suggests that information can remain in STM for up to 30 seconds. If the information in STM is not transferred to LTM then it decays. This means that the memory trace fades.

According to the theory, we must repeat or rehearse the information that is in short-term memory. This is called **maintenance rehearsal** and it allows information to be moved into **long-term memory**. The encoding in short-term memory is mainly **auditory**. Shiffrin also suggested that as well as maintenance rehearsal, elaborative rehearsal is also important for information to pass from STM to LTM. Elaborative rehearsal involves thinking about the meaning of the word or what is being memorised rather than just repeating it over and over.

For example, imagine your friend is telling you details of a party he is having. The information enters your ears as sound waves and travels to the sensory store. If you are paying attention to your friend and focus on the information he is telling you about the party, then the information will move to your short-term memory. If you rehearse that information, it will then move into your long-term memory so you can retrieve it later when you need it – remembering to go to the party!

Research has shown that the capacity of STM can be increased by chunking information. For example, when you are trying to memorise a phone number it is easier to 'chunk it': 01632 345 967.

Long-term memory

Long-term memory (LTM) has both unlimited capacity and **duration** is potentially forever. This means that there is no limit to the amount of information that it can store and no limit to how long it can hold the information there.

The encoding in long-term memory is mainly semantic. This means we think about the meaning of the information. Encoding can also be **visual** and auditory.

> **DIY**
>
> Try a quick experiment to see if chunking really works.
>
> Before you start (**Ethics**):
> - Have you got informed consent?
> - Have you briefed your participants?
> - Are their individual results confidential?
> - Are there any other ethical issues you should take into account?
>
> Using an **independent measures design** you will have two groups. In your **experimental group**, read out a long number sequence in chunks. In the **control group**, read out each number in one long string with no breaks. See the table on the next page. The number groups have already been created for you.
>
> What do you predict will be the difference between the two groups? Write a hypothesis with your prediction.

OCR GCSE Psychology

After you have read out each number, immediately ask your participants to write the number down in the correct order. Count up how many fully correct number groups each participant has recalled.

For more information on ethics and research methods see page 179.

Time for some maths

Once you have done this for each group, calculate the **mean, median** and **modal** scores for each group. Has chunking the numbers increased the recall? Compare the mean scores for the chunking and not chunked groups. Do your results support your hypothesis? Create a **bar chart** for your mean scores – don't forget to label your axes and give your chart a title.

	Chunked (Read three numbers, then pause and read the next three and so on)	Not chunked (Read all of the numbers without pausing)
1	765 949 238	765949238
2	197 475 490	197475490
3	293 601 247	293601247
4	943 782 416	943782416
5	549 295 839	549295839
6	436 431 973	436431973
7	750 429 026	750429026
8	509 271 839	509271839
9	305 814 975	305814975
10	613 790 423	613790423

	Participant scores (the number of numbers sequences they recalled correctly) /10	
	Chunked group	**Not chunked group**
1		
2		
3		
4		
5		
6		
7		
8		
9		
10		
Total		
Mean		
Median		
Mode		

Chapter 5 Memory

Challenge

Can you complete the table without checking? Did the rehearsal you used in the previous task help you memorise the information?

Store	Duration	Capacity	Encoding
Sensory			Via the individual senses
Short-term	Up to 30 seconds		
Long-term			Mainly semantic

Criticisms

- **The Multi-store Model of memory is too simple.** It suggests that short-term memory is a single store, but other research has suggested that it is much more complex and can deal with multiple sensory information at one time, by using separate sections. For example, if you were having a spa day your brain would be able to encode the relaxing sound of the spa music, the smell of the essential oils and the feel of the back massage that you are having.
- **Neuropsychology has also suggested that long-term memory is also made up of more than one store.** Evidence suggests that different types of memories are stored in different parts of the brain. This contradicts what the Multi-store Model says. For example, there is evidence to suggest that the hippocampus is responsible for autobiographical memories, whereas the cerebellum is responsible for procedural memory like knowing how to do things.
- **The model places too much importance on the role of rehearsal versus meaning.** It suggests that in order for information to be passed into long-term memory, it must be rehearsed. However, not all information is rehearsed. If something is very shocking, it does not need to be rehearsed for it to enter long-term memory. We also don't tend to rehearse sensory information like taste and smell.
- **Other psychologists have suggested that thinking about the meaning of what you are trying to remember (semantic processing) is more important in transferring it to long-term memory than simply repeating it.** By thinking about the meaning, it processes the information more deeply and therefore embeds it more deeply in long-term memory. Shiffrin realised that semantic processing was also important and added it to the Multi-store Model as elaborative rehearsal.

STUDY HINT
The third and forth criticisms listed here can be combined to deal with an issue referred to on the specification: rehearsal versus meaning in memory.

Rehearsal versus meaning

A criticism of the Multi-store Model of memory, whereby meaningful information is recalled despite not being rehearsed.

Challenge

Create a 3D model of the Multi-store Model of memory using 'junk modelling'. Use old cardboard boxes, string and other recycled material to create your model. Don't forget to label the parts. Include evaluative points. What are the weaknesses of this model?

Check your understanding

1. Why is rehearsal important?
2. What is the duration of short-term memory?
3. How is information encoded in long-term memory?
4. Why has the role of rehearsal been criticised by other psychologists?
5. What happens when too much information enters short-term memory?

Types of forgetting

Decay

Decay happens if we do not pay attention to the information that enters the sensory store. This means that the sensory information breaks down and the memory is no longer available. In short-term memory, according to the multi-store model, decay occurs if information is not rehearsed. As the duration of short-term memory is limited to up to 30 seconds, information will decay quickly if it is not rehearsed. Some psychologists believe that decay can also occur in long-term memory especially if there is a long gap between creating the memory and recall.

Displacement

As short-term memory has limited capacity it can only hold a small amount of information (seven items, plus or minus two). Therefore, when it is 'full', new information pushes out the old information, which, if it has not been rehearsed, will be forgotten. This is called **displacement**. Displacement does not occur in long-term memory as the capacity is thought to be without limit.

> **Displacement**
> Information that is already in short-term memory is pushed out by new information, once the store becomes full.

DIY

You can test the theory of displacement. Create a list of 24 words (they should all be of a similar length and difficulty). Put them onto a PowerPoint presentation, with one word per slide. Time the slides so that they are shown for one second each.

Get your participants to watch the presentation. After it is finished, ask them to write on a piece of paper as many of the words as they can recall.

You now need to analyse the data. Group the words that were recalled into three. The first eight words that were presented are group one, the next eight are group two and the last eight are group three. Count up how many words each participant recalled in each group of words.

Now work out the mean score for all the participants' scores in group one, two and three.

Previous research would suggest that participants will recall most words in group one and three. In group one, the words that were presented first, participants will have had time and opportunity to rehearse them, so they will have been transferred to long-term memory (this is called primacy effect). In group three, the words are still in short-term memory, so should be recalled (this is called recency effect). In group two, the words are most likely to be displaced by the final eight words, so are least likely to be recalled. Present your results on a graph.

Don't forget to make sure your research is run ethically! Ensure you have gone through all the **ethical guidelines** before you run the study. How have you ensured that you have met each guideline? Why is it important that we follow the ethical guidelines when conducting research?

Did your results support the theory?

What do you think would happen to participants' recall if they had to do a distractor task (something that diverts participants' attention away from the list of words they were just shown) for three minutes before they recalled the words, instead of recalling immediately after the words were shown?

> **STUDY HINT**
> You may be asked to apply types of forgetting to a source. You may be told about different characters who experience forgetting and be asked why. Look for the clues in the source. For decay, look for lack of rehearsal or use. For displacement, look for overload of information. For retrieval failure, look for changes to cues.

Chapter 5 Memory

Retrieval failure (lack of cues)

One theory of forgetting is that, although the memory is accessible, we lack the necessary **cues** to recall the memory. Cues are things that can trigger your memory. For example, if you smell candyfloss, it might trigger a memory of a visit to a fair when you were little.

Have you ever gone upstairs to get something only to completely forget what you went up to get as soon as you get to the top of the stairs? This is an example of **retrieval failure**. If you go back downstairs to where you were when you had the idea to go upstairs, then you are likely to remember what it is you wanted. Some psychologists are interested in why this happens. They suggest that the reason you can't remember what you went to get is because you are lacking the **cue** you need to trigger the memory. By going back downstairs, you are in the same context that you were when you had the thought and so it acts as a trigger to give you access to the memory. This is called a **context cue**.

State cues, such as being in the same psychological or physical state as when the memory was encoded, can help you retrieve the memories. For example, you might recall more words from a list if you are feeling happy both when you learnt them and recalled them. Miles and Hardman (2010) found that participants who learnt a list of words when riding an exercise bike recalled more words when on the bike than at rest: they were in the same **physiological** state.

▲ Ever got to the top of the stairs and forgotten what you have gone up for?

Retrieval failure
The inability to recall something because the cue needed to trigger the memory is not present. The cue could be internal (like an emotion, i.e. you were feeling sad when the memory was encoded but are happy now) or external (perhaps a certain smell would help you recall).

Lack of cues
The absence of triggers to help retrieve memories.

Cues
Things that can trigger your memory, such as going back to the place where you grew up which might trigger memories of your childhood.

Context cues
These are 'external' cues and refer, for example, to being back in the same place where the memory was encoded, in order to trigger the memory.

State cues
These refer to 'internal' cues such as your emotional state when the memory was encoded. Being in the same emotional state can act as a trigger for the memory.

Physiological
Relating to physical biology.

> **Check your understanding**
> 1. What is decay?
> 2. What happens to information held in short-term memory if it runs out of capacity?
> 3. What can help us retrieve memories that we cannot access?

The Multi-Store Model of Memory Research Study: Wilson, Kopelman, & Kapur (2008) – Prominent and persistent loss of past awareness in amnesia: delusion, impaired consciousness or coping strategy?

Background

People who have **amnesic syndrome** often experience varying degrees of memory loss. This can include forgetting who they are, how old they are, what the date is and where they are.

When people are unable to be aware of what time or date it is and where they are, this is usually associated with brain injury, severe amnesia or the more advanced stages of **dementia**.

However, according to Kopelman (2002), for someone to completely forget who they are and everything about themselves is extremely rare in **neurological disease**.

With some neurological conditions, people may not be aware how old they are. For example, they may think that they are younger than they are.

According to Wilson *et al.*, there are two types of **distorted memories**:

1. Faulty episodic memories. These are memories of past events that are incorrectly recalled. They might be recalled as being in a different time or place or they may remember things that never actually happened. For example, someone with flawed episodic memory might remember their last holiday but remember it as being in Cornwall when in fact they went to Scotland.
2. Faulty semantic memories. Knowledge and understanding of things can be inaccurate. In the case of Clive Wearing, who had severe retrograde amnesia (see below) when he was shown a picture of a scarecrow, he described it as a 'worshipping point for certain **cultures**'.

Delusions

Delusions are defined as false beliefs that the person who is experiencing them fully believes in, and will not listen to others who argue that it cannot be correct. Delusions are also generally preoccupying, meaning that the person who has the delusion tends to be very focused on it.

When considering people who have damage to their memory, delusions can be seen as part of faulty semantic memory.

Consciousness

Damasio (2000) defined consciousness as an 'organism's awareness of its own self and surroundings and its ability to respond to environmental factors'.

▲ Clive Wearing and his wife Deborah.

Amnesic syndrome

A general term to describe any memory problems caused by brain damage, illness or psychological trauma, such as post-traumatic stress disorder.

Dementia

A degenerative disorder. This means that the longer you have it, the worse your symptoms get. Symptoms of dementia include loss of memory, problems with thinking and problem solving.

Neurological disease

Diseases which affect the brain, spine and the nerves that connect them. An example of a neurological disease is dementia.

Distorted memories

Memories that have been changed or altered in some way.

Delusions

False beliefs that the person fully believes in, even if someone argues that it cannot be correct. They are often bizarre and the person will be very preoccupied by them.

Chapter 5 Memory

Aim
Wilson, Kopelman and Kapur (2008) aimed to report on the case of a man called Clive Wearing who suffered from a severe and very rare case of both anterograde and retrograde amnesia. The researchers recorded neurophysiological assessments of Clive's brain as well as his psychological experiences.

Sample
Clive Wearing (CW) was born in the UK in 1938. He was an outstanding musician and a gifted musical scholar and was leader of the London Sinfonietta.

Method
Research method/design
A longitudinal single case study covering 21 years. The research gathered both **qualitative** and **quantitative data**.

Materials
The researchers used both **neuropsychological tests** such as **IQ tests**, tests of verbal fluency, and a digit span test which tested his short-term and long-term memory. They also used **MRI** scans to see the amount and location of damage in his brain.

Outline of the study
- In March 1985, CW developed an influenza-type illness. Symptoms included headache and fever. Several days later, he was admitted to hospital where he was diagnosed with herpes simplex viral encephalitis (HSVE). He was given medication which probably saved his life. However, the virus had already destroyed large parts of his brain.

Neuropsychological assessment
- CW was referred to Barbara Wilson in October 1985. He had already been assessed and the report found that he was experiencing 'extremely severe episodic memory deficits, some semantic memory impairments but his immediate memory span was normal'. This means his memory for autobiographical events was very damaged. He was unable to recall many details about his life before the illness. He was also unable to create new memories. His memory for facts and knowledge (semantic) had some damage but his ability to remember a small amount of information over a short amount of time (a few seconds) was normal.

- CW was assessed in November 1985. His verbal and performance IQ tests were found to be within the 'average' range. However, CW was an extraordinarily gifted man before his illness so this score is likely to be poorer than he would have scored before his illness.

- His short-term memory was found to be normal but his long-term memory was 'severely impaired'.

- He also still showed impaired semantic memory. When asked 'what is a scarecrow', he responded 'a bird that flies and makes funny noises'.

Magnetic resonance imaging (MRI) scanning
- In 1991, CW had his first MRI scan. The scans were rated by three independent experts who all agreed that there were significant abnormalities in **hippocampal formations**, amygdala, mammillary bodies, temporal poles and substantia innominate. There were also other abnormalities in many other brain areas such as the left fornix and the left medial frontal cortex.

- CW was given a second MRI scan fifteen years later, in 2006.

- This second scan showed there had been very little change. It also revealed that CW had extensive damage to his temporal **cortices**. As the scans show, the damage was greater on the left than the right.

- Over the 21 years of the study, CW was given numerous assessments.

Patient | Normal

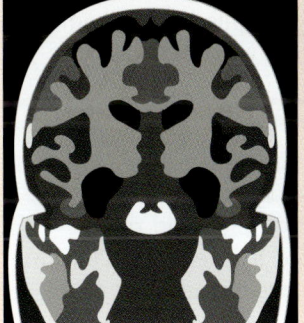 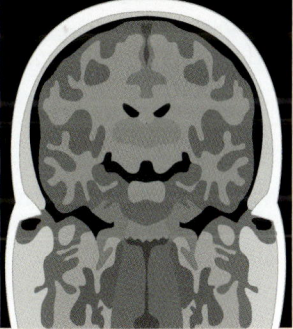

▲ CW's brain scan from 1991 with comparison normal brain

- Results showed that he always scored zero on tests of delayed recall. This means that if he was given new things to learn, he was completely unable to recall them after a delay, showing that he could not form new semantic memories. This is evidence for anterograde amnesia.

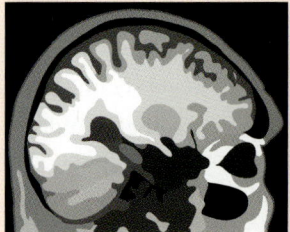
Right

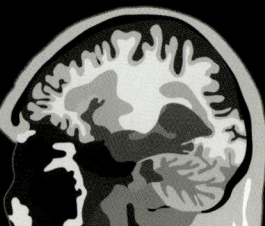
Left

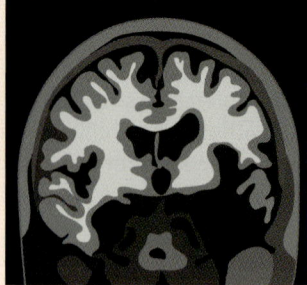
Coronal view

▲ CW's brain scan from 2006

- He was, however, still able to talk, read, write, sight-read music and conduct an orchestra.
- Evidence for his retrograde amnesia can be seen in his inability to recall facts and autobiographical information from before the accident. For example, when he was shown pictures of eighteen well-known people, he did not recognise any of them. He thought that Prince Philip was a member of his choir.

MRI

Magnetic resonance imaging is a type of scan that uses strong magnetic fields and radio waves to produce detailed images of the inside of the brain and other parts of the body.

Hippocampal formations

A general term to describe the hippocampus.

Cortices

Plural of cortex.

- He did, however, recall who he was, where he went to school, where he studied music and that he had married his wife.
- In summary, his memory remained largely unchanged over the 21 years of the study.

CW's auditory hallucination

In 1990, CW developed an auditory hallucination. His wife, Deborah, reported that CW thought he could hear his music being played. This hallucination persisted and he still 'hears' his music played several times a week. It is quite common for auditory hallucinations to be familiar songs that are repeated over and over. This suggests that left over memory traces play a part in the creation of hallucinations.

Results

CW was found to have:

- severe brain abnormalities
- both retrograde and anterograde amnesia
- the inability to form new memories
- decreased performance and verbal IQs (although these were classed as 'normal', CW was exceptionally talented before his illness)
- some loss of semantic memory
- a severely damaged episodic memory.

Delusions?
CW's beliefs about his consciousness

According to Wilson *et al.*, CW did not appear to accept that he had a problem with his memory. Instead CW insisted that his memory problems were due to the fact that he had not been conscious since his illness.

When he was challenged on his belief about his consciousness, for example, by being shown previous entries in the diary that he kept, or a videotape of him conducting his choir (which he was recorded doing for a television documentary after his illness), he would say that he wasn't conscious at the time of doing it.

Wilson *et al.* questioned whether CW was suffering from a delusion. However, they decided against this, as he wasn't experiencing other psychiatric features of delusions.

Lacking autobiographical consciousness

According to Damasio (2000) consciousness is made up of three parts. The first part is the proto self, that we are not consciously aware of. The second part is the core consciousness which only requires short term memory where a person is aware that their thoughts are their own and can respond to emotion. The third stage – and highest form of consciousness –

is the autobiographical self, which is linked to long term memory and a person's memory of their past experiences.

Wilson *et al.* suggest that CW has core consciousness – he is aware that his thoughts are his own. However, the severe brain damage has meant that he was virtually unable to create new autobiographical memories. For example, if his wife came to visit him, he was unable to create this as a memory so that each time he saw her it was as if it was the first time since his illness. His memories of his past life before his illness are also very limited. Therefore, according to Damasio's theory of consciousness, CW has very limited 'autobiographical self'.

Conclusions

- CW's sense of 'self' was disrupted by his memory disorder.
- The viral infection herpes simplex encephalitis can result in brain damage.
- Brain damage can result in both retrograde and anterograde amnesia.
- Brain damage can significantly affect memory. Provides support for the Multi-store Model. It suggests that both short-term memory and long-term memory have separate stores. The Multi-store Model would also suggest that CW is unable to use elaborative rehearsal or maintenance rehearsal in order for the information to pass into LTM.

Challenge

Create a timeline of CW including his illness, when he was tested, what those tests were and what the results were.

Criticisms

- **CW was repeatedly tested over 21 years, which may have caused him psychological distress.** The authors state that CW was given neuropsychological tests on many occasions over the 21 years of the study. Although CW would have been unable to remember these tests, was it **ethical** to use him repeatedly as a test subject? Although CW might have been able to provide **consent**, given the extent of his brain damage, he may not have truly understood what they were planning to do and how often.
- **The tests that Wilson *et al.* describe were not designed to actually help CW or to find ways to help him.** They were simply used to repeatedly test his memory ability to gain a better understanding of retrograde and anterograde amnesia. Therefore, CW didn't actually gain anything from taking part in this research.

- **CW was irritated at having his belief in his own consciousness questioned.** This obviously caused him some **psychological harm** at those brief moments in time. It can be argued that it was unethical to cause him irritation even in those short moments, given how difficult life must be for him.

- **Confidentiality was not maintained.** Although the authors refer to the participant as CW, they do identify him by his full name and give enough personal background details to make it very clear who CW actually is. Therefore, his identity was not kept private.

- **It is hard to generalise the results to other people because of the extent of the damage to his brain.** Obviously, CW's case is highly unusual. Considering the extent of the damage to his brain, it is difficult to pin-point how the exact areas of the brain that were damaged were linked to his retrograde and anterograde amnesia. Wilson *et al.* mention a patient of Damasio, known as David, who had similar brain damage to CW. However, David did not report thinking that he had just woken up or had not been conscious before. Therefore, the results of Wilson's single case study may not be useful for generalising to the wider population to understanding how our memories work.

Extension

Listen to the radio programme to hear more about Clive's experiences with amnesia. You will hear both Clive speaking as well as his wife Deborah. The page also gives you links to further reading about Clive. www.radiolab.org/story/91578-clive/

Something to think about

CW's wife has said that new information entering his brain is like 'snow alighting on warm ground.'

What do you think his wife meant? Could you imagine what it would be like to live without the ability to make new memories?

Further reading: Forever Today by Deborah Wearing

STUDY HINT

You don't need to know the function of all of the damaged parts of CW's brain, but the definitions will help you to understand why the damage affected his memory.

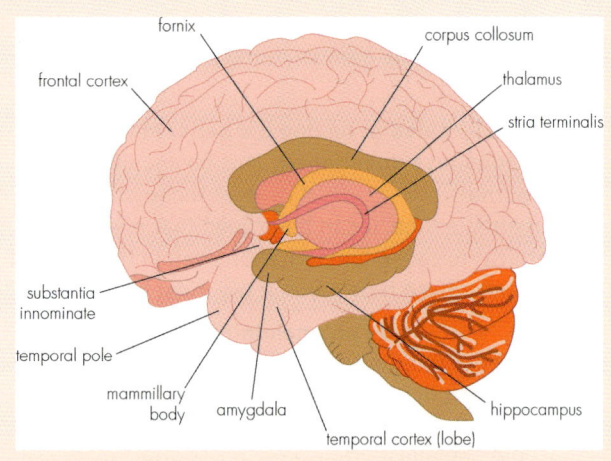

▲ Parts of CW's brain that were affected. All of these areas are related to different types of memory function. For example, the temporal cortex is thought to be linked to the ability to access autobiographical memories, whereas the mammillary bodies are thought to be important in creating and recalling memories.

For more information about ethics see page 179.

Check your understanding

1. Name three areas of CW's brain that were damaged.
2. Give an example of how CW's semantic memory was damaged.
3. What were the results of the tests of CW's verbal and performance IQ tests?
4. What was CW still able to do?
5. What is anterograde amnesia?

The structure and process of the theory of reconstructive memory

The concept of schemas

It is tempting to think that memory is like a film, recorded accurately like camera footage, but the reality is quite different. Psychologist Frederick Bartlett (1932) theorised that people reconstruct their memories based on prior experiences called **schemas**. This theory does not support the idea of memory being like a computer processing, as it recognises that our memory is far from being an accurate reconstruction of our experiences.

Bartlett described a schema as being 'an active organisation of past reactions or experiences'. This means that things we feel, see and hear frequently give us a mental picture of what they are. So if we see an animal and it has soft fur, purrs, meows and has whiskers, we know from previous experiences that it is a cat.

> **Something to think about**
> What are the implications for society if someone is wrongly convicted of a crime due to an incorrect eyewitness? Can you find any examples of when this has happened?

Bartlett states that we don't just recall our schemas in **chronological order**, but that we can be flexible with our schemas and access what is most relevant at that moment in time from our memory. He also states that we can reconstruct our schemas based on new information that we see, hear or feel. Therefore, if we saw a bald cat, we would add the fact that they can have fur or no fur to our 'cat schema'.

> **STUDY HINT**
> Like many case studies, this study offers lots of interesting details on CW. However, you won't be expected to recall all of this in an exam. Your job is to focus on key results and conclusions which summarise what the researchers found out.

Schema

A mental representation of an object or situation. It is based on prior experience.

Reconstructive memory

A theory which suggests that our memory is influenced by our prior experiences and schemas and is not an exact representation of what actually happened.

Chronological order

Time order. Things being presented or recalled in the order that they actually occurred.

He tested his theory by giving participants a story to remember, called 'The War of the Ghosts'. It was a North American folk tale and some of the words and the style of the story were unfamiliar to the participants who were British. He found that when participants recalled the story, it was lacking in detail compared to the original and words that were culturally unfamiliar tended to be left out. For example, 'hunting for seals' was changed to 'fishing' which would have been more consistent with their existing schemas. Bartlett suggested this was because it did not fit with the participants' existing schemas.

The role of experience and expectation on memory

Our perceptions and memories are shaped by prior **experiences**. This means that our memory of events may not be accurate as we might imagine. When recalling an event, what we might actually recall is aspects of two different events that our memory has reconstructed as one event. This would explain why two people's memory of the same event may be different. Imagine that you went on a camping holiday as a child. If you went on another camping holiday the next year, your memories of the first holiday might interfere with memories of the second holiday, so that when you remember them you might confuse the two.

Our schemas are designed to help us quickly interpret the huge amount of sensory information that we perceive. These **expectations** help us make swift judgements about how to act in different situations. Our expectations may not always be correct but without them we would not be able to respond quickly. For example, if there is a new teacher at school who looks very stern, students might assume that he is very strict and won't be kind, so they don't react positively towards him. However, once they get to know him, they realise that their expectations were wrong and he is actually very kind and supportive.

The process of confabulation

Confabulation means making things up. It is not the same as lying, as when people confabulate, they don't do it with the intent to deceive people nor do they believe that what they are saying is incorrect. Bartlett suggested that people make up details or use aspects of other memories to fill in the blanks in their schema. This is so that it creates a more consistent reconstruction of the memory.

Distortion and the effect of leading questions

Distortion refers to a memory that differs from the event which took place. Researchers Loftus and Palmer (1974) have demonstrated that memory can be deliberately altered (distorted) by simply changing a verb. They showed participants clips of car crashes then asked them 'how fast were the cars going when they...' Participants were given one of five verbs, including 'contacted' and 'smashed'. Results showed that participants who received the verb 'smashed' estimated the speed of the cars as significantly higher than those who had received the verb 'contacted'.

The implications for this research are very important for the police when dealing with eyewitnesses. It is possible that if they use **leading questions** when interviewing witnesses, they could influence their testimony.

▲ We might have to change our cat schema if we saw one like this

Experience (on memory)

The idea that our memory is influenced by our prior experiences, meaning that our recall of an event may not be entirely accurate.

Expectation (on memory)

Our schemas are designed to help us deal quickly with a huge amount of sensory data. They influence what we expect to happen in certain situations.

Confabulation

Making up details to create a more complete memory. It is not done with the intent to deceive people.

Challenge

Get together with a close friend or family member. Think of a key event that you both shared at least one year ago like a birthday or perhaps a school trip. Don't discuss the event. Each of you write down your recollection of the event. Then compare the two. Do you remember things in the same way? Do your memories differ? Are you both convinced that your versions are the true recollection?

Criticisms of the theory

- **The theory is reductionist.** It focuses on how we create schemas and reconstruct our memories but fails to explain how these processes actually happen in the brain.
- **The theory doesn't actually explain *how* memories are processed.** Bartlett describes memory as being an active process but doesn't offer an explanation for how this actually happens.
- **Critics have said that the concept of schema is too vague and hypothetical to be useful.** Schema cannot be observed. Scans can only show **brain activity**, not exactly what an individual is processing.
- **The research evidence Bartlett used to support his theory was not conducted in a systematic way, so many extraneous variables could have affected the results.** Bartlett used his 'War of the Ghosts' research as evidence to support his theory. However, he did not use standardised instructions and his research was not tightly controlled, which could have affected how the participants responded. It might be that the errors and omissions they made were due to **demand characteristics** and therefore the research does not offer valid support for the theory.
- **The Reconstructive model of memory is very complicated.** It makes it very hard to determine which aspects of memory will be recalled and which won't. This makes it very hard to test and therefore it is difficult to predict how people will recall information.

> For more information on the reductionism/holism debate see page 34.

Leading questions
Questions which suggest a certain answer or type of answer.

Brain activity
The action of neurons firing within the brain as they send chemical messages from one neuron to the next.

> **STUDY HINT**
> If using a research study to criticise the theory, it must be explained why this is a problem with the theory – criticising the study on its own is not enough!

Check your understanding
1. What is meant by a schema?
2. Give an example of a schema.
3. What is confabulation?
4. What is distortion?
5. What does it mean if we recall things in chronological order?

Reconstructive memory research study: Braun, Ellis, & Loftus, (2002) – Make my memory: How advertising can change our memories of the past.

Challenge
Search the internet for 'Walt Disney World Vacation Planning VHS 25th Anniversary 1996 video' and watch the first three minutes. What do you think was the aim of this advertisement? Why might it make people want to go back to Disney World®?

Background
According to Braun *et al.*, advertisers use **autobiographical advertising** to manipulate consumers to focus more on the 'feelings evoked' by the memories of their **childhood**, rather than focusing on the 'rational product information', such as details of what the product does and costs.

For example, Braun *et al.* reported that when Disney World® in Orlando celebrated their 25th anniversary, they used an advertising campaign that included vintage-style home movies of people enjoying themselves.

Braun *et al.* suggest that because nostalgic advertisements might act as a cue for consumers' memory of their personal past events, the advertisements themselves might alter what consumers actually remember as they reconstruct their memory of the event.

They propose that autobiographical adverts might encourage consumers to picture themselves in the scenario that is presented in the advert and this could result in them thinking that the event actually happened to them personally.

Loftus and Pickrell (1995) suggest that older memories are more vulnerable to alternation. By using suggestion, presenting false cues and getting participants to use their imagination, it is possible to create false memories about childhood events in a significant minority of participants.

Advertising companies use something called 'experiential information'. This is a type of promotion which is designed to immerse consumers in the advertisement as they learn about the advertisement by 'experiencing it'. Another technique used by advertising companies is using 'dramatic narratives', which uses a story to convey the message of the advertisement. Both of these advertising methods are thought to trigger the consumers' memories.

Challenge
An example of this is the advertising campaign to promote the Sanctuary Spa™ range of products at Boots PLC. They had a pop-up spa tour of seven cities across the UK, where consumers could have mini makeovers and collect free product samples. The pop-up spas were placed close to the Boots PLC store so that consumers could go and buy the products easily. Can you find another advertising campaign that has used experiential information?

Experiment 1

Aim
To see whether autobiographically-focused advertising could directly affect how consumers remember a prior childhood experience.

Hypotheses
1. If the advertisement is part of how the consumer's memory is reconstructed, then elements or images of the advertisement may appear as part of the consumer's reconstructed memory of their visit, regardless of whether or not the events actually happened.
2. If the advertisement causes the consumer to visualise their childhood memory, then the process of imagining the memory will lead consumers to believe the section of the advertisement that showed someone shaking hands with Mickey actually happened to them (this is called 'advertising inflation').

Method
Research method and design
This was a **laboratory experiment** with an independent measures design, where participants only took part in one condition.

For more on the independent measures design, see page 173.

Read the study and think about how these issues might relate directly to this study.

Both quantitative and qualitative data was collected using **questionnaires** and **self-report**.

Autobiographical advertising
Adverts that are intended to bring back people's memories of their past to influence how they feel about the product that is being advertised.

The **independent variable** was whether participants were shown the Disney™ advert or the **control** advert.

The dependent variable was the difference in score between week one and week two on the Life Events Inventory on the target item, which was 'met and shook hands with a favourite TV character'.

Sample

107 undergraduates (64 female and 43 male) from a Midwestern university in the USA.

Participants received a course credit for their involvement.

Materials

- A questionnaire containing twenty childhood events. It was called the Life Events Inventory. The target event, 'met and shook hands with a favourite TV character at a theme resort' appeared fourth on the list. These were rated on a 100mm line where 0 definitely did not happen and 100 definitely did happen.
- Disney™ resort advert.
- A questionnaire rating the advert using attitude scales such as 'unfavourable/favourable'.
- A questionnaire rating on a scale of 0 (strongly disagree) to 100 (strongly agree) how involved they felt in the ad using empathy measures such as 'I got really involved in the feelings provoked by the ad.'
- Two distraction tasks.
- Questionnaire about their personal memories of Disney™.

Procedure

Week one

Participants were **randomly** assigned to either the experimental group, who received the Disney™ advert, or the control group, who received the control non-Disney™ advert.

During the first week, participants were given the Life Events Inventory. Participants were also given a number of other experimental tasks. This was to minimise the opportunity for participants to work out the aim of the research and change their behaviour (demand characteristics).

Participants were then asked to return the following week to finish one of those experiments.

Week two

Participants were given either the Disney™ or the control advert by a second experimenter. Participants were asked to try to visualise the advert and imagine themselves experiencing the situation described. They were given five minutes to write down what the video made them feel and what it made them think about.

Afterwards, participants rated the advert using the attitude scale and the empathy measures.

They were then given a five minute distraction task. After they had completed the task, the experimenter from week one entered the room, looking 'panicked' and saying there had been a problem coding the autobiographical data from the Life Events Inventory which they completed in week one. He asked if they could fill out the questionnaire again.

Participants then did a second distraction task which lasted fifteen minutes. A third experimenter then gave participants another questionnaire which asked participants if they had ever visited Disney World® and, if so, to describe their memory of the event. They were asked a number of questions about their memory of the event, such as how well they remembered it (one = not at all, seven = perfectly).

Finally, participants were asked what they thought the aim of the experiment was, to test them for demand characteristics. They were also asked whether they believed that their memories of Disney™ had been affected by the advert.

Results

The participants' reactions to the adverts and their statements recalling their personal experience of Disney World® were rated by two independent judges who did not know what the **alternative hypothesis** was. This was so that their ratings would not be **biased** by the predictions of the experimenters.

A **correlation** analysis showed that their **inter-rater reliability** was 0.83, meaning that their ratings were similar.

Autobiographical effects of the advertising

30 out of the 46 (65 per cent) participants in the experimental group who received the autobiographical advert mentioned memories of Disney World®.

34 (74 per cent) reported that the advert had caused them to imagine the experience.

29 (63 per cent) mentioned that they would visit Disney World® in the future.

Even those participants who had not previously visited Disney World® were able to imagine what it would be like to visit.

Imagination inflation

One of the key aims of Experiment 1 was to see whether reading an advertisement and imagining the event can increase the confidence of the participants that they had had their own childhood experience with the product.

Significantly more participants in the experimental (Disney™) group showed an increase in their score on the Life Events Inventory in week two for the critical question ('met and shook hands with a favourite TV character at a theme resort'): 90 per cent versus 47 per cent in the control group.

The mean difference scores of the Life Events Inventory were analysed. The experimenters found that the Disney™ group showed a significantly more positive change, with a mean average of 37.05, compared to the control group mean of -1.5. This shows that the Disney™ group were much more confident that the event had happened to them.

There were no other significant differences between the two groups across the other eighteen items on the questionnaire.

Disney™ memory

Out of those participants who had reported previously visiting a Disney™ Park, significantly more of the experimental (Disney™) group recorded positive thoughts about Disney™ compared to the control group (Disney™ mean = 3.6. Control mean = 2.8).

There were no significant differences in negative thoughts about Disney™.

Significantly more elements of the advert, such as use of the words 'magical' and 'cool rides', were used by the Disney™ group compared to the control group (Disney™ mean = 2.38. Control mean = 1.47).

> **Time for some maths**
> Calculate the difference for the pairs of means listed in the results. Can you justify why there are significant differences?

Demand characteristics

The experimenters asked the participants to try to guess what the aim of the experiment was, in order to see whether their responses had been influenced by working out the purpose of the experiment.

However, no one was able to guess that the aim was to see whether the advertising could alter their childhood memories.

Therefore, they found no demand characteristics.

Experiment 2

Aim

To see whether false information in an advertisement could make participants think that those events had happened to them as a child.

Design

Independent measures.

Sample

167 undergraduate psychology students from an American university (104 female/63 male).

Materials

Same as Experiment 1 with a few amendments:

- Ad 1: suggested they had shaken hands with Bugs Bunny.
- Ad 2: suggested they had shaken hands with Ariel.
- Ad 3: factual – given to control group. Life Events Inventory modified so that the critical question was: 'shaking hands with a cartoon character in a theme park' with a 10-point scale 'definitely did not happen'/'definitely did happen.'

Procedure

Participants were given two different types of false information. The first suggested that they had shaken hands with Bugs Bunny at Disney World®. Bugs Bunny is not a Disney™ character, so it is impossible that this could have happened.

In the second advert, it was suggested that they had shaken hands with Ariel. Ariel *is* a Disney™ character, but the character wasn't introduced until later, so they also could not have met her as a child.

The experimenters used the same basic procedure as Experiment 1. However, this time both the experimental and the control group were given a Disney™ advert. This was to see whether just the mention on the Disney™ name was enough to trigger autobiographical memories.

The experimental group received the autobiographical ads with the false information. The control group received a Disney™ advert that contained factual content, giving information on a new ride and how to book tickets.

Results

The autobiographical adverts were rated as being more involving. It was scored on an 8 point scale, with a lower score meaning less involvement.

	Mean score /8
Ariel	4.8
Bugs Bunny	5.1
Non-autobiographical	3.8

▲ Table 5.2

All of the groups showed an increase in confidence that they had shaken hands with the characters on the second Life Events Inventory. However, those in the experimental group showed a greater increase.

	Percentage increase
Ariel	76%
Bugs Bunny	78%
Non-autobiographical	62%

▲ Table 5.3

> **Time for some maths**
> Create a graph to represent these results.
> Don't forget to label the axes and give it a title.

Conclusions

- Autobiographical advertising can influence how consumers recall their past.
- Autobiographical advertising can make consumers more likely to believe an event happened to them as a child, even if the event would have been impossible.
- Autobiographical advertising can create false memories.
- The results support the theory that memory is reconstructed as participants' memory of events were influenced by the advertisements.

Criticisms

- **There was age bias.** Both studies used undergraduate students from the USA. This is a biased sample as they may not represent how people of different ages respond to autobiographical advertising.
- **It is not ethical to manipulate people's memory.** Many participants reported that they were more likely to visit Disney World® and could have therefore been manipulated to spend a considerable amount of money on a holiday that might not have taken otherwise. It also affected how the participants recalled their past.
- **The study lacked ecological validity.** The study took place under laboratory conditions. It may not have reflected how people think about autobiographical advertisements in real life situations. For example, participants were directly instructed to imagine themselves experiencing the situation. In real life, people do not generally get given direct instructions on how to perceive an advertisement and therefore may be less likely to have their childhood memories altered.

> **For more information on ecological validity see page 202.**

> **STUDY HINT**
> When you are criticising a study, you need to contextualise your answer. This means, if you are using low ecological validity as a criticism, you need to say exactly why and how you think the study has low ecological validity.

Check your understanding

1. Who were the participants in the first Braun *et al.* study?
2. What was the name of the questionnaire given to participants about their childhood?
3. What was the key question on the questionnaire?
4. In the second study, what were the two impossible events suggested to participants?

Chapter 5 Memory

> **Challenge**
>
> Discuss in groups which adverts you can recall from your childhood (before the age of ten). What was it about those adverts that made them memorable? Did they actually make you want to purchase the product? How do the advertisements make you feel now?

> **Challenge**
>
> Can you think of an advertisement that acted as a cue for you? Was it a context or state cue? Was the advertisement effective? If the cue triggered a memory of the product, did you actually then buy it? Discuss in class or with groups of four.

Overload

The result of too much information entering a memory store.

> **DIY**
>
> Watch five video advertisements, either on your television or the internet. Watch them once and at the end of each advertisement, pause the recording and write down all the information that you can recall. Watch each advertisement again and see if you missed any details. If so, how important were they? How much information was the consumer given? Can you link your results to Miller's Magic Number Seven (page 123)? Was there between five and seven pieces of information to recall?

Application: techniques used for recall

Research into how people recall advertisements and what influences their recall provides extremely important information for advertising companies, many of whom spend millions of pounds on advertising campaigns for their products. It is therefore essential to the company that their advertising is as effective as possible. Autobiographical advertising provides an emotional context to the advertisement which triggers positive childhood memories when the product is recalled. This positive association helps boost sales of the product.

The use of cues, repetition and avoiding overload in advertisements and the use of autobiographical advertising

Cues

Advertisers use cues to create a certain context or feeling when advertising their products. This links to the cue dependent theory of memory. When the consumer is in the same situation or emotional state, then the advertisement will act as a cue to trigger their memory of the product.

For example, an advertising company might show someone feeling sad who is comforted by drinking their soup, which is hot and tastes good. Then, if the consumer is feeling sad themselves, they might recall the soup and purchase it, hoping that it will offer them the same comfort.

Advertisers sometimes use non-verbal cues in their advertisements. For example, if there is a brand logo or a key message shown, then having a model in the advert actually looking directly at it can 'trick' consumers to also look at what the model is looking at; it is human nature to want to see what someone else is seeing. This will then increase the consumers' awareness of the brand.

Repetition

Advertisers use repetition in their advertising to help build a familiarity with their brand. It helps the memory of the product stay in the consumers' long-term memory and prevents decay.

Psychologists use repetition to promote positive feelings about their product. Research has shown that consumers can feel negatively about new products, simply because they are unfamiliar. By repeating them frequently, they become more familiar to the consumer and this encourages more positive feelings. In addition, simply repeating a slogan or a message (when an advert ends) will increase the likelihood of it entering and staying in long-term memory.

Avoiding overload

Overload in advertising can occur when consumers are exposed to too much information within an advertisement. This can result in key information being displaced out of short-term memory. Therefore, it is important when designing advertising campaigns that slogans are kept short and the essential product details are kept to a minimum to avoid overload.

The use of autobiographical advertising

Advertisers and companies use autobiographical advertising to increase consumer opinion of their product. Braun *et al.* state that this type of advertising is used mainly with 'baby boomers'. These are people who were born after the Second World War, from around 1946 to 1964. The nostalgic advertising is thought to remind them of a time in their life when they were young and free such as the Christmas advertisement for Coca cola with the holiday truck. The idea is to link these positive memories to the advertised product and make the consumers more likely to buy it.

> **STUDY HINT**
> It is important to know how to apply your knowledge to a scenario, such as how memory research helps advertisers sell their product. Imagine a scenario where a company wants to promote its new chocolate bar. Describe how they could use memory research to make their product sell better.
> To improve your answer, make sure you contextualise it. In other words, you need to ensure your answer refers to the chocolate bar mentioned in the question. Don't just give a generic answer.

The development of neuropsychology for measuring different memory functions, including the Wechsler Memory Scale

Neuropsychologists use different tests, such as the **Wechsler Memory Scale**, in order to evaluate the extent of brain damage in patients who might have had a brain injury or suffer from an illness like dementia. It is important for the neuropsychologists to be able to accurately identify what cognitive problems the patient has and how bad they are, so they can offer them the best and most appropriate treatment. The Wechsler Memory Scale was created to test whether different types of memory are functioning properly. It can be used on people aged between 16 and 90. It has seven different subtests: spatial addition, symbol span, design memory, general cognitive screener, logical memory, verbal paired associates, and visual reproduction. Results are presented in five different sets looking at different aspects of memory: auditory, visual, visual working, immediate and delayed memory.

Wechsler Memory Scale

A diagnostic tool used by psychologists to evaluate how much brain damage patients have after injury or illness.

SUMMARY

This chapter has shown us that our memory is not reliable and even if we think we are remembering something correctly, it does not mean that it is correct. The cognitive approach also compares our mind to a computer where information is input, encoded, stored, retrieved, then output. There are different theories of how our memory works and the simplest one – the Multi-store Model – theorises that there are only three separate stores, which differ in their capacity, duration and encoding. However, this theory has been found to be far too simplistic and relies too much on the role of rehearsal. The theory of reconstructive memory suggests that our memory is not accurate and that we piece together our memories based on our existing schemas. If we have gaps in our memory, Bartlett suggests that we make things up to fill in the blanks and provide us with a more consistent reconstruction of the memory.

The case of CW shows how brain injury can have devastating effects on memory; he is unable to create new long-term memories and any he retains are very damaged.

The research by Braun *et al.* shows that advertising can affect our memory of our own past events and childhood. Advertising sometimes uses context and state cues to trigger memories of a product when the consumer is in the same state. They are using theories of memory to help sell their products.

This chapter has shown us theories about how our memory works, as well as looking at brain structures and how they are linked to different types of memory. Although there is still a lot we don't know about how memory works, the advances in neuropsychology take us a step closer to finding out.

Practice questions

The questions in this textbook have been written by the authors, Mark Billingham and Helen Kitching. They have not been produced or endorsed by OCR.

1

> **Accidents and Memory**
> Suman had an accident where he fell off his motorbike and hit his head. Luckily he was wearing a helmet, so the damage was not too severe. However, he can't remember the accident at all. Emelia fell from a balcony and hit her head. She has trouble making new memories.

Using the source

a Name the type of amnesia Suman has. [1 mark]

Retrograde.

Correct. One mark.

b Name the type of amnesia Emelia has. [1 mark]

Anterograde.

Correct. One mark.

2 Outline **one** difference between sensory store and long-term memory, according to the Multi-store Model. [3 marks]

In sensory store memory, information lasts for a matter of seconds, whereas in long-term memory it is potentially there forever.

Two marks awarded here. The answer gives an accurate feature of each store but to earn a third mark it would need to be more explicit about what is being compared.

3 Describe the procedure of **either** of the experiments carried out by Braun, Ellis and Loftus (2002) in their study of how advertising can change our memories. [5 marks]

In week one, participants were assigned to either the experimental group, who received the Disney advert, or the control group, who received the control non-Disney advert. During the first week, participants were given the Life Events Inventory. They were also given some other experimental tasks. Participants were then asked to return the following week to finish one of those experiments.

In week two, participants were given either the Disney or the control advert by a second experimenter. Participants were asked to visualise the advert and imagine themselves experiencing the situation described. They were given five minutes to write down what the video made them feel and what it made them think about. Afterwards, participants rated the advert. They then had to fill in the LEI again.

Then participants had to fill in another questionnaire about whether they had ever visited Disney World and to describe their memory. They also had to answer questions about how well they remembered the event.

This response accurately describes lots of the procedure's features, but makes assumptions about the reader's knowledge and leaves 'gaps' by not explaining certain aspects of the experiment. For example, what was the purpose of watching the adverts, and what does the Life Events Inventory measure? It is an answer that demonstrates knowledge rather than understanding and, as such, earns three out of the five marks.

4 An advertisement company wants to promote a new fizzy drink.

Using your knowledge of psychology, explain how they could do this. **[6 marks]**

The advertiser could use cues to promote their fizzy drink. The cue-dependent theory of memory says that if the advertisers create a certain context or feeling when advertising their fizzy drink, it will act as a trigger when consumers are in the same situation. Therefore, the advertiser could make an advert where people are shown drinking it when they are out with friends having a good time. This would cue people to buy the drink when they are out with their friends, triggered by the positive feelings of enjoying themselves in good company.

The advertisers could also use repetition to help make consumers more familiar with their fizzy drink. The more familiar they are, the more positive they will feel about the drink — they will buy it to be associated with it.

The advertiser would need to avoid overloading the consumer though. This means that the information that they include about the drink itself should be kept to a minimum, so that consumers can recall the key points. If the drink comes in different flavours, for example, the names of the flavours should be kept short so that the people have a chance of remembering them all.

This response demonstrates a wide range of knowledge and understanding by describing three different techniques. Each technique is clearly and explicitly considered in the context of the product. This very effective combining of psychological knowledge and practical application earns this response all six marks.

OCR GCSE Psychology

5 Describe and evaluate the theory of reconstructive memory. **[8 marks]**

The theory of reconstructive memory says that memory is not an accurate thing. Instead, it is based on schemas, which are mental pictures of things that we see, feel or hear frequently.

A criticism of the theory is that it doesn't explain how we actually process memories in our brain. Bartlett says memory is active but doesn't explain how this happens.

He does say we can change our schemas if we're presented with new information that is not part of our current schemas. So, if we've never seen a man pushing a pram before, we might update our schema of 'what men do' to count for this.

Then there is confabulation to fill in the blanks in memory. Confabulation is not lying, because people don't know they're doing it. They use information from other memories to create a more sensible memory of an event.

Bartlett used his War of the Ghosts research to support his theory. However, he didn't do this very scientifically.

Distortion is also part of this theory, where memories are distorted — again not on purpose. It's almost human nature.

But is human nature that holistic? It would be more useful if the theory was more reductionist to help us to pinpoint exactly how memory works.

The content of this response is all relevant and demonstrates an underlying understanding of the theory, it also shows descriptive and evaluative skills. However, the lack of coherency and structure make it difficult to make sense of the answer. Clearer explanation and expansion of key concepts would improve the response. As it stands, the answer is worth four marks.

6 Sleep and dreaming

Sleep is a very important behaviour to study. Why? It is something that everybody does – we would die if we didn't! The average person spends a third of their lives asleep. Dreaming is another universal behaviour which is part of sleep. Psychologists are interested in the reasons why we dream, assuming there is a reason for this very bizarre, but normal, experience.

> This chapter should enable you to:
> - develop awareness of the functions, features and benefits of sleep
> - know the stages of the sleep cycle and when dreaming occurs
> - know the role of the pineal gland and melatonin
> - develop knowledge of the causes of sleep disorders
> - know the difference between endogenous pacemakers and exogenous zeitgebers and their role in sleep
> - be able to explain and evaluate the Freudian Theory of Dreaming with specific reference to the unconscious mind, the role of repression, the concept of wish fulfilment, manifest and latent content of dreams; and the issue of subjectivity
> - be able to describe and evaluate Freud's (1918) dream analysis of the Wolfman
> - be able to explain and evaluate the Activation Synthesis theory of dreaming with specific reference to the role of REM sleep, the function and actions of the brain (including the limbic system) during sleep, the activity of neurons in the pons during sleep, the process of synthesis as a function of the cerebral cortex; and the reductionism/holism debate
> - be able to describe and evaluate Williams *et al.*'s (1992) study into Bizarreness in Dreams and Fantasies
> - understand the impact of neurological damage to the hypothalamus on sleep
> - understand features of insomnia, the role of the nervous system and its management through relaxation techniques, and the role of the physical environment in insomnia and its treatment through improved sleep hygiene.

▲ Most of us look forward to getting some sleep, it must be doing us some good!

The functions, features and benefits of sleep

Why do we sleep?

Sleep is a **universal** behaviour, meaning that everyone does it. It is also instinctive; we cannot stop ourselves from sleeping. This suggests that it is an evolved behaviour that aids survival.

- Sleep keeps us safe. Humans tend to sleep when it is dark, which makes sense for a number of reasons. When it is dark, we are more prone to predators as they can see us but we can't see them. Therefore, if we are asleep we are less easy to spot in the sense that we are not moving around or making much noise. Similarly, if we try to venture out in the dark, we are much more vulnerable to accidents as well as attacks, therefore it makes sense to be active during daylight hours.
- Sleep is good for a **healthy brain**. Research has shown that REM sleep resets the brain after all the synaptic activity that has taken place during the day. The process appears to be crucial for our brains to consolidate our memories from the day, as well as protecting established memories. There is also evidence that decisions are made when we sleep, as well as making creative connections. The space between brain cells increases when we sleep, allowing the brain to clear out toxins associated with neurodegeneration.
- Sleep is important for **physical repair**. A healthy body relies on **slow wave sleep**, particularly in the healing of cells, such as those in the cardiovascular system. It also helps to keep the balance of hormones in the body, such as those that regulate feelings of hunger and fullness, or increase blood sugar level. When we sleep, our immune system activity increases, killing bacteria and viruses in large numbers. Deep sleep can trigger the release of growth hormones, which boost muscle mass, and also repair cells and tissues in the body.
- Sleep plays a role in **emotional stability**. Getting a good night's sleep means we wake up feeling alert and re-energised. A well-rested body produces less of the stress hormone cortisol, meaning we should also feel calm and relaxed. Sleeping generally gives your brain the chance to get back into balance all of the necessary chemicals and hormones that affect our mental clarity and mood. For this reason, there is a strong link between sleep and feeling content and happy.

Healthy brain

A brain that functions normally.

Physical repair

Returning the body to a normal, healthy state.

Slow wave sleep

A type of deep sleep where brain activity is slow.

Emotional stability

Feeling normal and psychologically healthy.

> **Neuropsychology now**
>
> Look at how many references there are to the brain and associated chemicals when outlining the functions of sleep.

> **Challenge**
>
> Do some research on the **consequences** of not getting enough sleep. There are plenty of good websites that cover this, such as www.nhs.uk and www.sleepcouncil.org.uk. See if you can relate the effects of sleep deprivation to the reasons why we sleep.

> **Extension**
>
> Children sleep for longer than adults. Can you explain why by revisiting the functions of sleep?

Sleep stages

Distinct periods of sleep which make up a cycle.

STUDY HINT
REM sleep eventually comes up in two places in the specification. Once under 'Stages of the Sleep Cycle' and then again under 'Explanations of Dreaming'. This is because it is in the key stage where dreaming occurs.

REM (rapid eye movement) sleep

A stage at the end of the sleep cycle where sleepers' eyes jerk and brain activity is high, leading to more dreaming in this stage than others.

The sleep cycle

When we sleep, we go through set **stages**, which are repeated depending how long we are asleep. People usually go through five stages: 1, 2, 3, 4 and **rapid eye movement (REM) sleep**. A complete sleep cycle takes an average of 90 minutes.

Stage 1 involves light, drowsy sleep. People drift in and out of sleep and can be stirred quite easily. In this stage, the eyes move slowly and muscle activity slows down. Many people experience sudden muscle spasms followed by a sensation that they're falling. Brain waves are more synchronised and slower than when we are awake, and are called alpha waves. These slow to become theta waves. If a person is woken during this period, they will often say they have not slept at all.

In Stage 2, eye movement stops and theta brain waves become slower with occasional bursts of rapid brain waves. We lose conscious awareness of the outside world at this point. When a person enters Stage 3, extremely slow brain waves called delta waves alternate with shorter, faster waves. In Stage 4, the brain only produces delta waves. Stages 3 and 4 are the stages of deep sleep which means it is difficult to wake someone from them. In deep sleep, there is no eye movement or muscle activity, and more growth hormones are released into the body which helps with physical repair too.

In the REM stage, breathing is quicker and less regular. Our eyes move rapidly and limb muscles are temporarily paralysed. Brain waves during this stage are similar to levels experienced when a person is awake, and so are fast. Heart rate increases, blood pressure rises and body temperature can go up or down. This is the time when most dreams occur. If someone is woken up during REM sleep, they can normally remember their dreams. Most people experience three to five intervals of REM sleep each night. The first sleep cycles each night have relatively short REM sleeps and long periods of deep sleep, but later in the night, REM periods get longer.

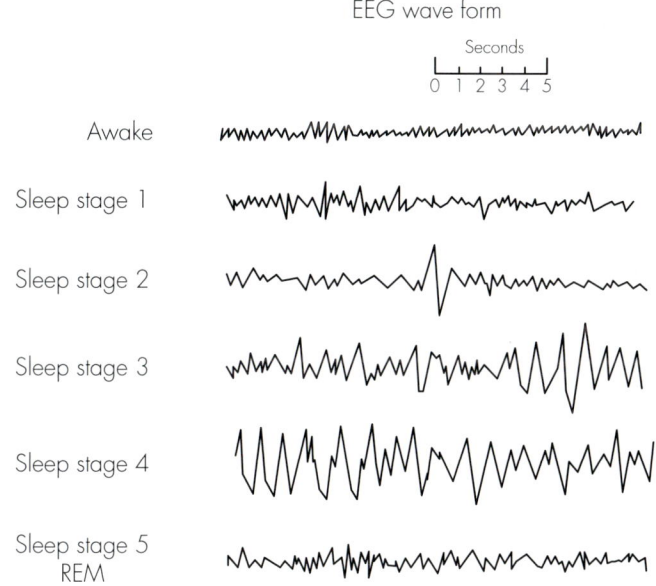

▲ These EEG readings show how brain activity is significantly different in each stage of the sleep cycle.

Adults spend approximately 50 per cent of the sleep cycle in Stage 2, about 20 per cent in REM and the other 30 per cent is divided between the other three stages.

Challenge

Re-read the paragraphs describing the stages of sleep and use the information to complete a copy of the table below.

Stage of sleep	Brain activity	Features of this stage	% of time in this stage
1	Slowing. Synchronised. Alpha waves becoming theta waves.	Drowsy. Easy to stir. People don't realise they have been asleep. Muscle spasms followed by sensation of falling.	10%
2			
3			
4			
REM			

Time for some maths

1. A person's sleep cycle lasts for 90 minutes. Based on research, how many minutes do they spend on average in Stage 1 sleep?
2. If a person's sleep cycle lasts for 110 minutes, based on research, how many minutes do they spend on average in REM sleep?
3. If an infant spends 2.5 times as much time in REM sleep compared to an adult, and their sleep cycle is 50 minutes long, then how many minutes does the infant spend in REM sleep?

The neuropsychology of sleep

Neuropsychology now
The brain plays a major role in sleep, which is why it often feels out of our control whether we sleep or not. You might find it useful to remind yourself of some of the basic structure and functions of the brain at this point.

The pattern of being awake during the day and asleep when it is night is a natural part of human life. Like other cycles in human beings (e.g. the feeding cycle, the menstrual cycle), it is thought to be governed by **endogenous pacemakers** and **exogenous zeitgebers**. These are, respectively, internal **cues** and external cues that regulate **biological** rhythms.

Endogenous pacemakers and exogenous zeitgebers in sleep

Both endogenous pacemakers and exogenous zeitgebers have a role in maintaining and controlling the 24 hour sleep waking cycle. A key factor in how we sleep is exposure to light or darkness. Light is an exogenous zeitgeber. When we are exposed to light, it stimulates a neural pathway from the retina in our eye to a part of the brain called the **hypothalamus**. Here, there is a special centre called the **suprachiasmatic nucleus** (SCN), which sends signals to other parts of the brain that control hormones, body temperature and various other processes that play a role in making us either feel sleepy or wide awake. The SCN is an endogenous pacemaker which obtains information about light via the optic nerve. One key thing that the SCN does is delay the release of a hormone called **melatonin** until it is dark.

STUDY HINT
Students sometimes get endogenous pacemakers and exogenous zeitgebers mixed up. It might help to take the 'ex' from exogenous to associate it with external cues.

Endogenous pacemakers
Internal biological clocks that manage bodily rhythms.

Exogenous zeitgebers
Features of the environment – either physical or social – that help to manage bodily rhythms.

Hypothalamus
A part of the brain that controls a number of key bodily functions.

Suprachiasmatic nucleus
A part of the brain that regulates circadian (24 hour) rhythms.

Melatonin
A hormone released in the brain that is responsible for regulating sleep.

Chapter 6 Sleep and dreaming

> **Challenge**
>
> A cave expert called Michel Siffre carried out research on himself by living in a cave for months at a time. Can you see why this is a good way of investigating exogenous zeitgebers? Do your own research on Siffre to find out how being in a cave affected his sleep wake cycle.

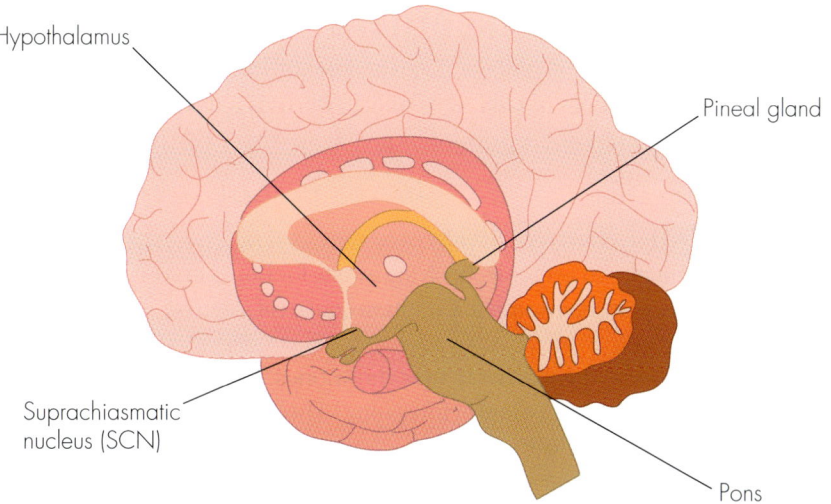

▲ This diagram shows that the parts of the brain involved in sleep are located deep in its structure. This is often the case with behaviours that we see in other animals as we have this part of the brain in common with them.

The role of melatonin

Melatonin is associated with sleep onset. It is a natural hormone made by the **pineal gland**, which is about the size of a pea and located just above the middle of the brain. During the day, the gland is inactive. However, as night falls, the pineal gland gets 'switched on' by the SCN and starts to produce melatonin, which is released into the blood. When melatonin levels increase, we begin to feel less alert and drowsier, eventually having the urge to sleep. Melatonin levels remain high for about 12 hours, generally until the start of a new day. During the day, it is hard to detect any melatonin in the body.

Pineal gland

An endocrine gland, found in the brain, which produces melatonin.

> **Something to think about**
>
> Have you ever been lucky enough to go on a holiday that requires a long haul flight? If so, you will know the downside is that you can suffer from jetlag. Can you see how jetlag links to exogenous zeitgebers and endogenous pacemakers?

▲ Shift workers often experience disruption to their circadian (sleep wake) cycle because their patterns of work do not follow patterns of light.

Causes of sleep disorders

Although sleep is a natural process, some people still have difficulty sleeping. When people's sleep does not follow normal patterns it is described as a **sleep disorder**. Two common sleep disorders are **sleep onset insomnia** and **sleep maintenance insomnia**.

Sleep onset insomnia

If someone struggles to get to sleep – lying awake for hours in some cases – this is called sleep onset insomnia. Common causes of sleep onset insomnia include:

- on-going anxiety which releases stress hormones
- too much caffeine or nicotine before going to bed
- eating a heavy meal close to bedtime
- playing computer games close to bedtime
- physical pain that keeps the sufferer awake.

Sleep maintenance insomnia

If someone falls to sleep, but then has a disturbed pattern of sleep where they wake regularly, this is called sleep maintenance insomnia. Common causes of sleep maintenance insomnia include:

- **depression**
- drinking alcohol
- restless legs syndrome
- sharing a bed or room with someone who snores
- menopause (for women).

> **Sleep disorders**
> Behaviours which affect the normal patterns of sleep.
>
> **Sleep onset insomnia**
> Problems falling asleep.
>
> **Sleep maintenance insomnia**
> Problems staying asleep.

> **Something to think about**
> Psychologists suggest that anxiety and depression may lead to insomnia. However, can you see why there may be issues establishing **cause and effect**?

> **Challenge**
> Use the information on causes of insomnia to produce a poster that gives advice on how to get a good night's sleep.

> **STUDY HINT**
> You only have to be able to describe causes of sleep disorders. Unlike other explanations on the specification, you do not need to be able to evaluate them.

> **Check your understanding**
> 1. What are the benefits of sleep?
> 2. How is REM sleep different from other stages of sleep?
> 3. What is the role of melatonin in sleep?
> 4. How do endogenous pacemakers and exogenous zeitgebers work together to regulate the sleep wake cycle?
> 5. What is the difference between sleep onset insomnia and sleep maintenance insomnia?

Theories of dreaming

In the same way that psychologists believe that sleep serves one or more functions, many psychologists also believe that dreaming serves a function too. Of course, what this function is depends very much on the perspective of the psychologist. As with much of psychology, there are a number of different theories to explain the nature of dreaming.

The Freudian Theory of Dreaming

Sigmund Freud is one of the most famous psychologists, and was one of the 'founding fathers' of psychology. Although many of his ideas may seem bizarre in this day and age, he has still had a great influence on the subject. One of his most notable works is his theory of dreaming, which some people still think is valid over a hundred years after it was first proposed.

Chapter 6 Sleep and dreaming

Freudian theory

A theory that looks at behaviour as a product of the dynamics of different parts of the personality

Unconscious mind

The part of the mind that people are not aware of but holds thoughts and memories.

Repression

The process of pushing unpleasant thoughts and experiences into the unconscious mind.

Wish fulfilment

Satisfying urges and desires.

Dreams

A series of thoughts, images, and sensations occurring in a person's mind during sleep.

> ### Challenge
>
> It is easy to find lots of examples of common images and themes found in dreams and what psychologists believe they really symbolise. Do some research on this to produce a matching quiz that you can try out with your classmates.
>
> To get you started, see if you can match the examples below.
>
> | Manifest content | Latent content |
> |---|---|
> | A person dreams they are falling through the air. | The person is feeling confident about an up and coming project. |
> | A person dreams they are late for an appointment. | The person is feeling like they are losing control of an aspect of their life. |
> | A person dreams they are flying through the air. | The person is worried about missing out on a key opportunity. |

A central idea of **Freudian theory** is that the human mind is mainly made up of the **unconscious mind**. This is a part of the mind that we are not consciously aware of, despite being the key drive behind many of our behaviours. Freud believed that actions do not happen **randomly**, and that they are motivated by unconscious urges and desires. For example, Freud was interested in mental illness and thought the best way to understand someone's psychology was through understanding what was happening in their unconscious.

Freud was faced with a problem. He wanted to investigate the unconscious mind, but this is part of the self into which people have no insight. However, Freud believed that dreams were a product of the unconscious mind. He decided that through analysing dreams, he would have a way of accessing what was happening in the unconscious mind.

A large part of the unconscious mind, according to Freud, is a division of the personality called the id. The id is primeval and presents all our instinctive urges, especially those related to **aggression** and sex. A lot of these urges are repressed into the unconscious mind to 'keep them in check', making sure that people do not say or do inappropriate or offensive things. However, the defence mechanism of **repression** only works to a degree and, according to Freud, these urges eventually need to be released, potentially through dreams. Dreams challenge the ego - a part of the personality that keep us in touch with reality - and are more likely to occur at a time when the ego's defences are weakened.

Freud believed that dreams act as **wish fulfilment**. People often cannot fulfil their deepest desires and so they are dreamt about instead. This becomes a way of releasing some of the anxiety around these urges. For example, an individual may be angry at their boss and consequently want to verbally attack them. However, they do not want to be seen to lose control (or their job!), and so this urge is repressed. Instead, they may have a **dream** about arguing with their boss and this then partly fulfils their wish, meaning they have a way of dealing with a potentially difficult situation.

Freud argued that dreams were rarely attempts to directly act out a wish. He talked about dreams having a manifest and a latent content.

The **manifest content** is the actual content of a dream and the **latent content** is the underlying meaning of the dream, what the dream really represents. For example, Freud proposed that objects like poles, swords and guns may make up the manifest content of a dream, but they are really phallic symbols. Consequently, a woman dreaming about these kind of objects may be experiencing penis envy. Similarly, Freud argued that dreams about dancing or riding horses were really dreams about sex.

> ### STUDY HINT
> If you are asked to describe the Freudian theory of dreams, you would want to try to include all of the key features. But would you remember them? Try using a silly, short story to help you remember the key words. For example – my *uncle* Sigmund *pressed* the doorbell when he arrived. When I opened the door, he said he *wished* he got there earlier, but the *man* who had picked him up from the station was running *late*.
>
> Uncle = unconscious. Pressed = repression. Wished = wish fulfilment. Man = manifest content. Late = latent content.

> **Challenge**
>
> Write a description of a dream you have recently had that you are prepared to share with others. Get a group of friends to do the same. Then pass the dreams around and get people to say what they think the dream really means. Compare people's different responses. If people's responses have anything in common this would suggest that there is some objectivity to interpreting dreams. Where there are differences, this is would be down to subjectivity.

▲ Dreams are not always what they seem. Freud suggested they need careful interpretation to get beyond the manifest content and into the latent content.

Manifest content

What is actually experienced in a dream in terms of visual, auditory and other information.

Latent content

The true meaning of a dream that is hidden in the manifest content.

Criticisms

- **This theory is considered too subjective.** Dream interpretation is very open to opinion. A number of people can hear the same description of a dream but have very different ways of explaining what it means. Why should we trust Freud's interpretation of a dream any more than someone else's? For example, what is the evidence that riding a horse symbolises having sex? Could it mean something else to somebody different?
- **Freud's dream theory is difficult to test.** This is partly because its concepts are not objective enough and partly due to the fact that dreams cannot be easily verified: how do we know people are recalling their dreams accurately? In addition, a big part of the theory relies on an unconscious mind, yet this cannot be observed or asked about.
- **The theory is based on unreliable research.** The evidence is mainly from case studies, and so making generalisations about the meaning of dreams for all may not be fair.
- **The theory has a narrow interpretation of dreams. It only relates them to wish fulfilment, and then it is mainly about sex and aggression.** Critics say that dreams can represent many aspects of our lives, including dreams that directly reflect what we have done that day, or things that we are worried about or looking forward to the next day. Also, it is hard to accept that nightmares have much to do with wish fulfilment!

> **Extension**
>
> These days, Freud's theories have largely been discredited. One of the main problems is that his theories are not scientific enough. Which of the listed criticisms relate to science and why?

- **The theory can be accused of cultural and historical bias.** Freud's themes, especially in terms of how dreams were interpreted, may have reflected the **culture** at the time. For example, at the time that Freud was writing, society had very strict and moralistic views about sexual intercourse and so the idea of repressing lust and desire makes sense. However, in this day and age, people have more liberal **attitudes** towards sex, but this does not necessarily mean that the manifest content of dreams is very different.

> **Check your understanding**
>
> 1. What is the role of the unconscious mind in dreaming, according to Freudian theory?
> 2. What is the role of repression in dreaming?
> 3. How might a dream show wish fulfilment?
> 4. What is the difference between the manifest and latent content of dreams?
> 5. Why is Freud's theory of dreaming criticised for being too subjective?

Freudian Theory of Dreaming Research Study: Freud (1918) – dream analysis of the Wolfman.

Background

Freud was writing at a time when psychology was a relatively new subject, therefore his work was original rather than based on previous research and theories. Freud's study of the Wolfman – a pseudonym for one of his patients – was an extensive piece of research. It started when the Wolfman approached Freud in 1910 to seek help with his depression. Freud was an early believer in the power of therapy, and was especially interested in the origins of mental illness. Freud's type of therapy was called **psychoanalysis**. As part of his aim to try to explain and treat the Wolfman's psychological problems, Freud began to develop this theory of dreams; dream analysis had a key role in Freud's therapy.

> **Psychoanalysis**
>
> A type of therapy that attempts to resolve psychological problems by accessing unconscious and unresolved conflicts.

Method

Design

Freud used the **case study** method to investigate the Wolfman's mental illness. Freud carried out a series of **interviews** between 1910 and 1914, which he analysed 15 years later, so this was a **longitudinal study**.

> **For more information on case studies see page 189.**

Sample

Although Freud used the pseudonym Wolfman to protect his patient's identity, he was later revealed to be a man called Sergei Pankejeff. Pankejeff was a man in his 20s from a wealthy Russian family. In 1906, his older sister had committed suicide, and his father did the same in 1907, having suffered depression for a number of years. These events led to Pankejeff's own depression. Pankejeff's problems included his inability to empty his bowels without the assistance of an enema and the fact that he felt like there was a veil cutting him off from the world.

Procedure

Freud's first publication on the Wolfman was *From the History of an Infantile Neurosis* published in 1918. Freud's treatment centred on a dream Pankejeff had had as a very young child, and was described to Freud as follows:

'I dreamt that it was night and that I was lying in bed. (My bed stood with its foot towards the window; in front of the window there was a row of old walnut trees. I know it was winter when I had the dream, and night-time.) Suddenly the window opened of its own accord, and I was terrified to see that some white wolves were sitting on the big walnut tree in front of the window. There were six or seven of them. The wolves were quite white, and looked more like foxes or sheep-dogs, for they had big tails like foxes and they had their ears pricked like dogs when they pay **attention** to something. In great terror, evidently of being eaten up by the wolves, I screamed and woke up. My nurse hurried to my bed, to see what had happened to me. It took quite a long while before I was convinced that it had only been a dream; I had had such a clear and life-like picture of the window opening and the wolves sitting on the tree. At last I grew quieter, felt as though I had escaped from some danger, and went to sleep again.'

Source: Sigmund Freud, 'From the History of an Infantile Neurosis' (1918)

▲ This is an artist's impression of what the Wolfman's dream scene may have looked like.

Results

Freud's eventual analysis of the dream was that it was the result of Pankejeff having witnessed a 'primal scene' – his parents having sex – at a very young age; it meant that the wolves watching the boy was a reversal of the boy watching the sex act. Freud believed that the wolf symbolised the father. Freud suggested that the tree in the dream represented a Christmas tree, as the dream had occurred at Christmas time, and where there would have been presents on the tree, there were wolves in their place. Freud also stated that the wolves were white, representing the white of the bedlinen and his parents' underclothes.

Freud's analysis of the dream led him to suggest that Pankejeff had an unconscious desire to be seduced by his father. This was related to the pleasure associated with receiving gifts at Christmas. In the dream, these gifts had turned into wolves, representing his father. Freud believed that Pankejeff had seen the look of pleasure on his mother's face during the sex act and wanted to experience this pleasure too. However, his mother had clearly been castrated by his father's actions because he could see she had no penis. Pankejeff therefore became very frightened of his father's power, leading to castration anxiety. The boy's castration anxiety was represented in the fear that the wolves would eat him. The fact the wolves were recalled as having big tails may also have symbolised their large penises, which were a threat to the young boy. Freud concluded that Pankejeff repressed his unconscious fear of his father, but displaced it onto wolves, which manifested itself in his dreams.

Challenge

Draw up a table with the headings 'Manifest Content' and 'Latent Content' and use the description of the study to show how these ideas can be applied to the case study of the Wolfman.

Conclusion

The case study of the Wolfman shows that the unconscious mind can have a significant effect on behaviour. It also illustrates the process of repression, where traumatic events are pushed into the unconscious mind as a safety mechanism. However, it also shows that these repressed memories can find their way back into the conscious through the dreams that people have and then recall.

STUDY HINT

Some of the criticisms of Freud's study are simply criticisms of using the case study method. You will need to learn these as part of Research Methods (Chapter 7). To earn good marks, remember to expand on these criticisms and relate them specifically to Freud's work.

Criticisms

- **The sample size is too small to make any generalisations.** It is not reliable to base a theory of dreams, which is supposed to apply to all, on the case of one person. It might be that other people do not use dreams as a way of symbolising traumatic experiences.
- **The Wolfman may only represent people with mental health problems.** Even if we accept we can make some generalisations based on the Wolfman's experiences, they may not apply to people with good psychological health. Everybody dreams but not everyone has mental health problems or traumatic life histories.
- **The study has a strong focus on the unconscious, yet this is an abstract concept that cannot be observed or reported on by the person.** Freud would have argued that analysing dreams is the way we test the unconscious, but dreams are quite abstract and do not provide hard evidence.
- **There is no way of knowing the accuracy of the dream recall.** Only the Wolfman experienced the dream, and so it relies on him to remember it as accurately as possible. It may be that Freud was analysing content that was never really in the dream.
- **The study is too subjective.** The results are accused of being one person's view on the dream, and therefore are very biased. A psychologist with a different theory could interpret the content of the dream in a completely different way.

STUDY HINT

There is some overlap between the criticisms of Freud's theory and his case study. This is not surprising as they both lack scientific rigour. Review the criticisms to identify this overlap. This should also make it easier to revise and recall these criticisms.

Check your understanding

1. Why was Freud interested in studying the Wolfman?
2. What explanation did Freud offer to explain the Wolfman's dream?
3. Why do psychologists often criticise the use of case studies such as Freud's?

The activation synthesis theory of dreaming

Hobson & McCarley (1977) came up with a neurobiological theory of dreaming., called the **activation synthesis theory**. They took the view that dreams occur when the mind tries to make sense (synthesis) of the **brain activity** happening during sleep (activation). In contrast to Freud, they believe that dreams have no real meaning.

> **Neuropsychology now**
>
> Hobson and McCarley are interested in the area of neuropsychology and so a lot of their research and theories focus on this.

Research shows that neuronal activity changes significantly just before and during REM sleep. At this point in the sleep cycle, powerful electrical signals pass through the brain like a wave. In readings from brain scans, they appear as sudden spikes. The signals arise from the **pons** in the **brainstem** and from the **neurons** that move the eyes, and then activate the **limbic system**, as well as travelling up to the occipital lobe in the higher part of the brain.

Hobson and McCarley's theory was that these spikes were sending a random surge of stimulation through the brain at frequent intervals. This activates the whole **cerebral cortex**, and as a result the higher brain tries to attach some meaning to what is happening. The effort to give the signals meaning is what leads us to dream. In order to produce synthesis, the brain draws upon its own stored memories. However, because the spikes activate many different brain areas at the same time, the outcome is often quite strange.

For example, the randomly produced spikes might be like those produced when running. A sleeping person could then **synthesise** those signals in their mind and dream of running. If, in addition, they'd had an argument with their neighbour that day then the brain might pick up on to that memory and produce a dream of running after or away from the neighbour! As the pons continues to fire random signals at the higher parts of the brain, they have to constantly try to make sense of them. This is why the content of dreams can shift so suddenly.

Activation synthesis theory
An explanation of dreams that focuses on the random activation of neurons and the brain's efforts to makes sense of this through synthesis.

Pons
A part of the brain that operates as a message station.

Brainstem
The central trunk of the brain that continues down to the spinal cord.

Synthesise
To make sense of and give meaning to dreams.

> **STUDY HINT**
>
> The processes of activation and synthesis are quite straightforward to understand and outline. A good description of the theory will need to include some of the technical detail about what is happening in the brain at the point of activation.

> **Something to think about**
>
> In what ways is Freud's theory more holistic than the reductionist approach of the activation synthesis theory?

Regions of the Human Brain

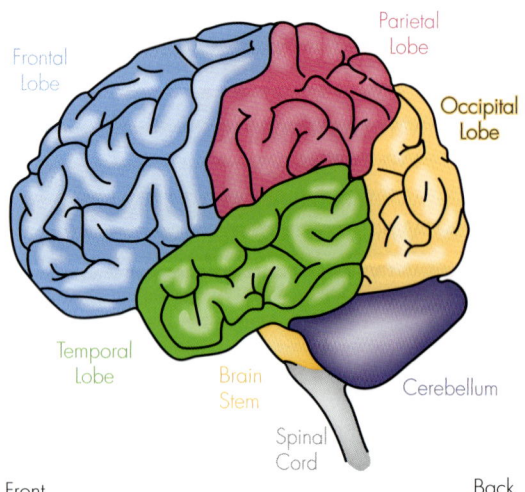

Reductionism

Viewing human behaviour from a simple perspective.

Holism

'The whole is greater than the sum of its parts'. Holism recognises that importance of seeing people as individuals and that not one approach or theory can fully explain human behaviour.

Criticisms

- **The theory is considered too reductionist.** Dreams are highly complex and, although bizarre, packed full of meaning. Critics therefore say it is wrong to try to reduce this down to simple neuronal processes. Compared to the more holistic Freudian theory, this is far too simplistic.
- **The theory is challenged by evidence that shows dreams are not as random as the neuronal activity in the brain.** Research suggests that dreams can be highly coherent and often have a direct relationship to experiences from the day.
- **The theory is challenged by evidence that shows there is some continuity to people's dreams.** Some people have recurring dreams, or dreams with similar themes. As well, when people wake and go back to sleep again, they sometimes pick up on the same dream. Patterns like this also go against the idea of randomness.
- **Dreams occur in non-REM stages of sleep.** Although brain activity is reduced in other stages of sleep, there is evidence of dreaming even if they are not as vivid. The fact we have better recall for dreams in REM sleep may be because we are more likely to wake from this state than from non-REM sleep.
- **Patients with damage to the brainstem do not stop dreaming, which contradicts the theory.** Even though the usual signals are not being sent in the brains of these patients, they will still have dreams. This is better explained by theories that suggest that dreams are about organising events from the day into memory, especially if the parts of the brain used for this are still functioning.

Check your understanding

1. What is the difference between the activation process and the synthesis process in the activation synthesis theory of dreaming?
2. How does brain activity happen during sleep?
3. In what way is the activation synthesis theory of dreaming a reductionist theory?

The Activation Synthesis Theory of Dreaming Research Study: Williams et al. (1992) – a study into bizarreness in dreams and fantasies: Implications for the activation synthesis hypothesis.

Background

The study was based on the assumption that the strange nature of some dreams correlates with the neurobiology of REM sleep. It quoted Mamelak and Hobson (1979), who concluded that in REM sleep the activated and disconnected brain sends random signals which will result in bizarre dreams. They also noted the challenges to this idea. For example, Foulkes (1985) reported that many children's REM sleep dreams lack bizarreness, and Reinsel et al. (1992) claimed that while REM dreams are bizarre, they are no more so than reports of either non-REM dreams or waking fantasy.

The researchers believed that two brain states – being awake and being in REM sleep – were so different **physiologically** that they must be different cognitively. Before this study, they had conducted a pilot study of bizarre cognition in dreams and daytime **fantasies** of twelve adult subjects. Their results showed that some distinction could be made between the two states in terms of the number of characters in dreams/fantasies and the remoteness of time and place. These measures were carried forward into the main study. The researchers predicted that the bizarre content of dreams would be different from the bizarre content of fantasies because of the activity associated with REM sleep.

> **Fantasies**
> Products of imagination where impossible or improbable occurrences are imagined.

Aim

The aim was to assess the bizarreness in dreams and fantasies as a way of showing support for the activation-synthesis hypothesis of dreaming.

Method

Design

The researchers used a **natural experiment** comparing people's experiences of dreams and fantasies (the **independent variable**) using a **self-report** method.

Participants

The participants were twelve students enrolled in a biopsychology course at Harvard University. Two subjects were male and ten were female; the age range was 23–45.

Materials

- Writing materials for participants to record experiences.
- A scale for measuring bizarreness of experiences.

Procedure

During one term, participants were asked to keep a written journal. They recorded any and all dreams that they remembered, whether waking in the night or in the morning. They also recorded any mental activity while awake if it related to fantasising. The researchers' definition of a fantasy was 'apparently spontaneous mentation of a narrative and/or perceptual nature without clear links to external stimuli or conscious intention.' In simple terms, this means that fantasies are something that 'pop' into people's minds and have no obvious connection with what is happening around them at the time.

A total of 60 dream reports and 60 fantasy reports were selected from the sample on the basis of length (longer than five lines) and because they described a **visual** experience. Therefore, 120 reports were selected for **quantitative** analysis.

> **For more information on quantitative data, see page 192.**

▲ 'Just had a really strange dream. I dreamt I was taking part in a study where the researchers asked me to keep a record of my fantasies and then they ended up rating them!'

The reports were divided into one-sentence units and were scored separately for bizarreness using a scale adapted from the two-stage system developed by Hobson. The first stage of the scoring system described the locus of the bizarre item and the second stage described the type of bizarreness, as shown in the table below.

▼ Table 6.1 Scales for categorising dreams.

Stage one: locus		Stage two: type of bizarreness	
Plot	A	Discontinuity	1
Thoughts of dreamer/ character	B	Incongruity	2
Emotion of dreamer/ character	C	Uncertainty	3
Ad hoc	D	Not bizarre	0

Williams, J. M., Rittenhouse, C., & Hobson, J.A. (1992) Bizarreness in Dreams and Fantasies: Implications for the Activation-Synthesis Hypothesis. Consciousness and Cognition, p.174

The example below shows an item that scored as A2 (Plot Incongruity), since it is unlikely that travellers would stuff sheep into their suitcases. The unit scored as A1 describes a sudden, unexpected change to a scene that has no relation to the previous one:

'The driver always returns with a sheep which we put in our suitcase. (A2) I remain silent throughout the trip and just watch the Indian man smile and joke. I worry about the sheep in my suitcase. I keep thinking that the sheep's blood is going to drip from the suitcase as soon as I pick it up and everyone is going to find out about me. I am at a swimming pool watching my sister compete in a swimming match. (A1)'

Sentence units did get more than one score if they contained more than one bizarre element while a unit that had no bizarreness got a score of 0.

A bizarreness density for each report was calculated by dividing the number of bizarre items scored by the total number of units. Total densities for each type of bizarreness (A1, A2, etc.) were determined for both categories – dreams and fantasies.

Using this scale, three judges scored all 120 reports for bizarreness. Judges did not know whether they were scoring a dream or a fantasy, though they were asked to decide what it was after scoring. They also worked independently of each other so that **inter-rater reliability** could be tested.

For more information on inter-rater reliability, see page 201.

Challenge

Here is your chance to use the ratings that Williams *et al.* used, as well as making a judgement on whether a report describes a dream or a fantasy.

1. Use the researchers' rating system to code the following dream. Compare your analysis with others to check for inter-rater reliability.

I am at a flea market, selling junk and clothing to a man who pays me in cash. My mom is there. I walk up to a booth which is Sotheby's in New York City. The antique watches on display for the auction are junk and few in number. The head of the watch department is hostile after an argument. The watch meeting rips apart the hotel, which is an immense glass structure with an orange glow to the interior. I am attending the meeting wearing a Harvard tee-shirt marked in Russian. George Kennan and his wife are on trial there, and we are plotting their escape. I fool the security guards by spraying nitrous oxide from a whipped cream can on the accused, and we elude the police by G.K. making a phone call to his wife to pretend to tell her to accept her fate. We walk out of the hotel casually.

2. Decide whether the following is an example of a dream or a fantasy. How have you reached this conclusion?

I see myself standing on top of a huge sphere. There is nothing else. It is shiny, deep bluish-green, seemingly somewhat translucent. When classes start each term, the sphere starts to move in all directions, starting, stopping, fast and slow. As long as everything else 'out there' is OK, I am fine and can handle it. It's almost, but not quite, fun. A challenge that feels good to handle. Then I see everything 'out there' building up, and I can barely balance – there is nothing physical to hold on to; it's just a shiny sphere. Just use skill, plan, keep control to hold on. It always eventually stops, when the semester ends.

Both extracts taken from original study by Williams et al. [Williams, J. M., Rittenhouse, C., & Hobson, J.A. (1992) Bizarreness in Dreams and Fantasies: Implications for the Activation-Synthesis Hypothesis. Consciousness and Cognition, 1 (2) 172-185.]

STUDY HINT

You may find it useful to summarise the key research studies using a spider diagram. You could start with lines for the background, method, results and conclusion. The method could be divided into categories, such as the sample and materials.

Results

Judges showed good inter-rater reliability; they agreed about 80 per cent of the time on both bizarre and non-bizarre items. Agreement on bizarre items alone ranged from 50 to 60 per cent. There was also a strong agreement between judges on bizarreness density scores for individual reports.

There was a highly significant difference between the **mean** density scores given for dreams and fantasies as shown in the table below.

▼ Table 6.2 Mean density scores for dreams and fantasies.

Bizarreness density scores for dreams	Bizarreness density scores for fantasies
0.223	0.089

Williams, J. M., Rittenhouse, C., & Hobson, J.A. (1992) Bizarreness in Dreams and Fantasies: Implications for the Activation-Synthesis Hypothesis. Consciousness and Cognition, p.176.

For more information on the mean see page 194.

In terms of more specific measures, the most significant difference between dreams and fantasies was on plot discontinuity. There were also differences on plot incongruity, thought incongruity and uncertainty, but not on the other measures.

Seven of the twelve participants had dreams with significantly higher bizarreness scores than their scores for fantasies. Only one participant had a significantly higher score for her fantasies – but this was someone who referred to her own magical powers in the fantasy reports!

The judges were able to assess whether a report was dream or fantasy with 88.7 per cent accuracy, showing there were some clear distinctions in bizarreness.

In this sample of 24 reports, dreams were always set in remote times or places (12/12) while fantasies were equally divided between remote or current environments (6/12). Fantasies involved the first person in only 4/12 reports while dreams always involved more than one character (12/12) and one involved more than eight characters.

Time for some maths
Use the 'Results' section to answer the following questions:
1. Construct an appropriate graph to display the mean bizarreness density scores for each condition.
2. What **percentage** of judgements were inaccurate when deciding whether a report was a dream or fantasy?
3. In its lowest form, what **fraction** of fantasies involved the first person?

Conclusions

- The researchers concluded from the evidence that dream bizarreness is the direct **cognitive** correlate of neuronal activity in REM sleep. In other words, the particular brain activity shown in REM sleep is associated with dreams being considered bizarre. In support of this, they referred to results that showed that dreams contain more bizarreness as well as other 'dreamy' features, such as remoteness of time and place compared to fantasies.

- In addition, both trained and untrained judges could distinguish dreams from fantasies with about 90 per cent accuracy, suggesting that dreaming and fantasising are two substantially different types of cognitive activity.

- However, the data did show some overlap of cognitive features between inattentive waking and sleep. The researchers explained this in terms of the parallels in brain activity in REM sleep and the wake-sleep boundary where neither register external stimuli, so that parts of the brain become *sensorially* disconnected and fire randomly.

Criticisms

- **The study relied on self-report, which means social desirability may have been a factor.** Participants may have been embarrassed about some of their dreams or fantasies, and so may not have reported them at all, or may have missed out or changed aspects in their description. If these things occurred, it makes comparisons unreliable.

- **The difference in scores may be down to variabilities in reporting techniques or the setting the reports were written in.** Participants were asked to report their dreams or fantasies as they happened but this may not always have been practical. This means that details may have been forgotten, or that participants took time to make sense of what they remembered, giving a more coherent – yet inaccurate – description.

- **There was a lack of control over the independent variable, which was supposed to be dreams versus fantasies.** Because the results relied on participants reporting from home, it is possible that they were writing about dreams that took place in non-REM sleep, rather than REM sleep. In addition, some fantasies may have taken place when people were feeling drowsy and so the brain functions like it does in non-REM sleep. Due to these **extraneous variables**, the differences between dreams and fantasies may have actually been greater than the results suggested.

- **The sample was difficult to generalise. Although a number of reports were analysed, they came from only twelve different people.** Also, the majority of these were females, which could affect the nature of dreams and fantasies, giving results which were gender biased.
- **The results may lack construct validity. This is because dreams and fantasies are complex phenomena.** Even if they were described accurately, the fact they were rated and reduced to numbers means that they are oversimplified. Critics argue that data on dreams should be qualitative rather than quantitative.

For more information on self-report, see page 183.

For more information on social desirability, see page 202.

For more information on independent variables, see page 172.

For more information on generalisation, see page 176.

For more information on construct validity, see page 202.

Check your understanding

1. Why were Williams *et al.* interested in the difference in the bizarreness of dreams and fantasies in their study?
2. In what way was self-report used in this study?
3. What were the two ratings used in this study?
4. Why was more than one judge used in the study?
5. According to results, what differences were found between reports of dreams and fantasies?

STUDY HINT
You only have to know about applications based on research into sleep. There is no need to look at applications for dreaming. Just as well really – it is easy to see how we might help people to sleep better, but how exactly would you help someone to dream?!

Insomnia
Inability to get to sleep or stay asleep.

Relaxation techniques
Strategies for making people feel more relaxed both physically and psychologically.

Sleep hygiene
Strategies that support a good night's sleep.

STUDY HINT
Remember, features of insomnia is required in the application part of the OCR specification.

Application: development of treatments for insomnia

We have established that sleep, and dreaming within it, is important for both our physical and psychological health. Therefore, if people suffer from sleep disorders it is important to try to develop treatments for them.

The impact of neurological damage to the hypothalamus on sleep

Neurological damage to the hypothalamus can happen after surgery; a disease or tumour; a trauma, such as an accident or a stroke; or degeneration due to old age. Because the suprachiasmatic nucleus (SCN) is part of the hypothalamus, this damage can result in **insomnia** among other problems. There is no way of undoing damage to the brain, so how can we help people in this situation? Because one of the problems is that melatonin production is not triggered in the normal way by lack of light, it can be addressed by giving patients a melatonin substitute at night-time. However, use of drugs is not a long-term option so the brain might need to be 'retrained' through other methods to help patients to sleep, such as **relaxation techniques** and **sleep hygiene** education.

Relaxation techniques

Using relaxation techniques before bedtime can help people to get to sleep more easily. These include the following strategies:

- **Clearing the mind**. People with insomnia are advised to set aside some time each day where they write down their worries. Once they've done this, they must try to stop themselves from worrying at any other time of the day.

Before getting ready for sleep, they then write down the worries they might have while in bed and set them to one side. When in bed, they should close their eyes and imagine these worries floating away in a balloon, leaving the mind free of worry.

- **Deep breathing**. This is best done in an upright sitting position, so people should do it before getting into bed. It involves people closing their mouth and inhaling through their nose for four seconds, then holding their breath for seven seconds and finally fully exhaling for about eight seconds. It is recommended to repeat this three or four times.
- **Relieving tension in the body**. This can be done in bed and involves people relaxing separate groups of muscles. The aim is to visualise each set of muscles being relaxed as they go through the exercise. Starting with the feet and working their way up their body, people tense a muscle by contracting and flexing it for a few seconds and then releasing it suddenly, relaxing, and allowing the body to go limp before moving onto the next set of muscles.

Relaxation techniques are particularly useful for people whose insomnia is predominately caused by anxiety. This is because relaxation techniques are an effort to rebalance the **nervous system**. In normal circumstances, stress and anxiety cause the **sympathetic nervous system** to respond, but this is balanced by the actions of the **parasympathetic nervous system**. However, if the stress is extreme and prolonged, it is more difficult for the parasympathetic nervous system to do its job and so relaxation techniques are an attempt to take some conscious control of this. For example, deep breathing normalises the heart and respiration rate as the parasympathetic nervous system should do.

Sleep hygiene education

There are many things that can be done externally to improve sleep. People are encouraged to 'clean up' their environment and their lives to help them sleep, and this advice sometimes comes under the heading of 'sleep hygiene'.

Sleep hygiene logically relates to what we know about sleep disorders. It therefore includes things such as reducing alcohol, caffeine and nicotine intake, as well as avoiding eating large meals just before bedtime. It also includes advice such as avoid taking naps, do regular exercise and expose yourself to enough natural daylight.

Sleep hygiene and the physical environment

The physical environment – literally the place we sleep in – can also be improved to promote good sleep. Ideally, bedrooms should be dark, quiet and neither too warm or too cold. This means trying to sleep with the light on or while listening to music is not conducive to sleep. The bed and bedding should be comfortable, bedrooms should be decluttered, and anything that is a reminder of the working day should be out of sight (computers, smart phones, work brought home, etc.). Additionally, if you have a clock, it should face away from you; otherwise it acts as a reminder that time is passing as you lay awake.

▲ Relaxation techniques, perhaps obviously, help us to relax. A relaxed person is going to find it much easier to fall to sleep.

Sympathetic nervous system

A division of the nervous system that controls the flight or fight response (whether someone escapes or faces danger) when faced with stress.

Parasympathetic nervous system

A division of the nervous system that regulates organ and gland functions during rest, and counters the response of the sympathetic nervous system.

Challenge

Time to get creative. Your task is to draw, make a collage or even build a model of a bedroom which has either good sleep hygiene or bad sleep hygiene. If you are feeling particularly industrious, you could attempt both types of bedrooms!

Chapter 6 Sleep and dreaming

> **DIY**
>
> Your brief is to design a **questionnaire study** that allows you to look at sleep hygiene. You need to devise a series of questions to help you to establish whether a person has good sleep hygiene or not. You also need to devise a scoring system as part of your questionnaire to show how good a person's sleep hygiene is.
>
> You are going to compare two distinct groups on sleep hygiene. You can decide what these two groups are, but an obvious one is to divide people into those who sleep well and those who do not, or those who sleep more than average and those who sleep less. Other options could be comparing genders or different age groups – or you might have lots of interesting ideas of your own!
>
> Once you have decided on your groups and then collected your data, you need to decide how you are going to analyse it. As you will have collected quantitative data, you will have the choice of measures of central tendency or other similar measures. Think about the best way to present your results. You may find it interesting to compare what you have found out with others.

Check your understanding

1. How can people be helped if their insomnia is due to neurological damage?
2. What strategies are used as part of relaxation techniques?
3. What should a person's physical environment be like if they are going to promote good sleep hygiene?

> **SUMMARY**
>
> Sleep and dreaming are something that everyone experiences, which tells us they are an important part of human life. Sleep and dreaming are instinctive behaviours which are under the control of our biology, and so the brain and body play a large part in it, such as by using endogenous pacemakers and exogenous zeitgebers. Sleep has many benefits and is essential for good physical and psychological health. This can be seen in the case of sleep disorders, which can lead to many serious problems for people who suffer from them. This is why psychologists and other professionals have carried out research to develop treatments for insomnia.
>
> There is more debate on the functions of dreams. Freudian theory suggests that they are a way of dealing with traumas from the past and this could be supported by Freud's own case of the Wolfman. Meanwhile, the activation synthesis theory of dreaming would argue that dreams are more about making sense of the random neural activity that happens when people are asleep. This would explain the results from Williams *et al.*'s study where they found the dreams had more bizarre content than daytime fantasies. Whatever their function, dreams are not something we can easily control and it seems like they will always be a part of human nature.

Practice questions

The questions in this textbook have been written by the authors, Mark Billingham and Helen Kitching. They have not been produced or endorsed by OCR.

1 Several parts of the brain associated with sleep and dreaming.
Look at the following diagram.
Draw lines to match the part of the brain to its correct definition. **[3 marks]**

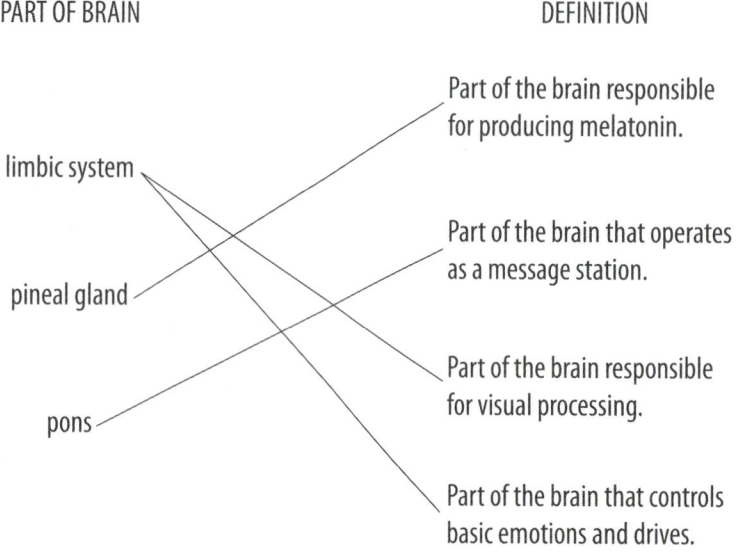

The candidate has correctly matched all three parts of the brain with their definition, but has also drawn an additional line from the limbic system to the false definition. This means they lose a mark and receive a total of two marks.

2 Using an example, explain what is meant by an exogenous zeitgeber. **[3 marks]**

An exogenous zeitgeber is a feature of the environment that help us regulate our sleep. It can be either physical or social. For example, if someone went camping they might go to bed early when it gets dark and be awoken early by the dawn. Their sleep would become regulated by the natural environment.

This is a good answer, worth three marks. The example of light is nicely illustrated through the camping example, and the student demonstrates a sound understanding of what an exogenous zeitgeber is.

3 Explain **one** criticism of the activation synthesis theory of dreaming. **[3 marks]**

One criticism of the theory is that it is contradicted by evidence that people have recurring dreams or dreams with similar stories. Sometimes people also carry on the same dream if they've been woken up and go back to sleep again. These patterns suggest that dreams are not just random neural processes.

This response provides a strong criticism, supported by two examples of evidence that contradict the theory. Importantly, it ends with a development that shows how the theory may be wrong. Three marks would be awarded.

Chapter 6 Sleep and dreaming

4 Eric is a 20 year old university student who suffers from sleep onset insomnia.

   a State what is meant by sleep onset insomnia. [1 mark]

   This is when someone struggles to get to sleep and may lie awake for hours.

Accurate statement – one mark.

   b Give **one** cause of sleep onset insomnia. [1 mark]

   Too much anxiety.

Accurate response – one mark.

   c Suggest ways in which Eric's insomnia could be treated. [6 marks]

   It depends what is causing Eric's sleep insomnia, but if he is suffering from too much anxiety, improving his sleep hygiene could help him get to sleep. For example, he could make sure that he turns off his computer and leaves his phone downstairs so that he is not worried about emails or messages coming in. He could turn his alarm clock to face the wall so that he is not constantly aware of what the time is, which might make him more anxious. He should make sure his bedroom is a calm, dark place where he can feel relaxed. He should keep it tidy and perhaps buy some blackout curtains to make it really dark.

   Another thing that Eric could try is using relaxation techniques just before bedtime. For example, he could keep a book beside his bed to write down anything that is worrying him. If he knows that his worries are written down, he doesn't have to think about them. This would then reduce his anxiety and help him sleep. He could also do deep breathing exercises once he has written his thoughts down, to help him relax even more. This involves inhaling through the nose for four seconds, holding that breath for 7 seconds and then exhaling for 8 seconds, then repeating it three or four times. This helps balance the nervous system by normalising heart and respiration rates, which can be a problem with anxiety.

   If Eric does all these things, it should help him sleep.

The candidate has sensibly identified a potential cause of Eric's insomnia, which has helped them to focus their answer. The response itself coherently offers both breadth and depth, suggesting a range of techniques that are well explained. This is easily good enough to earn all six marks.

5 Use your knowledge and understanding from across the psychology course to explain how far you agree with the following viewpoint:

'Freud's approach to explaining dreaming is too subjective.'

In your answer you should refer to **both** Freud's theory of dreaming and his case study of the Wolfman, and to another area of psychology that is considered less subjective.

[13 marks]

Freud was interested in understanding mental illness. He thought that the human mind was made up of unconscious thoughts, and that by understanding these he would be able to understand why people become mentally ill. He thought that the best way to understand what was happening in someone's unconscious mind was by analysing their dreams. This is because he believed that dreams were repressed urges from the unconscious mind being released. He saw this as wish-fulfilment of people's deepest desires that couldn't be fulfilled in real life. Freud used dream analysis to try to understand the case of Wolfman, who was a man suffering from depression. Freud spoke to the man and found that when he was a child he had had a dream about wolves. Freud interpreted this dream as the result of the man having witnessed his parents having sex when he was a boy, which lead to fear of his father and castration anxiety. For example, Freud analysed the wolf's long tails as representing the father's penis.

There are a number of reasons why this interpretation may be seen as subjective. For example, Freud was interpreting something that happened when the man was a young boy. The man's recall of the dream may therefore not be accurate. Even if he had written it down the next morning, he may not have remembered all of the details. This makes the data unreliable. It is qualitative data and hard to analyse objectively. Freud only analysed the dream of one participant. As the man was suffering from depression, it is unlikely that the results would be generalisable so again too subjective. The unconscious mind is an abstract concept and cannot be observed. There is no hard evidence to suggest that dreams actually do represent the unconscious mind.

Freud did not use other people to independently interpret Wolfman's dream, meaning that there could have been experimenter bias, where Freud interpreted the dream in a way that other people might not have. This makes it very subjective and therefore not scientific.

In contrast to Freud's research, Braun et al. carried out a laboratory experiment to test reconstructive memory.

Although memories are more conscious than dreams, they are still potentially subjective because they rely on people's recall. However, Braun et al. tried to deal with this by measuring recall as objectively as possible by using a rating scale and a 'hidden question'. They also checked for demand characteristics. In contrast to Freud, they used a sample of over 100 participants, making any generalisation much more reliable. A number of controls were also included in the experiment to make it easier to establish cause and effect. The results from Braun et al.'s study were primarily quantitative and so less open to interpretation.

To conclude, Braun et al.'s research shows that Freud's is not scientific enough. However, Braun et al.'s research has its own issues, such as a lack of ecological validity and a lack of construct validity. These limitations are often associated with being scientific.

In fairness to Freud, it is very hard to scientifically measure and analyse dreams. They take place whilst we are asleep, and it is therefore impossible to know for sure whether they have been recalled accurately. Any interpretation of the content of the dreams is likely to be subjective, but Freud could have made his study more reliable by using more than one person to interpret the dream.

This answer provides a clear and accurate descriptions of both Freud's theory and his case study of the Wolfman. The information presented is relevant and substantiated with reference to subjectivity. All six AO1 marks are earned.

There is a thorough analysis of Freud's approach, with Braun et al.'s study serving as an effective contrast from another area of psychology. Points are clear and pertinent, and the response reaches a substantiated judgement. All seven AO3 marks are earned here. In total, this excellent response is worth full marks.

7 Research methods

Psychologists are interested in many different areas of study, from child development to psychological problems, from investigating the brain to investigating the mind, from focusing on the past to looking at current patterns of behaviour. However, whatever their area of interest, psychologists approach research in a similar way, following certain procedures. These procedures can be divided into three main stages of investigation: planning, doing and analysing research.

This chapter should enable you to:
- develop knowledge and understanding of key features involved in planning psychological research, including formulating hypotheses, setting up and controlling variables, using experimental designs, sampling and considering ethics
- demonstrate the range of methods and techniques available for doing psychological research – experiments, interviews, questionnaires, observations, case studies, correlations - including their associated strengths and weaknesses, and objectives
- demonstrate how different types of data can be collected, analysed and presented in psychological research including considering issues of reliability, validity and bias
- develop the competence to select and apply key mathematical procedures and processes when doing psychological research with a focus on arithmetical and numerical computation, and handling data

▲ What causes us to experience stress? This is something that psychologists may be interested in researching.

Planning research

Before psychologists do their research, there are certain planning decisions to make, including what they are interested in studying. For example, a psychologist may be interested in what causes stress in people.

Hypotheses

Psychologists make predictions about what their results will be before they carry out their research. These predictions are known as **hypotheses**. For example, a psychologist may predict that noise is a cause of stress.

There are two main types of hypothesis: an **alternative hypothesis** and a **null hypothesis**. An alternative hypothesis predicts a pattern in results; whether that is a difference or a correlation.

> For more information on correlations, see page 189.

To predict a difference, a psychologist needs to set up at least two conditions or compare at least two groups. For example, they could measure participants' stress levels under noisy conditions and then under silent conditions.

The psychologist's alternative hypothesis could be:

'There will be a significant difference between the heart rates of participants when tested under noisy conditions compared to when tested under silent conditions.'

Hypothesis (pl. hypotheses)
A statement predicting what research results will show before it is carried out.

Alternative hypothesis
A statement that predicts a difference or correlation in results.

Null hypothesis
A statement that predicts no difference or correlation in results.

> **STUDY HINT**
> If you are asked to write a hypothesis, try to be specific about how a variable is measured. Note how this statement refers to heart rates rather than stress in general.

Chapter 7 Research methods

STUDY HINT
When predicting a difference, a hypothesis will always contain an independent variable (IV) and a dependent variable (DV). It is important to make sure that both conditions, or groups, are stated when you refer to the IV.

In a different example, a psychologist could compare the stress levels of people who work in noisy workplaces and people who work in quiet workplaces.

The alternative hypothesis could be:

'There will be a significant difference in how much job satisfaction people report, depending on whether they work in a noisy workplace or a quiet workplace.'

Rather than predicting a difference, the psychologist could predict a correlation between two variables.

In this case, the psychologist's alternative hypothesis could be:

'There will be a correlation between how loud a sound is played and how stressed participants rate themselves on a scale of 1 to 10.'

STUDY HINT
Start your hypothesis with 'There will be', and decide whether you are predicting a correlation or a difference. Then describe the variables and make your prediction. When predicting a difference, write the DV before the IV. The order does not matter for correlation predictions.

Extension
All of the examples of alternative hypotheses given in this section are non-directional. However, often psychologists can predict the direction of their results. What would the alternative hypotheses look like if they were directional?

A null hypothesis is the 'opposite' of an alternative hypothesis because it predicts no pattern or trend in results. Put simply, it predicts no difference or correlation. This means that in a piece of research, either the null or alternative hypothesis will be supported. The psychologist's job is to find out which hypothesis is correct, and reject the one that is not supported.

Using the alternative hypotheses from earlier, the psychologist's null hypotheses would be:

'There will be no significant difference between the heart rates of participants when tested under noisy conditions compared to when tested under silent conditions.'

and

'There will not be a correlation between how loud a sound is played and how stressed participants rate themselves on a scale of 1 to 10.'

STUDY HINT
Thinking of the word 'nil' might help you remember what a null hypothesis is. It predicts *no* pattern.

DIY
Carry out a piece of research to investigate which of the following hypotheses should be rejected.

Null hypothesis: *'There will be no difference in the speed at which participants complete a task under noisy and under quiet conditions.'*

Alternative hypothesis: *'There will be a difference in the speed at which participants complete a task under noisy and quiet conditions.'*

What is the task going to be? How will you set up the noisy and quiet conditions? What **controls** will you put into place?

STUDY HINT
If you are asked to write a hypothesis in the exam, check to see if you are asked to formulate a null or an alternative hypothesis. If you write the wrong type, you could end up with no marks even if it is really well constructed. The same is true if you predict a correlation when it should be a difference, and vice versa.

Check your understanding

1. What is a hypothesis?
2. What two patterns can an alternative hypothesis predict?
3. What is the difference between a null hypothesis and an alternative hypothesis?

Variables

Research often deals with variables: variables are anything that can change. Making changes or testing for changes is how psychologists and other scientists work out the cause of something such as the cause of stress.

Hypotheses that predict a difference contain two key variables: the **independent variable** (IV) and the **dependent variable** (DV). The IV is often made up of the two conditions or two groups (e.g. working in a group or working alone). This is what researchers manipulate (e.g. they make participants work in a group and then make them work by themselves). The IV is manipulated to see whether it has an effect on the DV. When something new or specific is being tested, this is sometimes called the **experimental group**. The other group is the **control group** and is there for comparison. Therefore, they measure, rather than manipulate, the dependent variable.

Think about it this way: a psychologist will predict that if they do 'so and so' then 'such and such' will happen. The 'so and so' is the IV (the thing the psychologist does). The 'such and such' is the DV (what the psychologist predicts).

STUDY HINT
You may be asked to identify an IV or DV in the exam. Students often get the IV and DV mixed up. Check by asking yourself whether the IV you have identified affects the DV. Double-check by asking yourself whether the DV depends on the IV. You could use a diagram like the one below to help you.

Independent variable
Something the researcher changes or manipulates.

Dependent variable
Something that is measured to see if it has changed (after an independent variable has been manipulated).

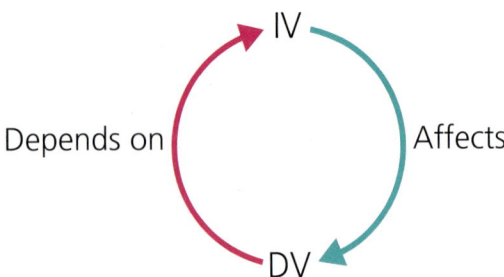

When researchers predict a correlation, there are no IVs or DVs. This is because correlations do not show **cause and effect**. Instead, they measure two **co-variables** to see if there is a relationship between them. For example, a psychologist may investigate whether there is a correlation between people's blood pressure and anxiety levels. Here, both blood pressure and anxiety levels are co-variables.

The best method to establish whether one variable affects another is to do an experiment. This is because in natural situations it is difficult to isolate a variable and state that it is definitely the cause of something else. Experiments allow psychologists to have control over **extraneous variables**.

Cause and effect
The process of one variable affecting a change in another.

Co-variable
Something that changes in relation to another variable.

Extraneous variable
A variable, apart from the independent variable, that can affect the dependent variable unless it's controlled.

For more information on experiments see page 181.

Standardisation

A way of controlling extraneous variables that keeps them the same across conditions.

Check your understanding

1. What is the difference between an independent variable and a dependent variable?
2. Why do experiments have independent and dependent variables?
3. What kind of investigation uses co-variables?
4. What is meant by the term 'extraneous variable'?
5. How can standardisation be used to control extraneous variables?

Experimental design

The way participants are allocated to conditions in an experiment.

Repeated measures design

An experimental design where participants take part in each condition.

Independent measures design

An experimental design where participants are different in each condition.

Challenge

Imagine you wanted to carry out an experiment where you test a group of people who have had eight hours sleep to compare their ability to solve problems with a group of people who have had four hours sleep.

List the extraneous variables you would want to control and outline how you would control each one. State how many of your controls use standardisation.

Make a list of what ethical issues you might have if you conducted this experiment. How could you overcome them?

Imagine a psychologist wants to investigate whether working in a noisy workplace causes more stress to workers than working in a quiet workplace. Although the IV is whether the workplace is noisy or quiet, there are lots of other things that could change (or differ) between the workplaces that could affect stress levels of workers, for example, the nature of their work, how many hours they have to work per day, what their manager is like and so on. All of these factors are extraneous variables. A common way to control extraneous variables is to keep them the same across conditions: this is known as **standardisation**. In the previous example, the psychologist could try to find two workplaces where the same type of work is done for the same number of hours per day. However, other extraneous variables may be difficult to control, for example, making sure that managers have the same personality or style.

STUDY HINT

If you are asked to identify an extraneous variable, look at the DV and ask yourself: what could affect this measure? For example, if the DV was **aggression**, what factors could affect this - sex? Age? Diet? Tiredness? However, make sure you don't come up with the IV! You are sometimes asked how you would control an extraneous variable you have identified so make sure it is one that you can deal with. Ask yourself whether it is possible to standardise it or not.

Experimental designs

Before a psychologist carries out an experiment, they need to decide on an experimental design. An **experimental design** refers to how participants are allocated experimental conditions. Many experiments have two conditions, for example, a researcher might be testing whether participants perform better when they are put in a crisis situation or in a calm situation. In terms of experimental design, the psychologist has two main options. The first option is to test all of the participants under both conditions: this is what is known as a **repeated measures design**. In other words, they would measure participants under one condition and then repeat the test under the other condition (e.g. under both calm and crisis conditions). The alternative to this is to test some participants in the calm condition and then the remaining participants in the crisis condition. The researcher could do this by **randomly** allocating each participant one of the two conditions, or by alternating between the two. The main point is that each condition will have a distinct set of participants. This is known as an **independent measures design**. The participants in one condition are independent from the participants in the other.

Sometimes a psychologist will not have a choice of experimental designs. For example, if they are comparing people with a mental illness and people without, then this has to be independent measures design; a psychologist cannot randomly allocate people to one condition or the other. Where psychologists do have a choice, it is not straightforward as one experimental design is not better than another. In fact, as the table on page 175 shows, the advantages of one tend to be the disadvantages of the other.

OCR GCSE Psychology

> **DIY**
>
> Carry out an experiment to test how many words from a list your participants can recall. The IV is whether the words are listed with or without images. The DV is how many words your participants can recall. As part of your planning, identify any potential extraneous variables and describe how you could control these.

> **STUDY HINT**
>
> It's not unusual for students to muddle up experiments with experimental designs. Look out for the word 'design' to remind you that you should be thinking about how an experiment is designed in terms of its participants and conditions.

▲ Repeated measures design involves using the same participants in both conditions. You need to watch out for order effects.

▲ Independent measures design involves using different participants in each condition. This can lead to individual differences becoming an extraneous variable.

Table 7.1 Strengths and weaknesses of experimental designs

	Strengths	Weaknesses
Repeated measures design	• Comparing 'like with like' so differences are not due to individual differences between participants. • Fewer participants need to be recruited, saving time and money.	• Participants may perform worse on the second condition due to the boredom or fatigue effect. • Participants may perform better on the second condition due to the practice effect. • Participants may work out the independent variable and change their behaviour accordingly (the effect of demand characteristics). • The task may need to be changed between conditions making it an extraneous variable.
Independent measures design	• No **order effects** (boredom/fatigue effect, practice effect, demand characteristics). • The same task can be used in both conditions because participants will not be familiar with it.	• Differences between conditions could be due to participant variables. • Potentially, more participants need to be recruited as they cannot be used more than once per condition.

Order effects

Factors that impact negatively on research findings because participants follow the same order of conditions in an experiment.

> **Challenge**
>
> Consider the strengths and weaknesses of the two experimental designs. Can you apply each one to an experiment where participants are tested on their task performance under crisis and calm conditions? For example, in a repeated measures design, the participants could get better at the task with practice.

> **Extension**
>
> The problem of order effects can be reduced when using a repeated measures design if a technique called **counterbalancing** is used. Investigate what this type of control is. Explain how it would address the issue of order effects in an experiment where crisis and calm conditions are compared.

> **Check your understanding**
>
> 1 What is meant by the term 'experimental design'?
> 2 What is the difference between a repeated measures design and an independent measures design?
> 3 What advantages does an independent measures design have over a repeated measures design?
> 4 What advantages does a repeated measures design have over an independent measures design?

Populations and sampling

As part of their planning, psychologists have to decide who they are going to do their research on. These people are called participants, but as a group they can also be called a **sample**. A sample is a smaller group drawn from a target population. A **target population** is everyone that a psychologist is interested in investigating.

Sometimes this may be all human beings (as with human memory) or may be more specific, such as children (as with **cognitive development**) or criminals (as with criminal behaviour).

> **STUDY HINT**
> The word 'sample' is used outside of psychology to mean a similar thing. For example, if you sampled a new food product in a supermarket, you would be trying a small bit of it. Hopefully it would tell you what the rest of the product was like; in other words, it would be representative.

Ideally, a sample would be **representative** of its target population. This means the participants who make up the sample will be a good cross-section of the population, because they represent a range of characteristics, such as sex, age and personality. When a sample is representative it means that research results have more **generalisability**. In other words, if a psychologist has a representative sample of adults and finds that most are caused more stress by their home life than their work life, then they can generalise and suggest that this is true of the rest of the adult population.

> **STUDY HINT**
> There are many other **sampling methods** used by psychologists, but only **random, opportunity** and **self-selected sampling** are on the OCR specification. This means these are the only ones that you can be asked about in the exam. However, when you are asked to design your own investigation in the exam, you can get credit for writing about other methods that you may know about from elsewhere.

Sometimes samples are not very representative because of a bias in the sample. For example, if a target population contained both sexes (as most do) then a sample made up of only men could be described as unrepresentative. In these circumstances, it would be difficult to make generalisations.

> **STUDY HINT**
> Students sometimes say things like 'random sampling is grabbing whoever is around'. Although this sounds quite 'random', you now know it is not. 'Grabbing whoever' sounds much more like opportunity sampling. Random sampling is much more technical than this.

> **STUDY HINT**
> In the exam, make sure you can distinguish between questions that ask you to describe or define a sampling method, and those that ask you how a particular sampling method could be carried out.

For more information on types of bias see page 204.

The larger the sample, the more representative of the target population it is likely to be. For example, if a psychologist studies 500 people from a population of 1000, it will be easier to make generalisations about the other 500. Very small samples are often accused of being unrepresentative.

Sample
A group selected from a larger population.

Target population
The entire set of people psychologists want to research.

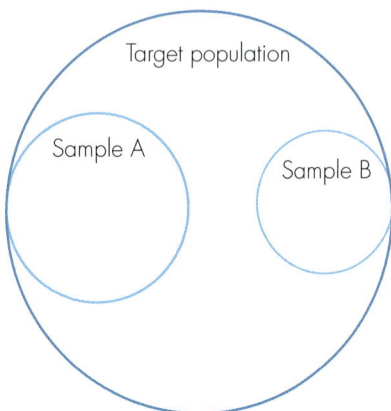

▲ Sample A is likely to represent the population better than Sample B because it is larger.

Representative
An accurate reflection of a larger group.

Generalisability
The ability to draw conclusions that apply to a larger group outside of research.

Random sample
A sample selected using chance.

Opportunity sample
A sample selected by convenience.

Self-selected sample
A sample selected through volunteers.

> **Something to think about**
> Are large samples always better than small samples? Think about that example again. If the sample of 500 contained no women but the sample of 50 contained both sexes, which sample would be more representative?

Chapter 7 Research methods

Sampling method
A technique for selecting participants from a population.

> **STUDY HINT**
> When evaluating sampling methods, try to use the words 'representative', 'generalise' and 'bias'. Appropriate use of psychological terms can sometimes get you higher marks in the exam, and is better than writing things like 'it applies to other people' or 'it is not a fair sample'.

Sampling methods

There are a number of **methods** that psychologists can use to select a sample. Three key methods are random sampling, opportunity sampling and self-selected sampling.

Time for some maths
Copy out the following table. Calculate the percentage of the target population represented in each sample. The first one is done for you as an example.

Target population (N)	Sample (n)	Calculations	Percentage of population in sample
1,000	100	100/1000 x 100	10%
200	40		
13,755	60		
677	50		

Decide which sample is most likely to give a representative sample. Justify your answer.

Challenge
Copy and complete the table below by filling in the last column using the examples listed here:
- By putting the names of a target population 'into a hat' and drawing out the required number for the sample.
- Using family or friends because the researcher has regular contact with them.
- Using random number generator software and choosing people whose numbers correspond to those selected.
- Advertising for participants (e.g. in a magazine/newspaper, through posters on a university campus).
- Using people that are in the vicinity, for example, university students, work colleagues, local residents.
- Posting a survey online to see who will respond.

Name of method	Definition	How it could be done
Random	Where everyone in the target population has an equal chance of being selected.	
Opportunity	Where participants are chosen because they are easily available.	
Self-selected	Where participants nominate themselves for a study without being directly approached.	

Strengths and weaknesses of sampling methods

One strength of opportunity sampling is that it is quick and convenient, particularly when you compare it with random sampling, which takes some effort to set up. However, a weakness is that it tends to be biased (and unrepresentative) for a number of reasons. For example, studying people who are available because they live close by may result in a group of similar people, in terms of age, education, ethnic group or social class.

One strength of self-selected sampling is that the psychologist does not have to put much effort into selecting participants as they volunteer themselves. The psychologist can also be sure that they have the full **consent** of the participants as they've come forward willingly. However, a weakness is that it tends to be biased as certain types of people are more likely to volunteer to take part in psychological research and therefore will be over-represented in the sample.

One strength of random sampling compared to the other two methods is that it is very likely to give a representative sample. This is because there is no bias in the selection and it is left to chance; most types of people will be represented in the right proportions. However, there is a chance of a freak sample where certain types of people are over-represented and others are under-represented or missing from the sample.

Consent

When a person agrees to being studied or agrees on someone else's behalf.

DIY

Use your classmates to test how often random sampling gives a representative sample compared to a freak sample.

Your classmates are the target population, so first you need to choose three or four characteristics that you can use to divide them up (for example: sex, month they were born, tutor group or what area they live in) and record these. Find out the percentage of each characteristic, for example, females to males may be 60 per cent and 40 per cent.

Now, write your classmates' names and the groups they belong to on separate pieces of paper. Put all of these names into a container and draw out half of them so that your sample is 50 per cent of the target population. Analyse how well the different groups are represented.

Carry out this test at least five times. Remember to put the names back in each time!

What conclusions can you draw? Do you tend to get a representative sample most of the time? How common are freak samples?

Something to think about

What types of people do you think are more or less likely to be in a self-selected sample and why?

Extension

Review the samples used in key studies that you have learned about so far. See if you can rank them from the most representative samples to the least. Justify the decisions that you make.

STUDY HINT

In the exam, you may have to evaluate a sample that a psychologist has used. The strengths and weaknesses you have learned about here would be your starting point but you would also earn marks by applying them to the particular study being referred to. For example, as well as saying that an opportunity sample tends to be biased, you would need to look at the study to see what types of people were selected and how that would impact on the results specifically.

Check your understanding

1. What is meant by the term 'sample'?
2. What is meant by the term 'target population'?
3. What is the link between representativeness and generalisability?
4. How do the following sample methods work?
   - random sampling
   - opportunity sampling
   - self-selected sampling.
5. What is a strength and a weakness of each of the sampling methods listed in Question 4?

Ethical guidelines

An important issue to consider before carrying out research is how participants will be personally affected by taking part. Psychologists should ensure that participants are treated appropriately, and there are **ethical guidelines** to help them to do this. In the UK, the guidelines are known as **The British Psychological Society's Code of Ethics and Conduct**.

Ethical issues

There are a number of issues that can arise in research that psychologists should try to avoid, unless it can be justified.

Psychological harm

Psychological research can potentially have an effect on people's minds and behaviour, as that is what is studied. Although it is not possible to guarantee that there will be no effect on the participant from taking part in the research, psychologists should not cause participants distress, discomfort or embarrassment. In other words, participants should be protected from **psychological harm**. As well, participants should generally leave a study in the same state as which they entered it, although not all psychologists agree with this point. Some argue that participants may actually benefit from taking part in their study, for example, they may actually feel better about themselves afterwards, or have learned a new skill. Overall, the general guideline is that psychologists should respect and be responsible for their participants. If they do not do this, their research may be described as unethical.

Deception

Psychologists should not unnecessarily deceive participants by misleading them about the aim of a piece of research or by making them think they have done something which they have not. However, sometimes this can be justified. If participants know the true aim of a study they could behave differently because they think they are helping the researcher. Sometimes, participants may need to believe they have done something they have not in order for the psychologist to test how they react. For example, a researcher may pretend to be in danger to see under what circumstances people would help him.

Lack of informed consent

Informed consent describes the situation in which participants have not only agreed to take part in a study ('consent') but also know what the study is about and what they are going to be expected to do ('informed'). As outlined above, it is not always appropriate to inform the participants of what is happening in a study, as they may not share their real thoughts or show their true behaviour. There are times when a participant may be under investigation without knowing it, so they cannot have given consent. This is normally acceptable when people are observed in public places because they would expect to be watched in public by all sorts of people for all sorts of reasons anyway. However, it would not be acceptable to observe someone when they think they are in a more private setting, such as their own home, or a toilet cubicle.

Additionally, some people are not in a position to give their own consent, such as children who are not considered old enough to understand why they are being studied. For this reason, ethical guidelines say that when participants are under the age of sixteen their parents or carers should be asked to give consent for them to take part in psychological research.

Ethical guidelines
Recommendations that consider the welfare of participants.

The British Psychological Society's Code of Ethics and Conduct
A set of criteria – under the headings of respect, competence, responsibility and integrity – that psychologists should aim to follow when carrying out research.

▲ Psychological research should be carried out to help people, so we need to make sure, as best we can, they do not experience suffering along the way.

> **Something to think about**
> Can you think of other people who may not be in a position to give their own consent?

Psychological harm
An ethical issue that relates to protecting participants from distress, discomfort and embarrassment.

Deception
An ethical issue that relates to being honest with participants about the purpose and process of research.

Lack of informed consent
An ethical issue that relates to participants agreeing to take part in research, knowing what that research is about.

Ways of dealing with ethical issues

Despite the guidelines, **ethical** issues will continue to arise in psychological research, so it is important they are dealt with in the best way possible. Examples of this are given below.

> **STUDY HINT**
> You may be asked to identify an ethical issue arising in a piece of research and how you would deal with it. It is important that you identify an issue that you know you can deal with, so you can describe the solution in some detail.

Debriefing

Debriefing involves informing participants of the aim of a piece of research *after the event*. Participants should always be debriefed at the end of a study, even when they have taken part in an investigation they have not been aware of. As part of the debriefing, researchers should make sure participants have fully understood the true nature of the study. Researchers should ask the participants about their experience, in order to check for any negative effects or misunderstandings. In some cases, counselling may need to be offered to ensure that participants leave in a healthy state of mind.

Right to withdraw

Participants should always have the **right to withdraw** from a study at any point and shouldn't feel pressured to continue, even if they've given informed consent. They should be informed of this right at the start of the study. Obviously, if participants have been studied without their knowledge then they cannot withdraw themselves. In these circumstances, participants should be offered the right to withdraw any data collected on them, and this would be done as part of the debriefing.

Confidentiality

Even if participants are willing to take part in research, it is the psychologist's responsibility to make sure they protect their **confidentiality**. As a lot of psychological research is quite private and sensitive, any data collected should remain anonymous – this is why participants are often referred to by numbers. Similarly, it would be unethical to take photographs or other types of recordings which could identify the participants. However, participants do sometimes have to agree that their personal data can be shared with other researchers.

> **Challenge**
> Produce a poster to summarise the 'dos and don'ts' of psychological research with reference to ethical considerations.

Ethics
What is morally right or wrong. In psychology, there are ethical guidelines which give psychologists an idea of what they should and shouldn't do when conducting their research. This is to protect both their participants and the psychologists themselves.

Debriefing
A way of dealing with ethical issues at the end of research, including an explanation of the study.

Right to withdraw
A way of dealing with ethical issues by ensuring participants know they can opt out of or stop a study at any point.

Confidentiality
A way of dealing with ethical issues by making sure that participants are not identifiable through use of names or other types of data.

> **Extension**
>
> Look at each of the ethical issues in this section. Explain how the three ways of dealing with them specifically addresses each of the issues. You may find it helpful to do this in a table.

> **Challenge**
>
> Imagine you are allowed to plan the most unethical piece of psychological research ever! Write an outline of what the research would involve. Then swap with a partner to see how many ethical considerations have been broken.

> **Check your understanding**
>
> 1. What is the purpose of ethical guidelines in psychological research?
> 2. What is meant by the following terms?
>   - psychological harm
>   - deception
>   - lack of informed consent.
> 3. How do the following deal with ethical issues?
>   - debriefing
>   - right to withdraw
>   - confidentiality.

Experiment
A method of collecting data which measures the effect of an IV on a DV by controlling other variables.

Interview
A method of collecting data that involves directly questioning people.

Questionnaire
A method of collecting data that involves people answering a series of pre-determined questions.

Case study
A method of collecting data that involves focusing on a small sample in detail.

Correlation
A method of analysis that looks for a relationship between two variables.

Doing research

Once psychologists have planned their research, the next stage is to conduct their study. This will involve collecting some data, which can be collected using a variety of methods, including **experiments, interviews, questionnaires, observations, case studies** and **correlations**.

Experiments

Experiments are commonly used in psychological research. They can collect data using a number of techniques, but they have certain features in common. The features of an experiment are as follows:

- an independent variable is set up (or identified)
- a dependent variable is measured
- there is an attempt to control extraneous variables.

Experiments are set up and controlled by a researcher, so they can investigate what causes something to happen or change. In other words, if they have identified the independent variable and controlled all others, then they know whether it has an effect on the dependent variable or not. This is the main strength of carrying out an experiment; no other method allows a researcher to *reliably establish cause and effect*. A common weakness is that experiments often *lack construct validity* because they tend to measure the dependent variable in a narrow way.

For more information on construct validity see page 202.

There are three types of experiments used in psychology:
1 **Laboratory experiment**: an experiment where the researcher directly manipulates the IV, and does this in a controlled environment (e.g. controlling noise, temperature, space).
2 **Field experiment**: an experiment where the researcher directly manipulates the IV, and does this in a natural environment (e.g. a school, a shopping centre, a psychiatric ward).
3 **Natural experiment**: an experiment where there is an IV but it is not directly manipulated by the researcher because it is pre-determined (e.g. comparing people with **depression** and those without) or it may not be naturally occurring and not open to control (e.g. comparing a new reading scheme being used in a school with an old one being used in a different school). Natural experiments can take place in laboratories or in the field.

STUDY HINT
You may be asked to describe what is meant by a laboratory experiment, a field experiment or a natural experiment. It is easy to focus on the 'laboratory', 'field' or 'natural' part but don't forget to also state what an 'experiment' is in general.

Strengths and weaknesses of experiments

- A strength of laboratory experiments is that they have more control over extraneous variables. This means that they are more reliable than field experiments so are easier to replicate. The fact that they are so highly standardised also makes them very objective, so there is less chance of experimenters influencing results.
- A weakness of laboratory experiments is that they have low ecological validity because of their artificial settings. They also tend to suffer from demand characteristics because participants are nearly always aware of being part of a laboratory experiment.

For more information on ecological validity see page 202.

For more information on demand characteristics see page 202.

- A strength of field experiments is that they tend to have higher ecological validity than laboratory experiments, because the environment is authentic, even if the IV is set up.
- A weakness of field experiments is that there is less control over extraneous variables, which could affect the **reliability** of results.
- A strength of natural experiments is that the experiment can be more ethical, because nothing is being manipulated. For example, you could compare people that already sleep badly with people that do not, rather than depriving someone of sleep on purpose.
- A weakness of natural experiments is that it may be difficult for researchers to match up the participants they are comparing if the IV is already in place. For example, people that sleep badly could be older than people who do not, and this becomes an extraneous variable.

Laboratory experiment
Where an IV is manipulated in a controlled environment to test its effect on a DV.

Field experiment
Where an IV is manipulated in a natural environment to test its effect on a DV.

Natural experiment
Where an IV is not directly controlled by the experimenter but its effect on a DV is still tested.

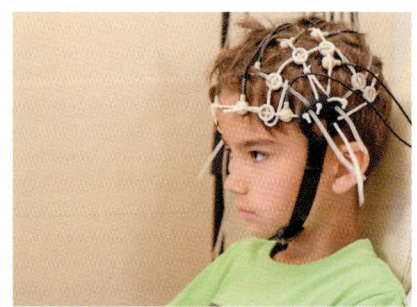

▲ How naturally does someone behave when they are being experimented on? Does it depend on the type of experiment?

STUDY HINT
Note that the strength of one type of experiment (e.g. field experiments have higher ecological validity) often gives the weakness of another type of experiment (e.g. laboratory experiments lack ecological validity) – so there are not as many different strengths and weaknesses to remember as you might think.

Chapter 7 Research methods

DIY

Imagine you are carrying out an experiment to test whether having personal space invaded affects stress levels. Draw up a plan for how this could be done using each of the three types of experiments.

STUDY HINT

When evaluating experiments make sure your strength or weakness is made explicit! For example, saying a laboratory experiment 'has a controlled environment' is actually descriptive but if you explain why this is a weakness or use a more evaluative term – 'has an artificial environment' – then this demonstrates the right skill.

Check your understanding

1. What are the three common features of all experiments?
2. What advantages do laboratory experiments have over field experiments?
3. What disadvantages do laboratory experiments have compared with field experiments?
4. What makes a natural experiment different from the other two types of experiments?

Structured interview

An interview with pre-determined questions.

Unstructured interview

An interview where questions vary depending on the interviewee's answers.

Interviews

Interviews use the **self-report** method, which means participants talk about their own thoughts, behaviour, or past experiences. The researcher directly asks questions of the interviewee and this is usually done face-to-face.

There are two main types of interviews:

1. **Structured interviews** use questions which are pre-set. This means everyone who is interviewed is asked the same series of questions.
2. **Unstructured interviews** do not have set questions. Instead, the interviewer asks questions based on the interviewees' responses. This means the interview is more like a conversation.

STUDY HINT

A common error is to think that the different types of interviews are to do with different types of questions, as in open and closed questions. However, it is to do with whether or not the questions are pre-determined.

DIY

Interview one older and one younger interviewee to see if they have different **attitudes** to social media. Do this using a structured interview. Repeat the research with a different pair of participants, but this time use an unstructured interview. Review both pieces of research to identify the strengths and weaknesses of each type of interview.

Strengths and weaknesses of interviews

- One strength of interviewing people rather than observing them is that it allows psychologists to access people's thoughts and feelings – something that cannot easily be seen but can be asked about.
- In contrast to most questionnaires, a strength of interviews is that interviewers and interviewees can clarify what questions and answers mean, therefore increasing the chance of more valid responses.
- A weakness of interviews is that people may lie or exaggerate when answering questions, which affects the validity of the results. Since the interviewer is actually engaged in the questioning, interviewees may feel obliged to give socially desirable responses, rather than being honest.
- Another weakness of interviews is that they rely on people being able to explain their thoughts and feelings. Some people may struggle to put their feelings into words, making it difficult for the interviewer to understand and find out what they want to know.

For more information on social desirability see page 202.

Check your understanding

1. How do structured interviews and unstructured interviews differ from each other?
2. What are the advantages and disadvantages of interviews?

Questionnaires

Questionnaires are another type of self-report method. They consist of a series of pre-set questions that are often written down. This means the questions are the same for everyone who takes part in the questionnaire.

Questionnaires can use **closed questions**, **open questions** or a mixture of both.

- Closed questions are questions with a fixed set of responses. These may be given in the form of multiple-choice answers or a **rating scale**. For example:

How anxious do you feel on a scale of 1 to 6?
Not anxious at all   1   2   3   4   5   6   Very anxious

- Open questions are questions where the respondent constructs their own answers. Such questions can often be answered in some depth. For example, 'to what extent do you agree with the use of drugs to treat anxiety?' or 'can you explain the kind of situations that cause you the most stress?'

Challenge

How many different ways can you think of for administering a questionnaire? Give yourself a minute and compare your list with someone else.

Closed questions

Questions which have set responses to choose from.

Open questions

Questions that have no fixed responses so participants can respond how they wish.

Rating scales

A way of answering a closed question that requires the respondent to select a number to represent their response.

Strengths and weaknesses of different types of questions

- A strength of closed questions is that they give quantitative data. This means it is easy to quantify participants' responses and is therefore easier to identify patterns. However, data can lack construct validity.
- A strength of open questions is that they give more qualitative data. This means that they allow more in-depth responses, which may give more valid results. However, data is difficult to analyse for trends.

For more information on quantitative and qualitative data, see page 192.

Time for some maths

Participants were asked to respond to the following closed question:

> **How often do you have bad dreams?**
>
> Every night   7   6   5   4   3   2   1   Never

Their results are shown below depending on whether they suffered mental health problems or not.

Rating	7	6	5	4	3	2	1
People with mental health problems	5	16	20	25	18	10	6
People without mental health problems	0	2	13	30	50	4	1

Analyse this data to decide whether people with mental health problems report having bad **dreams** more frequently than people without. There are a number of ways of doing the maths, so think carefully about what is the best way.

Extension

What is the ideal range of numbers to use on a rating scale? Does it depend? On what? Justify your response.

Challenge

Look at the following examples of closed questions and decide what is wrong with each one. There may be more than one problem.

1. How likely are you to help a stranger in difficulty, on a scale of 1 to 10?

   1   2   3   4   5   6   7   8   9   10

2. How would you describe your relationship with your family?

   Extremely good   ❏
   Very good   ❏
   Really good   ❏
   Mediocre   ❏
   Not so good   ❏

3. Do you agree that capital punishment should be re-introduced and that we should have stricter punishment in general?

   Yes   ❏
   No   ❏
   (tick one box)

Strengths and weaknesses of questionnaires

- A strength of questionnaires is that they can be used to access people's thoughts and feelings.
- Compared to interviews, questionnaires make it easy to survey a large sample quickly because they can be administered at the same time.
- Another strength is that it is possible to compare answers and look for reliable patterns and trends because all respondents are asked the same set of questions.
- A weakness of questionnaires is that respondents may misunderstand a question as they often complete them alone. In addition, the options for a closed question may not contain the answer they want to give, resulting in unanswered questions and unreliable responses.
- Another weakness is that questionnaires do not consider individuals. By asking everybody the same questions, researchers cannot explore more personal responses. This may affect the validity of responses.

> **Something to think about**
>
> Questionnaires can be anonymous in a way that interviews cannot. Some psychologists see this as a strength, others see it as a weakness. Can you work out why there are two views on this?

DIY

Look at the topics below. For each one, write a closed question and an open question that would allow you to find out something about it. Use at least one rating scale.

- Memory techniques used in everyday life
- Experiences of crime
- Attitudes towards mental illness
- Sleep patterns
- When people disobey

STUDY HINT

You may be asked to write an example of a closed or open question that relates to a study or investigation. If you have to write a closed question, make sure you include a rating scale or multiple choices. If you have to write an open question, consider including an opening answer phrase that will work with any open question, whatever it is about.

Check your understanding

1. How are questionnaires and interviews similar?
2. How are questionnaires and interviews different?
3. What are the arguments for and against using questionnaires in psychological research?
4. What are the weaknesses of using closed questions and of using open questions?

Chapter 7 Research methods

Observations

Naturalistic observation
Observing people in a real-life setting.

Controlled observation
Observing people in an environment that has been set up in some way.

Overt observation
Observing people with their knowledge.

Covert observation
Observing people without them knowing.

Participant observation
Observing people while also participating in their activities.

Non-participant observation
Observing people from a distance.

Something to think about
Could lesson observations be carried out in other ways? Is it possible for them to be controlled observations? Or covert observations? Or participant observations?

In very simple terms, observations involve the researcher watching the behaviour of participants. A strength of this method is that the researcher can see how someone behaves in a certain situation, rather than relying on them telling the truth about their experience, or being able to express their feelings.

There are many different ways of doing observations, as shown below.

1. Firstly, observations can be either **naturalistic** or **controlled**. In a naturalistic observation, participants are observed in a real-life setting. Meanwhile, a controlled observation is where participants are observed in a situation that has been set up. This is likely to be an experiment.

2. Secondly, observations can be **overt** or **covert**. An overt observation is where participants know they're being observed; psychologists are open about the fact they are carrying out an observation. In a covert observation, participants are not aware they are being observed; psychologists go 'undercover' to do their observation.

3. Finally, observations can be **participant** or **non-participant**. In a participant observation, a psychologist actually joins in with the group of people they are observing. Meanwhile, in a non-participant observation, they would 'stand back' from the group and not interfere with what they are doing.

STUDY HINT
Students can make the mistake of thinking that all participant observations are also undercover observations. This is not necessarily true. It is possible to join a group with or without them knowing.

Different types of observation can be combined to give a number of dimensions to a study. For example, an observation can be naturalistic, overt and non-participant. This is the case for most lesson observations.

▲ Would it be possible to carry out a covert, participant observation of a lesson?

> **DIY**
>
> Working in a research team if you can, decide what types of observations you would use to investigate each of the following aims. Justify your decisions for each of the aims.
>
> 1. To investigate whether pre-school children play more imaginatively than primary-school children.
> 2. To investigate how motivated different employees are, depending on the department in which they work.
> 3. To investigate how criminal gangs recruit new members.
> 4. To investigate non-verbal communication used by couples on a first date.
> 5. To investigate if **crowd behaviour** varies at different times of the day.

Strengths and weaknesses of observations

Each type of observation has its own strengths and weaknesses. A key weakness of each type of observation is identified below:

- **Naturalistic** – There is a lack of control over extraneous variables, making it difficult to reliably establish cause and effect.
- **Controlled** – Situations can be artificial, so people do not behave naturally, meaning results lack ecological validity.
- **Overt** – There may be an observer effect where participants behave differently because they are conscious of being observed, therefore affecting validity.
- **Covert** – This can be seen as unethical as participants are not aware of being observed and therefore cannot have given consent.
- **Participant** – It is more difficult for the psychologist to be objective as they may become too involved in who or what they are studying.
- **Non-participant** – The psychologist may miss important details or lack insight as they are not involved in what is being studied.

A general weakness of all types of observations is that they can be prone to **observer bias**. There is always a risk that a researcher will only see what they want to see, particularly as many behaviours are open to interpretation. This can be addressed by using more than one observer to give inter-rater reliability.

> **Extension**
>
> Another weakness for some types of observation is that it can be difficult to accurately record data. Can you identify which types of observations this applies to and why?

> **Challenge**
>
> The weakness of one type of observation tends to give the strength of its opposite (e.g. covert is unethical, but overt is ethical).
>
> Work through the list of weaknesses of the different types of observations and use these to outline the strength of each type of observation.

For more information on observer bias see page 204.

For more information on inter-rater reliability see page 201.

> **Check your understanding**
>
> 1. What is the difference between the following types of observations?
>   - naturalistic and controlled
>   - overt and covert
>   - participant and non-participant.
> 2. What advantage does each type of observation have?
> 3. What are the benefits and the limitations of using observation as a way of studying people?

Case studies

Case studies use other methods such as interviews and observations, but their key function is to collect detailed information on one person or one group. Case studies are often carried out on individuals or groups that are unusual in some way. For example, a case study of a person with brain damage may tell psychologists a lot about the functions of different areas of the brain, or a case study of a cult group may tell psychologists a lot about the processes involved in social influence.

Strengths and weaknesses of case studies

STUDY HINT
As a case study can use interviews and observations, do consider the strengths and weaknesses of these methods when evaluating the use of this method.

Qualitative data
Descriptive data.

- A strength of case studies is that they provide rich, in-depth **qualitative data** which will be high in validity, because they go into a lot of detail and are likely to get closer to the truth. It may also be possible to study individuals or groups that could not be manipulated. For example, ethically speaking, a psychologist could not purposefully cause brain damage or set up a cult.

For more information on qualitative data see page 192.

- A major weakness of case studies is the fact that they are based on small samples, often because cases are rare. This means their results and findings may not represent larger populations or 'normal' people, and it therefore is hard to generalise. In addition, case studies are very in-depth studies and so the psychologist may find it difficult to remain objective, leading to **subjective** findings and results.

Check your understanding

1. What are the main features of a case study?
2. What are the reasons for carrying out a case study in psychology?
3. What are the drawbacks of carrying out a case study?

Challenge

'Genie' is a very famous psychological case study, examining the effects of neglect and social isolation. She was discovered at the age of thirteen, having been locked away by her parents for most of her life. She had been completely isolated during her developmental years and so it was interesting for psychologists to see what she could do as a result of **nature**, and what she could not do due to her lack of **nurture**.

Carry out your own research on this case study. You will find lots of useful information on the internet. Decide whether the above strengths and weaknesses apply to this case study and to what extent.

Correlations

Correlations measure two co-variables to see if there is a relationship between them. Like case studies, correlations use other methods to collect data – mainly questionnaires and observations. However, unlike case studies, they use **quantitative data**.

Quantitative data
Numerical data.

For more information on quantitative data, see page 192.

STUDY HINT
Students often confuse experiments and correlations. Remember that correlations measure two variables whereas experiments just measure the dependent variable. The other variable in an experiment is an independent variable and this is what allows an experiment to establish cause and effect. Correlations can only show relationships.

OCR GCSE Psychology

When a correlation is carried out, there are three possible outcomes:

o   a positive correlation
o   a negative correlation
o   zero correlation.

> **STUDY HINT**
> Do not make the mistake of thinking that a negative relationship shows no correlation. A negative correlation can be just a strong and significant as a positive relationship.

With a positive relationship, as one variable increases or decreases, the other variable does the same. This is measured by a positive **correlation coefficient** with +1 representing a perfect positive correlation. For example, +0.85 shows a correlation is strong and positive.

In a negative relationship, as one variable increases then the other decreases, or vice versa. This is measured by a negative correlation coefficient with −1 representing a perfect negative correlation. For example, −0.35 shows a correlation is weak and negative.

With a zero correlation, there is no relationship between variables.

Correlations can be represented on a scatter diagram, which allows researchers to see the strength and direction of their correlation. Here are some examples:

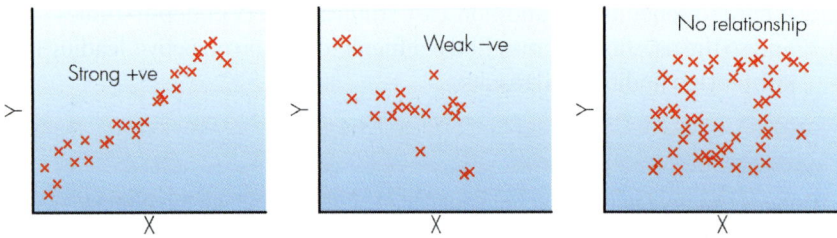

▲ As well as referring to direction, correlations can be described as strong, moderate or weak.

For more information on scatter diagrams, see page 200.

Positive correlation
When two variables travel in the same direction.

Negative correlation
When two variables travel in the opposite direction.

Zero correlation
When two variables show no relationship.

Correlation coefficient
A score that measures the strength and direction of the relationship between two co-variables.

> **Time for some maths**
> A psychologist investigated how many stressful incidents participants reported in a four week period and correlated this with a stress score based on a number of physical and psychological measures. The higher the stress score, the more stress a participant was experiencing.
> Plot the data from the study using a scatter diagram and decide what type of correlation is shown.
>
> | Participant | 1 | 2 | 3 | 4 | 5 | 6 | 7 | 8 | 9 | 10 |
> |---|---|---|---|---|---|---|---|---|---|---|
> | Number of stressful incidents | 15 | 12 | 8 | 4 | 23 | 15 | 9 | 10 | 18 | 7 |
> | Stress score | 12 | 10 | 5 | 7 | 19 | 14 | 3 | 8 | 20 | 5 |
>
> Remember to label your axes and give your graph a title!

> **STUDY HINT**
> Do not make the mistake of putting participant numbers on the axes of the scatter diagram. The axes are for the two co-variables being measured. Participant numbers are not measuring anything – they are just a way of labelling participants.

Strengths and weaknesses of correlations

- A strength of correlations is that they allow psychologists to carry out a *statistical investigation of behaviours that could not be experimented on*. For example, it would not be that practical or ethical to manipulate hormone levels to see if they made people feel more or less depressed. However, it is possible to measure people's depression levels and correlate these with their existing hormone levels.

- Another strength of correlations is that they have *high levels of ecological validity* compared with experiments as nothing is set up or manipulated.

- A major weakness of correlations is that although they inform researchers about the relationship between variables, *it does not tell them about a causal relationship*. Only experiments can do this reliably. For example, if a psychologist finds a positive relationship between depression levels and hormone levels, they cannot be sure whether depression affects hormone production or whether hormone production affects depression.

- Another weakness of correlations is that they need to use quantitative data, which can lead to a *lack of construct validity*. For example, although it might be reliable to measure hormone levels, some psychologists would ask whether it is valid to measure something like depression in terms of numbers.

Challenge

Look again at the study in the 'Time for some maths' activity on the previous page. How well do the strengths and limitations apply to this correlation study?

Check your understanding

1. What are the differences between a correlation and an experiment?
2. What is the difference between a positive and negative correlation?
3. What is meant by the term 'negative correlation'?
4. Why does a correlation need to use quantitative data?

STUDY HINT

You can be asked to design an investigation using any of the six methods listed in this section. Make sure you know the difference between them as you will limit your marks if you design the wrong one! However, be aware of the overlap between methods too.

Analysing research

Once data has been collected, psychologists then need to analyse it to draw conclusions. However, psychologists also need to be aware of any flaws in their research and how this has affected their results.

Types of data

Research data can be divided into two main forms: quantitative data and qualitative data.

1. Quantitative data is numerical data. If a psychologist takes a measurement, they will have quantitative data. It can come in the form of averages, percentages or raw figures, for example.
2. Qualitative data is descriptive data. This means it is normally in the form of words, but can also be in other formats such as video images or pictures.

STUDY HINT

Not surprisingly, students can easily confuse quantitative and qualitative data. If it helps, think about the letter 'n' in qua<u>n</u>titative and associate it with the word <u>n</u>umber.

Challenge

Copy and complete the following table by ticking the column to show whether each example gives quantitative or qualitative data.

Example	Quantitative	Qualitative
A summary of how a teacher dealt with disruptive behaviour in his lesson.		
The journal entries of a person who has been held hostage.		
The case notes on a boy raised as a girl by his parents.		
The mean number of times male drivers stop at a red light.		
The number of items recalled in two minutes.		
A tape recording of interviews with high security prisoners.		
How long (in milliseconds) participants take to respond to an image on a screen.		

Chapter 7 Research methods

Strengths and weaknesses of quantitative and qualitative data

A strength that quantitative data has over qualitative data is that it is easy to identify patterns and trends.

A strength that qualitative data has over quantitative data is that it provides richer, more in-depth data that may make results more valid.

Primary data
Information collected first-hand.

Secondary data
Information used but collected by another (second-hand).

Data can also be divided into **primary data** and **secondary data**. Most data in psychology is primary data as it has been collected by the researchers themselves. A strength of this is that the psychologist can trust the data and knows it has not been misquoted or misinterpreted by someone else. Secondary data is when researchers use data collected by someone else. For example, they may use statistics from a piece of research carried out by the government as part of their own investigation. The strength of this is that it saves time and money, and the psychologist may have access to data that they would not be able to collect otherwise.

Extension

Secondary data also allows psychologists to study people who they would not be able to access themselves but might be interested in investigating, perhaps through looking at material produced by the subject. Can you think of any examples where this may apply?

Check your understanding

1. What is the difference between quantitative data and qualitative data?
2. What is the difference between primary and secondary data?
3. What is a strength of each type of data?

STUDY HINT
The maths that you need to know about for GCSE Psychology is the kind of stuff you would do in GCSE Mathematics. The trick is making sure that you can apply it to data that comes from psychological research. For example, a mean or a percentage is calculated in the same way whether it applies to data from a design project, from a sports match or from a memory test.

Descriptive statistics

A lot of the data collected in psychological research is quantitative data. This can be summarised using what are known as descriptive statistics. Rather than presenting the raw data (actual scores), descriptive statistics describe the data in more general terms, so that patterns and trends can be easily identified.

Measure of central tendency
An average taken from a data set.

Measures of central tendency are a good example of this. If a researcher wanted to compare the scores of females and males in a literacy test, he would look how each group did on average rather than looking at each individual score in turn. A measure of central tendency gives the researcher a score that represents the data set that it comes from.

Extension

Sometimes it is not possible or appropriate to use the mode to analyse data. Can you think of situations when this would be the case?

Ways of calculating a measure of central tendency:

- Using a **mode**. The mode is simply the most commonly occurring score. It represents the data set by being the most 'popular'.
- Using a **median**. The median is calculated by putting the data in numerical order and finding the middle score. If there is an even number of scores in a data set, then you work out which score would fall in the middle. For example, in the data set {3 4 7 12 15 18}, there is no actual middle score, but 9.5 is the median as it falls between 7 and 12. It represents that data set by showing what is happening around the centre.
- Using a **mean**. To find the mean, add together all of the scores in a data set to find the total. Divide this total by the number of scores in the data set. The final figure represents the data set as it is what each participant would get if the total score was shared out equally.

As well as calculating a measure of central tendency, it is often useful to know the **range** of a set of data. The range is calculated by subtracting the lowest score in a data set from the highest one. This tells a researcher whether data is very spread out around an average, or very close to the average. Look at the data set below which compares the stress scores of out-going and shy people.

Stress scores for out-going people	6 7 7 9 10 11 12 13 14 15 17 17 18 18
Stress scores for shy people	9 9 9 10 11 12 12 12 12 13 14 14 14

The out-going people and the shy people have very similar stress scores on average: the out-going group have a median of 12.5 and the shy group have a median of 12. However, the range of scores for the out-going people is 13 and the range for shy people is only 6. This shows that the out-going people's scores are very wide ranging around the median whereas the shy people's scores are much more consistent. Their experience of stress differs more than the measures of central tendency would suggest.

A **ratio** can also be useful for comparing measures taken from groups or conditions. For example, imagine one group had a mean score of 15 on a memory test and another group had a mean score of 5. The ratio of the means can be written as 15:5 and then simplified to 3:1 by dividing by the highest common factor (5 in this example). This shows the first group's mean was three times more than the second group's. Ratios can also be expressed as single numbers by dividing one number by the other, e.g. 3 ÷ 1 = 3.

Percentages are often used with quantitative data. They are particularly useful when comparing two groups or conditions of different sizes. For example, if six participants passed a test in one condition and six passed the same test in another condition then it might appear that there is no difference between them. However, if there are twenty participants in the first condition and ten in the second then there actually is a difference. This means 30 per cent passed the test in the first, and 60 per cent passed it in the second. Percentages are

Mode
A measure of central tendency that uses the most common score or scores in a data set.

Median
A measure of central tendency that uses the middle score from a data set once it has been ordered numerically.

Mean
A measure of central tendency that is the result of adding all scores in a data set together and then dividing that total by the sum of scores.

Range
A measure of how spread out scores are that compares the highest score with the lowest score in a data set. This is calculated by taking the lowest score away from the highest score.

> **Something to think about**
> Some researchers believe that it is not appropriate to use the mean when there are extremely high or low scores in a data set because they skew the measure. However, other researchers argue this is exactly why it should be used as it represents the full set of data. What point of view do you agree with and why? Try to think about it in terms of psychological research.

Ratio
A measure that shows the relative sizes of two or more values.

Percentage
A proportion of something expressed as a number out of 100.

Fractions

A value that represents the smaller part of a whole.

> **STUDY HINT**
> You may be asked to present a figure to a certain number of decimal places. Remember to round up digits of 5 or over, and round down digits below 5. You may need to decide for yourself how many decimal places to present a figure to. In this case, ask yourself how many digits you need in order to be able to see patterns or differences between participants and conditions.

Decimal

A value that is expressed in terms of a series of digits to the right of a point that separates the fraction from its whole number.

Decimal place

The position of a digit to the right of a decimal point.

Significant figures

The amount of digits (starting from the first non-zero digit) that carry meaning in terms of showing how accurate a number is.

Standard form

A way of writing very large or small numbers using the digits 0–9.

calculated by dividing the fraction by the whole and then multiplying by 100 to give a figure between 0 and 100, e.g. $(6 \div 20) \times 100 = 0.3 \times 100 = 30$.

Fractions can do a similar job to ratios. For example, a psychologist could state that the ratio of males to females in a sample is 1:4 or they could state ¼ of a sample are males. They also do a similar job to percentages. For example, a psychologist could state that 50 per cent of their sample followed orders or they could state that ½ of their sample did as $^{50}/_{100}$ simplifies to ½ – the fraction in its lowest form.

When researchers use statistics such as means and percentages, they sometimes find they have to work with **decimals**. Indeed, a ratio or fraction can also be expressed as a decimal. This is necessary when handling data that is not in whole numbers. For example, it might be important to distinguish between a participant who responds to an image in 1.531 seconds and one who responds in 1.895 seconds. If these were rounded to the nearest whole number (2) it would look like they had responded equally when they had not. However, in this example, you could report the times to two **decimal places** so that 1.531 becomes 1.53 and 1.895 becomes 1.90.

Sometimes, numbers are presented to a degree of **significant figures**. This is a way of rounding off a number so that it is approximate but accurate enough. It can involve digits that occur before or after a decimal point. In the previous example, the time of 1.53 seconds is rounded to three significant figures. We know this because it has three digits in it.

The zeros in a decimal are counted as significant figures, so the time of 1.90 seconds is also presented to three significant figures. However, this is not the case when the number is not a decimal. For example, the number 125 000 000 is presented to three significant figures, whereas the number 125 000 000.0 is presented to ten significant figures. The first version may be an approximate number, whereas the inclusion of the decimal point tells us that the second version is precisely 125 000 000.

Zeros before a number are not significant. For example, 0.0000043 is rounded to two significant figures and 0.000000777 is rounded to three significant figures. However, when zeros occur between other digits they are always significant because they are place-holders. For example, 605 is rounded to three significant figures, because the zero tells us there are no tens in this number. Similarly, the number 7.0106 is rounded to five significant figures, because the zeros tell us where decimal points occur and do not occur.

Although decimal numbers are often used in psychology, very small and very large numbers are rarer. However, where they do arise, it is sometimes helpful to use **standard form**. Standard form describes values in terms of a number expressed in units and decimal places multiplied by 10 to the power of a particular digit (the index). Examples of this are given in the table below.

▼ Table 7.2 Examples of standard form.

Raw value	Standard form	Raw value	Standard form
4,000	4×10^3	0.0000043	4.3×10^{-6}
125,000,000	1.25×10^8	0.000000777	7.77×10^{-8}

The index shows how many places a decimal point needs to be moved. If it is positive, the decimal moves to the right. If it is negative, it moves to the left.

> **STUDY HINT**
> Make sure you can both interpret values in standard form and convert values to standard form.

A lot of statistics assume that a data set follows a **normal distribution**. Below is an example of a data set that follows a normal distribution and one that does not (a **skewed distribution**).

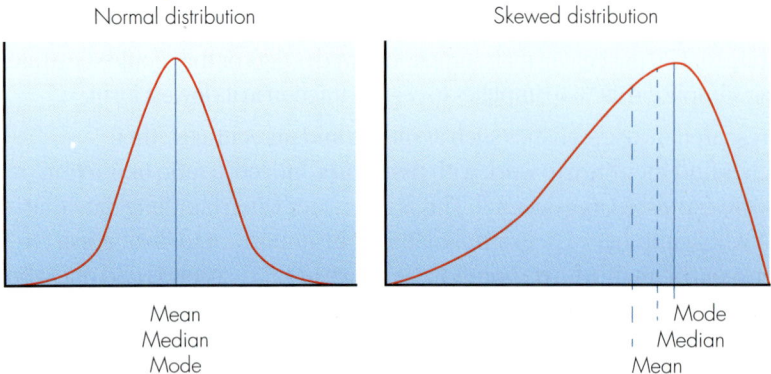

Normal distribution

Where data is distributed so that it follows a symmetrical 'bell shaped' curve, with middle scores being the most frequent.

Skewed distribution

Where data has an assymmetric distribution because scores are clustered towards one of the extremes.

Normally distributed data follows the same kind of pattern whatever is being measured. It means that extreme scores (high and low) are rare with middle scores having the highest frequency – it basically means that 'most people are average'.

Extension

Statistics are often reliable in psychological research because many human characteristics follow a normal distribution. For example, for characteristics like height most people are considered average, with very tall or very short people being rare. This can also be applied to psychological characteristics. For example, most people have average **intelligence**; super intelligent people are very rare. Can you identify any psychological characteristics that wouldn't follow a normal distribution?

Although descriptive statistics can give very exact measures of patterns and trends, it is sometimes appropriate for researchers to make **estimations** from data collected (if you had 56 plus 26 you might estimate 60 plus 30). For example, if just looking at the pattern of data shows there is no evidence of a correlation, then a researcher may decide to not do unnecessary calculations to show this. A researcher may decide to not continue with a piece of research if early estimates show that the results are not going to be as expected.

Estimation

A process where we roughly calculate or judge a value, quantity or pattern in data.

STUDY HINT

It is possible that you could be asked to work out a measure of central tendency, a range, a ratio, a percentage or a fraction in psychology. That's why it makes sense to take a calculator into the exam with you. You may also be asked to interpret any of these values so do make sure you understand what they show you.

Check your understanding

1. What do measures of central tendency show about a data set?
2. What does a range show about a data set?
3. What does it mean when a set of data is normally distributed?

Chapter 7 Research methods

Time for some maths
Have a go at these multi-choice questions. Choose one answer each time.

1. What is the mean of the following data set?
   Products recalled from commercial break: 3, 6, 7, 6, 1, 1, 2, 5, 4, 2, 3, 2
   A 2   **B** 3   **C** 3.5

2. What is the range of the following data set?
   Aggression ratings for boys: 3, 5, 9, 11, 11, 8, 2, 15, 18, 16
   A 10   **B** 14   **C** 17

3. The ratio of criminals to non-criminals in a family was 45:15. What does this simplify to?
   A 3:1   **B** 6:1   **C** 9:1

4. The ratio of jumbled up faces recognised compared to normal faces was 1:6. How else can this ratio be expressed?
   A 0.125   **B** 1/7   **C** 60 per cent

5. 7/23 passers-by helped a pedestrian. What percentage of passers-by (to two decimal places) helped?
   A 30 per cent   **B** 31 per cent   **C** 32 per cent

6. Twenty males and twenty females were tested to see how many would obey in a given situation. 3/5 of males obeyed and 7/10 of females did. What fraction of participants obeyed all together?
   A 13/20   **B** 10/15   **C** 20/40

7. The mean personal space required with strangers was 33.10 cm, but with familiar people it was 29.45 cm. What was the difference between the two means to two significant figures?
   A 3.6   **B** 3.7   **C** 4.0

8. The sample was drawn from a target population of 125,000. What was the size of the sample expressed in standard form?
   A 1.25×10^5 **B** 12.5×10^4 **C** 125×10^3

9. The difference between the mass of two neurons was 1.1×10^{-8} grams. What is this difference expressed in decimal form?
   A 0.000000011 grams   **B** 0.00000011 grams   **C** 110,000,000 grams

10. Two hundred participants rated their self-confidence on a scale of 1 to 10 (10 being high self-confidence). Their scores followed a normal distribution. Which of the following scores would be the modal (most frequent) score?
    A 3   **B** 5   **C** 7

Tables, charts and graphs

Quantitative data can be represented visually by using techniques such as tables, charts and graphs.

Tables are used to collect raw data during investigations and can also be a useful way of summarising results for others to see. An example of this is a **frequency table** also known as a **tally chart**.

▼ Table 7.3 A frequency table to show students' preferred way of learning.

WAY OF LEARNING	FREQUENCY
Alone	卌 卌 卌 卌 II
In pairs	卌 III
In groups	卌 卌 卌 卌

This data can also be presented graphically using a **bar chart** or a **pie chart**, as shown below.

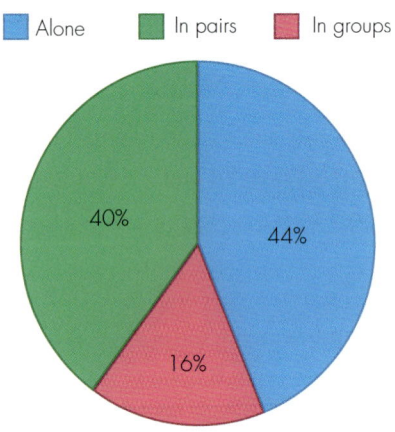

A bar chart to show students' preferred way of learning

A pie chart to show students' preferred way of learning
- Alone 44%
- In pairs 40%
- In groups 16%

Both bar charts and pie charts can be used when participants are put into categories rather than given scores. Bar charts offer more flexibility as a number of different sets of categories can be placed on one chart. In addition, bar charts don't have to have bars that add up to 100 per cent so are useful, for example, where individual participants appear in more than one category.

> **STUDY HINT**
> Tables, charts and graphs often appear in reports on psychological results. When they do, you may be asked to interpret them in some way. This normally involves drawing a conclusion, which means looking for a pattern in the chart. Quite often you have to justify this conclusion. This involves making reference to the data that you can see.

Frequency table/tally chart
A way of recording and presenting how often different measures occur.

Bar chart
A chart that presents data by using bars to represent the different frequencies of categories.

Pie chart
A chart that presents data using segments of a circle to represent different proportions by category.

Chapter 7 Research methods

Time for some maths
The data in the line graph (right) could also be summarised in a bar graph. There would be a bar for each condition, which would show the average recall. Construct a bar graph to compare average recall between the two conditions, using an appropriate measure of central tendency.

Line graph
A graph that presents data using a line to show changes in the frequencies of scores.

Histogram
A graph that presents data using a series of bars to show changes in the frequencies of scores or sets of scores.

When participants are given scores rather than put into categories, it may be more appropriate to use a **line graph** to summarise data, as in the following example:

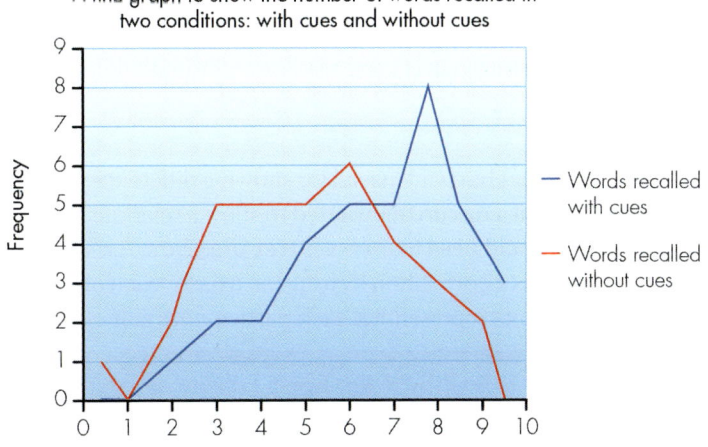

A histogram is a good way to represent continuous data. They are particularly useful when there is a wide range of scores – especially if the frequencies for each score are low and would not show a pattern. This is because histograms allow scores to be grouped in what are known as intervals.

Look at the table of data below.

▼ Table 7.4 How many days participants were able to resist eating chocolate.

Days	No	Days	No	Days	No	Days	No	Days	No	Days	No
1	4	6	4	11	4	16	3	21	3	26	1
2	4	7	6	12	3	17	4	22	2	27	1
3	3	8	5	13	3	18	3	23	1	28	4
4	4	9	5	14	2	19	2	24	2	29	5
5	3	10	6	15	4	20	1	25	2	30	5

It is more appropriate to plot this data as a histogram than a line graph. This can be seen below:

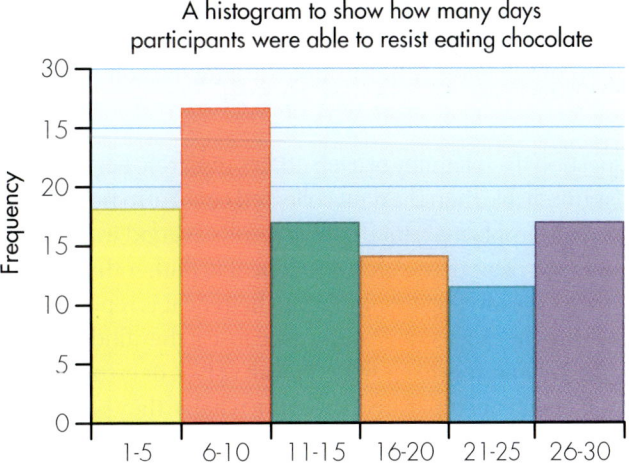

OCR GCSE Psychology

> **STUDY HINT**
> Bar charts and histograms are sometimes mixed up. When looking at them, the difference is obvious. On a bar chart, the bars have gaps between them, whereas on a histogram they touch. Bars on bar charts represent categories, and categories are separate from each other. Bars on histograms represent scores or intervals of scores, so follow a scale (scales do not have gaps).

Histograms, line graphs and bar charts are useful for showing differences between conditions. However, if a researcher wanted to show a relationship between two variables, they would need to use a **scatter diagram**. A scatter diagram shows whether there is a correlation by using an axis for each of the co-variables and then plotting points representing each participant's pair of scores.

Scatter diagram

A graph that presents data by plotting scores to see if there is a relationship between two variables.

> **For more information on scatter diagrams, see page 190.**

> **STUDY HINT**
> You may have to sketch a chart or graph. Presentation matters, but accuracy is more important. The more accurate your chart or graph is the more marks you earn. There will also be marks available for a clear title and for correctly labelled axes.

> **DIY**
> Draw up a table to list the different types of charts and graphs you should know about for the exam. For each one, outline when it would be appropriate to use it.

> **Check your understanding**
> 1. What is a frequency chart used for?
> 2. What does a pie chart show?
> 3. When would a researcher use a line graph rather than a bar chart?
> 4. What do a histogram and a line graph have in common?
> 5. What method is associated with a scatter diagram?

Reliability and validity

Analysing data does not just involve presenting data and looking for patterns. Researchers should also consider how **reliable** and **valid** their results are.

Reliability

Psychologists often question the reliability of each other's research. For example, if a method is unreliable then the data collected could also be unreliable. This means that people may not trust the results. A good way of checking the reliability of a piece of research is to repeat it. Rather than a researcher repeating their own investigation, it is even better if it is repeated by a different researcher, using the exact same sample, because if they find similar results it suggests the findings are less likely to be a result of bias or errors. The more times the research results are replicated, the more reliable they become.

Reliability

A measure of how consistent or replicable something is.

Validity

A measure of how true or accurate something is.

Chapter 7 Research methods

> **STUDY HINT**
> The word 'reliability' is used outside of psychology and has the same kind of meaning. For example, a student who is reliable will consistently get their work done, but an unreliable car might occasionally break down. Therefore, we trust the student but not the car!

Internal reliability

Where a measure is consistent within itself.

External reliability

Where a measure is consistent beyond itself, on another occasion.

Internal reliability measures how consistent something like a questionnaire or test is *within* itself. For example, if an **IQ test** has easier questions at the start and then harder questions at the end then this test does *not* have internal reliability. If an aggression questionnaire, using rating scales, gives participants the same score on each question then this has high internal reliability. This means the overall score can be trusted as a measure of that one construct.

> **Extension**
> Internal reliability can be put to the test using a technique called the 'split half' method. Research what this technique involves and how it helps to establish internal reliability.

External reliability refers to consistency across time or situations. For example, a measuring ruler has very high external reliability; if a researcher measured the height of the same adult on two different occasions, they would get the same result. If a psychological measure (e.g. the IQ test and the aggression questionnaire) gave the same score to the same person on two different occasions then it would also have high external reliability. Because psychological measures are not as precise as physical measures (e.g. like rulers and clocks), psychologists may argue that a set of similar scores are good enough to show external reliability. They may also have to allow for the fact that a test has been done once before and so, on something like an IQ test, scores may improve slightly through practice.

> **Time for some maths**
> Look at the following data taken from a leadership test that was given to ten participants on two different occasions. Decide whether the test has external reliability. How can you analyse the data to make this decision?
>
> | Participant | A | B | C | D | E | F | G | H | I | J |
> |---|---|---|---|---|---|---|---|---|---|---|
> | 1st score | 18 | 13 | 10 | 9 | 12 | 15 | 5 | 11 | 16 | 7 |
> | 2nd score | 17 | 5 | 5 | 14 | 8 | 11 | 10 | 11 | 12 | 10 |

Inter-rater reliability

Where two or more researchers agree on a set of results.

Unreliable results may be due to psychologists' different perspectives on what is being studied. This is why it is useful to have more than one psychologist involved in a study. They can then check they agree on what they are observing, or on what is being measured. If there is agreement, then results have **inter-rater reliability**. This makes results more objective.

Validity

The aim of all research is to produce valid results that reflect the truth. This is where there is a link with reliability. In scientific terms, if an experiment repeatedly gets the same results, the probability is that it is true or valid. However, this is not always the case. For example, if a researcher makes a mistake in his investigation it will make his results invalid, but if he keeps making the same mistake on similar investigations, he could still get the same results. These results are technically reliable, but for the wrong reason.

If a set of results are valid, it means a researcher has measured what they intended to measure. There are different types of validity that psychologists are interested in achieving when they do their research:

- **Ecological validity**. If this is low or lacking it means psychologists are not measuring things in a realistic way. For example, the artificial setting of a laboratory experiment often causes this problem: a participant's memory may be better without distractions and results may not generalise to real-life.
- **Construct validity**. If this is low or lacking it means psychologists are not measuring something in its entirety. Quantitative measures often have this problem as they take a narrow measure of the subject under investigation. For example, how often children kick an object is a very narrow measure of aggressive behaviour.
- **Population validity**. If this is low or lacking it means psychologists have not measured a representative sample of the target population. Small or biased samples are an example of this, for example results from American students cannot be generalised to the human population.

> **Challenge**
>
> Draw up a table with a column for each type of validity. In each row, place the core studies. For each of these, decide whether each type of validity is high or low. You could do this retrospectively as a revision exercise or fill in the table as you learn about each new study.

One of the challenges for psychologists is that they are studying people rather than physical matter, such as particles and chemicals. People are often conscious of the fact they are being studied and this is likely to affect how they think and behave. If participants end up behaving differently from normal then this has clear issues for the validity of results. The following are related to this problem:

- **Demand characteristics**. These are often an issue in experiments that are set up so participants identify clues or **cues** that potentially give away the aim of the research. When participants think they know the aim, they may behave differently. Even if they are trying to help the researcher, it still means their responses are not valid.
- **Observer effect**. This describes the situation where participants behave differently because they know they are being watched. For example, they may exaggerate behaviour or stop doing certain things. Either way, their responses are not valid.
- **Social desirability**. This occurs in self-report studies where participants answer questions in a way they think they should, rather than giving their honest responses. For example, they may want to 'look good' in the eyes of the researcher. Although they may come across in a more socially acceptable way, their responses are still invalid.

Ecological validity
How far a research setting mirrors real-life.

Construct validity
How far a variable is measured in relation to the whole concept.

Population validity
How far a sample represents the target population.

Demand characteristics
Cues from the procedure that suggest what the research is about.

Observer effect
The effect on behaviour when people know they are being observed.

Social desirability
The pressure to respond to questions in a way that is expected and acceptable.

> **STUDY HINT**
> There is sometimes confusion around what demand characteristics are. These are the clues that give away the aim. Behaviour changes as a **consequence** of demand characteristics.

DIY

As a psychologist, how would you deal with each of the following issues? Outline your plans for the research.

1. You want to carry out an experiment to investigate how different people will help a stranger in need. However, you are concerned about the effect of demand characteristics.
2. You want to carry out an observation of the way that teachers deal with disruptive behaviour in the classroom. However, you are concerned about the observer effect.
3. You want to carry out a survey to ask teenagers about their use of social media in relation to bullying. However, you are concerned about the issue of social desirability.

Check your understanding

1. What is the link between reliability and validity?
2. What is the difference between internal and external reliability?
3. What does inter-rater reliability measure?
4. What is meant by each of the following?
   - low ecological validity
   - low construct validity
   - high population validity.
5. How do each of the following affect the validity of results?
   - demand characteristics
   - observer effect
   - social desirability.

Bias

When certain types of people are over-represented while others are under-represented.

Sources of bias

Validity and reliability are related to the idea of **bias**. If a piece of research has been influenced by a psychologist's beliefs, it is unlikely to be reliable. When another researcher repeats it, the results may be different. Research should ideally be free of bias to make it objective. This means it is more likely to produce facts rather than opinion, and therefore be valid.

The table below identifies different types of bias that can be found in psychological research.

Table 7.5 Different types of bias in psychological research.

Type of bias	Definition	Example
Gender	To favour one gender over another.	To have a sample containing only women but then generalising to both sexes.
Cultural	To favour particular cultures over others.	To assume that mental health problems are universal, after only studying a sample of British people.
Age	To favour certain age groups over others.	To design a memory experiment where the content is targeted at a teenage audience.
Experimenter	To favour one psychological theory over another within their own research.	To measure a variable (aggression) in a way that is going to give results that supports a particular theory (that children from single parent families are more aggressive).
Observer	To interpret and record a behaviour to favour one view over others.	To rate an offender's body language as defensive because there is an assumption that she has something to hide.
Questioning	To phrase a question to favour one view over others.	To ask a question like 'Don't you think you need more sleep?' that suggests a particular response.

Check your understanding

1. When might a sample be gender, age and culturally biased?
2. What is the difference between **experimenter bias** and observer bias?
3. Why is **bias in questioning** a problem?

Challenge

Can you come up with a second example of each type of bias that is distinct from the ones already given in the table? You might have examples from the core studies that you can use to help with this activity.

Experimenter bias

To favour one theory over another when conducting research.

Bias in questioning

To phrase a question to support one view more than another.

SUMMARY

This chapter has shown there are number of factors involved in conducting research. First of all, there are a range of methods that a psychologist can choose to collect their data – from experiments to case studies, from observations to questionnaires. Each method will have its own strengths and weaknesses and so one method is not better than another. The choice of method depends on a psychologist's priorities and also what they are investigating.

Psychologists also have to make similar decisions about features such as the sample, and how they are going to measure and control variables. In experiments, they also have to choose their experimental design. Psychologists also need to start their research with a hypothesis: a prediction of what they think will happen. When planning research, ethical guidelines need to be considered as well. The type of research carried out will also affect the type of data that is collected and this, in turn, will affect how data is analysed in terms of descriptive statistics and how results can be presented. Finally, psychologists are also obliged to evaluate their own research and come to a conclusion about how reliable and valid their results are.

Practice questions

The questions in this textbook have been written by the authors, Mark Billingham and Helen Kitching. They have not been produced or endorsed by OCR.

A psychologist carried out an experiment to investigate the effect on perception of two different types of adverts: one that used a celebrity and one that used an ordinary person. The adverts were produced in the same way, used the same script and had the same duration.

The psychologist used a self-selected sample who signed up for the study while doing their supermarket shopping. While in store, they were taken to a booth to view one of the two adverts. An independent measures design was used where 30 participants were shown the first advert, and another 30 were shown the second. Afterwards, they were asked whether they would be likely to buy the product, a new brand of crisps, with the choice being 'yes' or 'no'.

The results of the study are shown in the bar chart below.

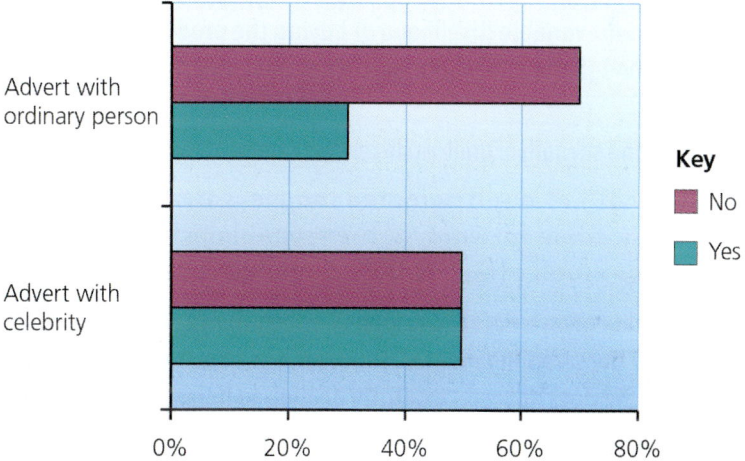

A bar graph to show the percentage of participants who would and would not buy the product after viewing their advert.

1 Write a hypothesis for this study. [2 marks]

There will be a difference in whether participants want to buy a product or not, depending on whether they have seen an advert featuring a celebrity or an ordinary person.

The candidate has the choice of writing a null or alternative hypothesis and has gone for the alternative hypothesis. Importantly, they recognise that it is an experiment and therefore is investigating a difference (as opposed to a correlation). One mark is awarded for the first part of the hypothesis (the stem) and then a second mark for correctly identifying the variables being tested. Here, the IV and DV are clearly stated. Overall, the hypothesis is well written and easily understood, so both marks would be given.

2 Identify the dependent variable. [1 mark]

Perception of a product.

The candidate knows what the dependent variable is in a broad sense – it is something to do with the product rather than the advert. However, because it is the DV they have been asked for, they need to be precise about how it was measured. Perception of the product was actually measured in terms of whether participants would buy it or not. This is what the candidate needs to state to get the mark. No marks would be awarded here.

3 Explain how **one** extraneous variable was controlled in this study. [3 marks]

If the adverts were different lengths, this would have been an extraneous variable. If one advert was longer than another, the participants might have got bored and this is why they may have not wanted to buy the product. To control for this, the two adverts were kept the same length.

The candidate shows knowledge of extraneous variables by firstly identifying a relevant one, and understanding by showing they know it would affect the dependent variable (likelihood of buying the product). This is worth two marks. Although the straightforward, they have clearly stated the control for a third mark.

4 Outline **one** strength of using a self-selected sample in this study. [2 marks]

A strength of a self-selected sample is that participants willingly come forward, so the psychologist does not have to put in so much effort as they would do with other methods.

The candidate gives a detailed response, which shows that they understand a strength of the sampling method. However, the question says 'in this study' and the candidate does not refer explicitly enough to it. Just using the words 'the psychologist' does not really make it relevant to the study. For example, they could have written about how the participants' willingness to take part might mean they are likely to watch the whole advert and not drop out. Consequently, this answer would earn one of the two available marks.

5 Explain one limitation of using an independent measures design in this study. [3 marks]

A limitation is that the difference in results may be due to participant variables because the psychologist did not compare 'like with like'. For example, one group of participants may be more health-conscious than average and this could be why they did not choose to buy crisps, rather than because of the advert.

This is a good answer. The first mark is for knowing a general limitation of the experimental design: the problem of participant variables. The candidate then applies this to the study by identifying a way in which participants may vary from each other, earning another mark. The final mark is given because the candidate considers how the limitation may impact on the results. The candidate would earn all three marks.

6 How many participants in total reported that they would buy the product? Show your working. **[3 marks]**

50 per cent of 30 = 0.5 × 30 = 15

30 per cent of 30 = 0.3 × 30 = 9

15 + 9 = 24 participants

One mark for the right answer: 24. Although there are other ways of getting there (e.g. taking the mean of the two percentages and then multiplying by 60), the calculations are suitably detailed to be able to award both the marks for showing working. All three marks would be awarded.

7 What fraction of participants in the condition featuring a celebrity said they would not buy the product? Show your working. **[2 marks]**

1/2

There is only one mark for showing working here as the maths is more straightforward. However, the candidate does not show the working at all and so only one mark can be awarded. Even if the candidate was able to do the calculation 'in their head', they still needed to show how they got to this fraction.

8 Evaluate the use of an experiment in this study. **[5 marks]**

Experiments allow us to establish cause and effect because they are highly controlled. In this experiment, any difference in perception of product is likely to be due to the different types of adverts. However, a weakness is the lack of ecological validity. We don't typically watch adverts in booths.

This is a fair effort. This answer identifies both a strength and a weakness of using an experiment. However, the application to the study is quite brief. The candidate needs to expand on both points by showing more clearly that they understand what each means. They could also have elaborated more on how they applied to the study. For example, what are the differences between booths and the places we normally view adverts? This is a middle band response which would be awarded three out of five marks.

You have been asked to carry out interviews to investigate addiction to social media. The theory is that people who have fewer interests and hobbies are more likely to be addicted to social media.

1 a Name the type of interview you would use in your investigation. **[1 mark]**

A structured interview, which would involve asking all participants the same set of questions.

This answer earns 1 mark for naming a relevant interview. The candidate now needs to be careful that they continue to refer to this type of interview in their other answers. Note that the outline of the type of interview was unnecessary – all they had to do was name it.

   b Outline one strength of using this type of interview in your investigation. **[2 marks]**

As everyone gets asked the same questions, it is easier to make comparisons.

This is a strength of a structured interview and therefore earns a mark. However, the second mark is not awarded as the strength has not been linked to the investigation itself. For example, the candidate could have written about being able to compare levels of addiction between participants.

   c Outline one weakness of using this type of interview in your investigation. **[2 marks]**

It is not possible to explore new lines of enquiry. For example, if a participant mentioned a reason for his addiction that I had not thought of, I would not be in a position to pick up on it.

This response earns both marks. It starts with a general weakness of structured interviews earning the first mark. This is then applied to the investigation, so the second mark is earned too.

2 a Write one example of a question you would use in your interview. **[1 mark]**

How much time would you say you spend on social media? Too much? About the right amount of time? Not as much as you would like?

This question is really testing whether the candidate can write a question that is relevant to the investigation. It is also important to note that it is one part of the question so hopefully the candidate has chosen to write a question that allows them to write a good answer for part (b). This question is reasonably well constructed and is appropriate for the investigation. One mark is given.

   b Identify the type of question you have used and give one reason why. **[2 marks]**

This is a closed question. I have used it so I can offer multiple choice answers.

The candidate is right to identify this as a closed question. However, just one mark is earned here. The second part of the answer is not really a reason for using a closed question - if anything, it is a description of a type of closed question. The candidate needs to ask themselves what are the benefits of having multiple choice answers.

Chapter 7 Research methods

3   Identify the type of data your investigation would collect.   **[1 mark]**

Tick one box to show your answer.
Primary data ✓
Secondary data ☐

One mark for ticking the correct box. The 'researcher' is collecting their own data so it is first hand (primary).

4   Outline the procedure you would use in your investigation.   **[4 marks]**

I would carry out my interview using students from my year group; they are convenient but also likely to have experience with using social media. I would interview each participant individually so they are more likely to give me honest answers. I would make a judgement on how much social media they use by giving them a score out of ten and then correlate this with a score for their interests and hobbies, again using a score out of ten.

The candidate should always be prepared for a question like this. It is important for the examiner to have an overview of the investigation but also it is the candidate's opportunity to write about things they have put into their plan that they have not been asked about elsewhere in the section. This candidate makes good use of this opportunity by outlining who would be interviewed, how, and what would be done with information arising from the investigation – none of these things have been asked elsewhere. The answer is a top band response offering three clear features of the procedure with two being justified along the way. Given the breadth and depth of the answer, the candidate can be awarded all four marks.

5   Name one type of bias you would want to avoid in your investigation and outline how you would do this.

Age bias. I would avoid this by interviewing a wide range of ages, from teenagers through to people in their 80s.

Just one of the two marks is awarded here. The type of bias identified is valid and can be credited. The second part of the answer would be feasible but it actually contradicts an earlier part of the plan where they suggest they are going to interview students from their year group. This shows how an examiner would be looking for coherency in the planning.

6   Write a debriefing that could be used as part of your investigation.   **[4 marks]**

Thank you for taking part in my investigation. I would like to remind you that all data will remain confidential, but if you would like to withdraw then you can do so now. The aim of this investigation was to see how addicted you are to social media. If you are very addicted I can organise some counselling for you.

This response is worth three of the four marks. It is relevant and covers a number of points. It is also written in an appropriate style. However, some of the statements are a little simplistic and it would need to be a bit more sophisticated for full marks.

Glossary

ABC Model (including activating events, beliefs and consequences) A theory that views depression as being the result of irrational thinking.

Accommodation New information is used to either alter an existing schema or create a new one.

Acquisitive offences Crimes where capital or belongings are acquired through illegal means, e.g. theft.

Activation synthesis theory An explanation of dreams that focuses on the random activation of neurons and the brain's efforts to makes sense of this through synthesis.

Active learning The idea that children should not just be sat at a desk and given information but should be actively engaging with their environment to learn from it.

Adolescence From age thirteen to nineteen years.

Adulthood From 20 years until death.

Age bias To favour certain age groups over others.

Agentic state An individual does not feel responsible for their actions as they are acting under orders from an authority figure.

Aggression Spoken or physical behaviour that is threatening or involves harm to someone.

Alternative hypothesis A statement that predicts a difference or correlation in results.

Altruism Helping others selflessly without expecting to gain personally.

Amnesic syndrome A general term to describe any memory problems caused by brain damage, illness or psychological trauma, such as post-traumatic stress disorder.

Animism Giving thoughts and feelings to inanimate objects.

Anterograde amnesia The inability to form new memories after damage.

Anti-depressants Medication that is used to help people who are depressed.

Anti-psychotics Medication designed to help people who are experiencing psychotic episodes such as with illnesses like schizophrenia.

Anti-social behaviour 'Behaviour by a person which causes or is likely to cause harassment, alarm or distress to one or more persons not of the same household as the person' (Antisocial Behaviour Act 2003 & Police Reform and Social Responsibility Act 2011).

Anti-social offences Criminal acts that cause harassment, alarm or distress to people who do not share a home with the perpetrator.

Arousal Activation of the nervous system making individuals awake, alert and attentive.

Assimilation New information is incorporated into an existing schema.

Attention This allows us to select information, which is then encoded.

Attitudes Feelings of like or dislike towards something.

Auditory What we hear.

Auditory cortex The part of the brain that processes information it receives from the ears.

Authoritarian personality A personality type that is very obedient to authority.

Authority figure Someone we perceive as having more power than ourselves.

Autobiographical advertising Adverts that are intended to bring back people's memories of their past to influence how they feel about the product that is being advertised.

Autobiographical memory Memories that we collect during our lifetime, of things we have done and places we have been.

Autonomic nervous system The system responsible for unconscious control of the body's internal organs.

Autonomous state Where the individual feels responsible for their own actions.

Bar chart A chart that presents data by using bars to represent the different frequencies of categories.

Bias When certain types of people are over-represented while others are under-represented.

Bias in questioning To phrase a question to support one view more than another.

Biological Relating to brain and body.

Brain activity The action of neurons firing within the brain as they send chemical messages from one neuron to the next.

Brain dysfunction When the brain is not working as normal.

Brain function The role or activity of the brain.

Brain imaging Machinery that allows us to scan people's brain to see what activity is occurring or see differences in structure.

Brain structure This refers to the different parts of the brain.

Brain volume The amount of space the brain occupies measured in 3D.

Brainstem The central trunk of the brain that continues down to the spinal cord.

The British Psychological Society's Code of Ethics and Conduct A set of criteria – under the headings of respect, competence, responsibility and integrity – that psychologists should aim to follow when carrying out research.

Capacity The amount of space available to store information.

Care in the community Administering health and social care outside of hospitals and instead treating people in their homes and living in their normal communities.

Case study A method of collecting data that involves focusing on a small sample in detail.

Cause and effect The process of one variable affecting a change in another.

Central nervous system A system consisting of the brain and spinal cord, to which sensory impulses are transmitted and from which motor impulses pass out.

Cerebellum This part of the brain can be found at the back of the skull. It is responsible for the ability to learn sequences of movements and our motor control. It is important for procedural and semantic memory.

Cerebral blood flow Supply of blood to the brain at any one given time

Glossary

Cerebral cortex The outer layer of the brain, which is important for conscious awareness.

Childhood From birth to the age of twelve.

Chronological order Time order. Things being presented or recalled in the order that they actually occurred.

Classification system A system of categorisation e.g. for diagnosing disorder.

Clinical characteristics Symptoms or features of a disorder.

Closed questions Questions which have set responses to choose from.

Co-variable Something that changes in relation to another variable.

Cognitive Mental processes of memory, perception, judgement and reasoning.

Cognitive development How our thought processes change over time throughout childhood. This includes language, memory and perception.

Collectivist culture The needs of the group are seen as more important than the needs of the individual, and the individuals in the society view themselves as interdependent or connected to other people.

Community sentence Time that has to be given back to the community in the form of unpaid work.

Concrete operational The third stage of Piaget's Theory of Cognitive Development. Children in this stage achieve the ability to conserve.

Conditioning Learning by association and outcome.

Confabulation Making up details to create a more complete memory. It is not done with the intent to deceive people.

Confederate Someone who appears to be a participant in an experiment but is actually working for the researcher to manipulate the experiment.

Confidentiality A way of dealing with ethical issues by making sure that participants are not identifiable through use of names or other types of data.

Conflict A serious disagreement.

Conformity Yielding to group pressure.

Consent When a person agrees to being studied or agrees on someone else's behalf.

Conservation The ability to understand that even though something might change it's shape or form, it's volume, mass or length remain the same.

Consequences The result of something, usually negative. For example, the consequences of being ignored by your friends might be feeling depressed.

Construct validity How far a variable is measured in relation to the whole concept.

Context cues These are 'external' cues and refer, for example, to being back in the same place where the memory was encoded, in order to trigger the memory.

Control A way of ensuring other variables do not affect the results of a study.

Control group A group of participants for whom the independent variable has not been manipulated. Psychologists use control groups to compare against the experimental group.

Controlled observation Observing people in an environment that has been set up in some way.

Correlation A method of analysis that looks for a relationship between two variables.

Correlation coefficient A score that measures the strength and direction of the relationship between two co-variables.

Cortices Plural of cortex.

Counterbalancing To even out trials/tasks so they do not occur in the same order each time.

Covert observation Observing people without them knowing.

Criminal personality A set of relatively fixed traits that are associated with people that commit crimes.

Cross-sectional study A study carried out at one point of time and comparing distinct groups of people.

Crowd and collective behaviour The actions of people who have gathered together for a particular purpose. The behaviour of crowds can often be spontaneous and unplanned. For example, people might find themselves acting in a way that they wouldn't normally do.

Cues Things that can trigger your memory, such as going back to the place where you grew up which might trigger memories of your childhood.

Culture A collective set of norms and values that determine the way of life of a group of people.

Debriefing A way of dealing with ethical issues at the end of research, including an explanation of the study.

Decay The fading of information that is not paid attention to until it is forgotten.

Decentration This is the ability to be able to focus on more than one aspect of a situation. For example, putting individual letters together to make a word.

Deception An ethical issue that relates to being honest with participants about the purpose and process of research.

Decimal A value that is expressed in terms of a series of digits to the right of a point that separates the fraction from its whole number.

Decimal place The position of a digit to the right of a decimal point.

Deindividuation When people are in a crowd and they lose their sense of individuality and feel more anonymous. This can also happen if someone is wearing a uniform or costume.

Delinquency Actions that go against accepted standards or laws.

Delusions False beliefs that the person fully believes in, even if someone argues that it cannot be correct. They are often bizarre and the person will be very preoccupied by them.

Demand characteristics Cues from the procedure that suggest what the research is about.

Dementia A degenerative disorder. This means that the longer you have it, the worse your symptoms get. Symptoms of dementia include loss of memory, problems with thinking and problem solving.

Dependent variable Something that is measured to see if it has changed (after an independent variable has been manipulated).

Depression A loss of interest and enjoyment in everyday life, with increased tiredness and reduced activity.

Glossary

Determinism   The idea that how we think and behaviour is determined by outside forces such as genetics or environmental influences such as our upbringing.

Deterrent   Something that reduces the likelihood of a crime being committed.

Development   How we change and mature across our lifetimes.

Deviation from norms   When an act or behaviour goes against the accepted standards of a society.

Direct reinforcement   When a behaviour is strengthened and likely to be repeated due to positive outcomes for the individual.

Discrimination   To treat people differently, normally less favourably, based on a perceived issue or problem.

Disengagement of individuals   When people withdraw from groups and activities.

Disinhibition   When people have a lack of control over their own behaviour because they are not concerned about what is expected.

Displacement   Information that is already in short-term memory is pushed out by new information, once the store becomes full.

Dispositional   How our own personality can affect whether or not we will obey or conform e.g. in a crowd situation.

Distorted memories   Memories that have been changed or altered in some way.

Dopamine   A neurotransmitter.

Dopamine hypothesis   The theory that an excess of dopamine causes schizophrenia.

Dopamine reward system   A neural network that is responsible for people experiencing pleasure.

Dopaminergic neurons   Nerve cells that produce the neurotransmitter dopamine.

Dreams   A series of thoughts, images, and sensations occurring in a person's mind during sleep.

Drug related offences   Crimes involving trading in or using illegal substances.

Duration   How long information can be stored for.

Early socialisation   The process where young children are conditioned to accept the norms and values of their family and wider society.

Ecological validity   How far a research setting mirrors real-life.

Education   A system of teaching, learning and assessment associated with schools, colleges and universities.

Effort   Determined attempt to do something.

Egocentrism   If a child is egocentric, they will assume that everyone views the world in the same way that they do.

Emotional stability   Feeling normal and psychologically healthy.

Encoding   Information is transformed into a format that we can understand. For example, sounds waves being transformed into music.

Endogenous pacemakers   Internal biological clocks that manage bodily rhythms.

Envy   A negative emotion created by seeing other people having things that you don't have but wish to have.

Episodic memory   Memories of places, events and people.

Estimation   A process where we roughly calculate or judge a value, quantity or pattern in data.

Ethical guidelines   Recommendations that consider the welfare of participants.

Ethics   What is morally right or wrong. In psychology, there are ethical guidelines which give psychologists an idea of what they should and shouldn't do when conducting their research. This is to protect both their participants and the psychologists themselves.

Ethnicity   Reference to a group of people with a common culture or nationality.

Evolutionary psychology   A branch of psychology that theorises that our behaviour has adapted over thousands of years to help us survive.

Exogenous zeitgebers   Features of the environment – either physical or social – that help to manage bodily rhythms.

Expectation (on memory)   Our schemas are designed to help us deal quickly with a huge amount of sensory data. They influence what we expect to happen in certain situations.

Experience (on memory)   The idea that our memory is influenced by our prior experiences, meaning that our recall of an event may not be entirely accurate.

Experiment   A method of collecting data which measures the effect of an IV and DV by controlling other variables.

Experimental design   The way participants are allocated to conditions in an experiment.

Experimental group   A group of participants for whom the independent variable is manipulated.

Experimenter bias   To favour one theory over another when conducting research.

External reliability   Where a measure is consistent beyond itself, on another occasion.

Extraneous variable   A variable, apart from the independent variable, that can affect the dependent variable unless it's controlled.

Extraversion   A trait measuring how out-going an individual is.

Fantasies   Products of imagination where impossible or improbable occurrences are imagined.

Field experiment   Where an IV is manipulated in a natural environment to test its effect on a DV.

Fine   A monetary charge imposed on an individual who has committed an offence.

Fixed mindset   Where people think their intelligence is innate and cannot be changed.

Foetus   The name given to the developing baby during pregnancy when it has reached eight weeks after conception (and all the major structures have been formed) until birth.

Formal operational   Piaget's fourth and final stage of cognitive development. During this stage, children develop abstract thinking.

Fraction   A value that represents the smaller part of a whole.

Free will   The idea that we have control over our own destiny and can change our behaviour and ways of thinking.

Frequency table/tally chart   A way of recording and presenting how often different measures occur.

Freudian theory   A theory that looks at behaviour as a product of the dynamics of different parts of the personality.

Glossary

Frontal lobe   A part of the brain that is its 'control centre' and is responsible for functions such as planning, organisation and making judgements.

Gender bias   To favour one gender or sex over another.

Generalisability   The ability to draw conclusions that apply to a larger group or outside of research.

Genetic inheritance   When genetic information is passed on from parents to child through the pairing of chromosomes at conception.

Group norm   Specific ideas or assumptions held by a particular group about what is considered acceptable behaviour within that group.

Growth mindset   Where people think that they can develop their intelligence over time.

Healthy brain   A brain that functions normally.

Hippocampal formations   A general term to describe the hippocampus.

Hippocampal volume   Volume of the hippocampus part of the brain.

Hippocampus   The part of the brain responsible for making new memories. It is important for forming semantic and autobiographical memories.

Histogram   A graph that presents data using a series of bars to show changes in the frequencies of scores or sets of scores.

Holism   'The whole is greater than the sum of its parts'. Holism recognises that importance of seeing people as individuals and that not one approach or theory can fully explain human behaviour.

Hypothalamus   A part of the brain that controls a number of key bodily functions.

Hypothesis (pl. hypotheses)   A statement predicting what research results will show before it is carried out.

Identification   The process where a person aligns themselves with another.

Imitation   A process where people recall behaviours and reproduce them in their own actions.

In-group   Someone who is part of your group. This could be someone who lives in the same area as you, or shares the same interests or is in the same class or team.

Independent measures design   An experimental design where participants are different in each condition.

Independent variable   Something the researcher changes or manipulates.

Individual differences   How people are unique and different from one another.

Individualist culture   The needs of the individual are seen as more important than the needs of the group, and the individuals in the society view themselves as independent.

Information processing   Taking sensory information and changing it, like a computer to produce an output.

Informational conformity   People conform because they want to be perceived as correct and so follow the lead of others.

Innate   Something you are born with.

Input   Where information enters the body through the senses.

Insomnia   Inability to get to sleep or stay asleep.

Intelligence   Our ability and potential to learn, think and problem solve.

Inter-rater reliability   Where two or more researchers agree on a set of results.

Internal reliability   Where a measure is consistent within itself.

Internalisation   The process whereby a behaviour becomes an integral part of an individual's personality due to continuous reinforcement.

International Classification of Diseases   A manual listing hundreds of mental disorders with their associated symptoms used by medical professionals to diagnose mental health problems.

Interview   A method of collecting data that involves directly questioning people.

Invariant   Something that does not change or vary.

IQ test   Intelligence Quotient test which is designed to measure people's intelligence.

Key stages   Age related stages of development used to organise the education of children.

Laboratory experiment   Where an IV is manipulated in a controlled environment to test its effect on a DV.

Lack of cues   The absence of triggers to help retrieve memories.

Lack of informed consent   An ethical issue that relates to participants agreeing to take part in research, knowing what that research is about.

Latent content   The true meaning of a dream that is hidden in the manifest content.

Leading questions   Questions which suggest a certain answer or type of answer.

Learning styles   The theory that students have different ways of learning and they would learn better if taught in the style that suits them.

Limbic system   A neural network that controls emotional expression.

Line graph   A graph that presents data using a line to show changes in the frequencies of scores.

Linguistic humour   Playing with words to create jokes or humour.

Locus of control   How much control a person feels they have over their own life, with reference to external and internal factors.

Long-term memory   This has unlimited capacity and duration is potentially forever, and is where information goes from STM to be permanently stored.

Longitudinal study   A study carried out over a period of time looking at the same group of people.

Maintenance rehearsal   This process refers to repeating information so that it stays in storage.

Majority influence   When the majority of a group tries to influence others in the group to conform to their beliefs.

Manifest content   What is actually experienced in a dream in terms of visual, auditory and other information.

Mean   A measure of central tendency that is the result of adding all scores in a data set together and then dividing that total by the sum of scores.

Glossary

Meaning for learning   The idea students should understand the meaning of what they are being taught, rather than just being drilled information.

Measure of central tendency   An average taken from a data set.

Median   A measure of central tendency that uses the middle score from a data set once it has been ordered numerically.

Melatonin   A hormone released in the brain that is responsible for regulating sleep.

Mental Health Act (1959)   A set of laws and declarations to address issues around mental health.

Mental health continuum   A way of defining mental health by looking at it on scale; individuals may feel more or less mentally healthy, rather than being mentally healthy or not, at different times and in different situations.

Minority influence   The idea that small groups of people can change the opinion and beliefs of larger groups of people.

Mindset   How a person thinks or their attitudes. People can have either growth or fixed mindsets.

Mode   A measure of central tendency that uses the most common score or scores in a data set.

Morality   Understanding what is right and wrong in how we think and behave. It includes being honest, truthful and responsible for your own actions.

MRI   Magnetic resonance imaging is a type of scan that uses strong magnetic fields and radio waves to produce detailed images of the inside of the brain and other parts of the body.

Multi-store Model   A theory which separates memory into three distinct stores: sensory, short-term and long-term.

Myth   A widely held but false belief.

Natural experiment   Where an IV is not directly controlled by the experimenter but its effect on a DV is still tested.

Naturalistic observation   Observing people in a real-life setting.

Nature   Relates to behaviours that people are born with or develop naturally.

Negative correlation   When two variables travel in the opposite direction.

Negative symptoms of schizophrenia   Thoughts or behaviours that the individual had before being ill and either no longer has or has to a lesser extent, such as feeling lethargic or social withdrawal.

Nervous system   A network of nerve cells and fibres that transmits impulses between parts of the body. The body's control centre.

Neurological disease   Diseases which affect the brain, spine and the nerves that connect them. An example of a neurological disease is dementia.

Neuron   A cell that transmits nerve impulses to send messages between the brain and other parts of the body.

Neuropsychological tests   These are tests designed by psychologists to measure how well the brain is functioning. They are often used with people who have experienced some form of brain injury to allow the psychologists to understand what damage has occurred to the patient's cognitive function i.e. how their thinking/memory has been affected.

Neuroticism   A trait measuring how anxious an individual is.

Neurotransmitter   A chemical that passes messages around the brain from neuron to neuron.

Non-participant observation   Observing people from a distance.

Normal distribution   Where data is distributed so that it follows a symmetrical 'bell shaped' curve, with middle scores being the most frequent.

Normative conformity   Where people yield to group pressure because they want to fit in and are concerned about being rejected by the others in the group.

Null hypothesis   A statement that predicts no difference or correlation in results.

Nurture   Refers to behaviours that people learn through experience.

Obedience   Following orders from someone we perceive as having more authority than us.

Object permanence   The idea that something still exists, even if it is hidden from view.

Observation   The process where people pay attention to behaviours and retain them in memory.

Observation method   A method of collecting data which involves watching and recording people's behaviours.

Observer bias   When a researcher sees what they expect to see implying a degree of subjectivity.

Observer effect   The effect on behaviour when people know they are being observed.

Open questions   Questions that have no fixed responses so participants can respond how they wish.

Opportunity sample   A sample selected by convenience.

Order effects   Factors that impact negatively on research results because participants follow the same order of conditions in an experiment.

Out-group   Someone who is not in your group. It could be that they support a different football team to you or are in a different class.

Output   Using the information that you have retrieved.

Overload   The result of too much information entering a memory store.

Overt observation   Observing people with their knowledge.

Parasympathetic nervous system   A division of the nervous system that regulates organ and gland functions during rest, and counters the response of the sympathetic nervous system.

Participant observation   Observing people while also participating in their activities.

Percentage   A proportion of something expressed as a number out of 100.

Physical repair   Returning the body to a normal, healthy state.

Physiological   Relating to physical biology.

Pie chart   A chart that presents data using segments of a circle to represent different proportions by category.

Pineal gland   An endocrine gland, found in the brain, which produces melatonin.

Placebo   A fake drug designed to have no effect (so it can be tested against a real drug).

Pons   A part of the brain that operates as a message station.

Glossary

Population validity How far a sample represents the target population.

Positive correlation When two variables travel in the same direction.

Positive symptoms of schizophrenia Thoughts and feelings that the individual does not normally have when they are well such as delusions and hallucinations.

Praise Expressing approval of something.

Prefrontal cortex The part of the brain that is located behind the forehead and is associated with making moral decisions.

Pre-natal From conception until birth.

Pre-operational The second stage of Piaget's theory of cognitive development, in which children start to learn to talk. Children in this stage are still egocentric.

Prevalence How common something is.

Primary Care Trust (PCT) A part of the National Health Service in England covering different parts of the country.

Primary data Information collected first-hand.

Prison A place where people are confined as a punishment.

Pro-social behaviour Behaviour that involves us being caring, helping and sharing. We may show pro-social behaviour because we are concerned about the well-being of others around us.

Procedural memory It is responsible for 'motor' skills. These are things like walking and being able to feed ourselves.

Psychoanalysis A type of therapy that attempts to resolve psychological problems by accessing unconscious and unresolved conflicts.

Psychological harm An ethical issue that relates to protecting participants from distress, discomfort and embarrassment.

Psychopath Someone who has a mental illness which is defined by having a lack of empathy for other people and a tendency to act immorally.

Psychotherapy 'Talking' therapy designed to help people with their problems using psychology rather than medicine.

Psychoticism A trait measuring how impulsive and aggressive an individual is.

Punishment When negative consequences follow a behaviour and reduce the chance of that behaviour happening again.

Qualitative data Descriptive data.

Quantitative data Numerical data.

Questionnaire A method of collecting data that involves people answering a series of pre-determined questions.

Random sample A sample selected using chance.

Randomly To leave to chance.

Range A measure of how spread out scores are that compares the highest score with the lowest score in a data set. This is calculated by taking the lowest score away from the highest score.

Rapid Eye Movement (REM) sleep A stage at the end of the sleep cycle where sleepers' eyes jerk and brain activity is high, leading to more dreaming in this stage than others.

Rating scales A way of answering a closed question that requires the respondent to select a number to represent their response.

Ratio A measure that shows the relative sizes of two or more values.

Readiness The idea that children are not ready to learn certain things until they have reached a particular stage of cognitive development.

Receptors Parts of the neuron that accept the neurotransmitter from another neuron. They help transmit the message between the neurons.

Reconstructive memory A theory which suggests that our memory is influenced by our prior experiences and schemas and is not an exact representation of what actually happened.

Recovery rate The number of people that get better after suffering a disorder.

Reductionism Viewing human behaviour from a simple perspective.

Rehabilitation The process of reintegrating a convicted person back into society, with the aim that they will no longer want to commit crimes.

Rehearsal versus meaning A criticism of the Multi-store Model of memory, whereby meaningful information is recalled despite not being rehearsed.

Rejection by society When the majority does not accept and actively excludes certain individuals.

Relaxation techniques Strategies for making people feel more relaxed both physically and psychologically.

Reliability A measure of how consistent or replicable something is.

Remote memory test This test looks at how accurate someone's memory is of their distant past.

Repeated measures design An experimental design where participants take part in each condition.

Representative An accurate reflection of a larger group.

Repression The process of pushing unpleasant thoughts and experiences into the unconscious mind.

Restorative justice A way of rehabilitating offenders by giving them the choice to be aware of the consequences of their actions.

Reticular activation system A neural network that mediates consciousness and alertness.

Retrieval Recalling information from where it is stored in memory.

Retrieval failure The inability to recall something because the cue needed to trigger the memory is not present. The cue could be internal (like an emotion, i.e. you were feeling sad when the memory was encoded but are happy now) or external (perhaps a certain smell would help you recall).

Retrograde amnesia The inability to recall memories from the past after damage.

Reversibility The ability to be able to think about things in reverse order.

Right to withdraw A way of dealing with ethical issues by making sure participants know they can opt out of or stop a study at any point.

Role model A person held in esteem by another.

Sample A group selected from a larger population.

Sampling method A technique for selecting participants from a population.

Scatter diagram A graph that presents data by plotting scores to see if there is a relationship between two variables.

Glossary

Schema   A mental representation of an object or situation. It is based on prior experience.

Schizophrenia   A psychotic disorder where people lose their sense of self and reality.

Secondary data   Information used but collected by another (second-hand).

Self-esteem   How much an individual values themselves.

Self-fulfilling prophecy   When an individual behaves in the way an assumption about them expects them to.

Self-report   A method that involves participants reporting on themselves through answering questions, as in interviews and questionnaires.

Self-selected sample   A sample selected through volunteers.

Semantic memory   Memory of facts, names, general knowledge, for example, knowing who the Prime Minister is. You don't have to know the time and place to be able to answer.

Sensori-motor   The first stage of Piaget's Theory of Cognitive Development, in which babies start to learn about their environment using their senses.

Sensory store   Where information goes first and is held there very briefly.

Seriation   The ability to be able to rank things in order.

Sexual offences   Crimes where a victim is forced to commit or submit to a sexual act against their will.

Sexual orientation   Describes the sex or gender that person is attracted to.

Short-term memory   This store has limited capacity and duration and is where information goes from the sensory store if attention is paid to it.

Significant figures   The amount of digits (starting from the first non-zero digit) that carry meaning in terms of showing how accurate a number is.

Single-Photon Emission-Computed Tomography   A type of nuclear imaging test that uses gamma rays to show how blood flows to tissues and organs.

Situational factors   How external influences affect our behaviour such as environments or others.

Skewed distribution   Where data has an asymmetric distribution because scores are clustered towards one of the extremes.

Sleep disorders   Behaviours which affect the normal patterns of sleep.

Sleep hygiene   Strategies that support a good night's sleep.

Sleep maintenance insomnia   Problems staying asleep.

Sleep onset insomnia   Problems falling asleep.

Sleep stages   Distinct periods of sleep which make up a cycle.

Slow wave sleep   A type of deep sleep where brain activity is slow.

Social construct   A concept that exists as the result of interactions between people who make up a society.

Social desirability   The pressure to respond to questions in a way that is expected and acceptable.

Social drift theory   The idea that individuals drift to the bottom of society when they have a mental health problem, as it takes away any status they may have.

Social Learning Theory   A theory that explains behaviour in terms of observation and imitation.

Social rank theory   This theory suggests that depression is an evolutionary adaptation that reduces conflict by stopping the loser in a contest from trying to compete again. This allows society to maintain a stable balance without too much conflict.

Standard form   A way of writing very large or small numbers using the digits 0–9.

Standardisation   A way of controlling extraneous variables that keeps them the same across conditions.

State cues   These refer to 'internal' cues such as your emotional state when the memory was encoded. Being in the same emotional state can act as a trigger for the memory.

Stigma   A strong sense of disapproval for something.

Storage   Where information is kept within the brain.

Structured interview   An interview with pre-determined questions.

Subjectivity   Based on personal opinion rather than fact.

Suprachiasmatic nucleus   A part of the brain that regulates circadian (24 hour) rhythms.

Symbolic play   This is where children play 'make believe', where a coat might be a Superhero cape, for example.

Sympathetic nervous system   A division of the nervous system that controls the flight or fight response (whether someone escapes or faces danger) when faced with stress.

Synapse   The gap between two neurons.

Synaptic transmission   The process where neurotransmitters are released by a presynaptic neuron and bind to and activate the receptors of postsynaptic neuron.

Synthesise   To make sense of and give meaning to dreams.

Target population   The entire set of people psychologists want to research.

Temporal lobe   Corresponding parts of the brain that are responsible for functions such as sensing information, understanding speech and generating language.

Unconscious mind   The part of the mind that people are not aware of, but holds thoughts and memories.

Universal   The same for everyone.

Unstructured interview   An interview where questions vary depending on the interviewee's answers.

Validity   A measure of how true or accurate something is.

Vicarious reinforcement   When a behaviour is strengthened by an individual observing the behaviour being rewarded in another.

Violent offences   Aggressive crimes resulting in physical harm or death to the victim.

Visual   What we see.

Wechsler Memory Scale   A diagnostic tool used by psychologists to evaluate how much brain damage patients have after injury or illness.

Wish fulfilment   Satisfying urges and desires.

Zero correlation   When two variables show no relationship.

Index

A
activation theory of dreaming 158–63
ABC model of clinical depression 76–9
accommodation 32
acquisitive offence 3
activation theory of dreaming, Hobson & McCarley (1977) 158–9
active learning 48
activity 121
adolescence 27–30
Adorno, Theodor 108–9
Adult Psychiatric Morbidity Survey (APMS) 56–7
adulthood 28–30
advertising
    autobiographical advertising 137–42
advertising, overload 141
age bias 18, 82, 140, 204
aggressive behaviour 9–13
alternative hypothesis 138, 170
Alzheimer's disease 30
amnesia 123–4, 130–4
amphetamine 71–3
analysing research 192–204
animism 33
anorexia nervosa 58
anti-psychotic drug 65, 71, 83–4
anti-social offence 3
anti-social behaviour 6, 17–22, 93, 97–8, 106–7, 109
anxiety 14–5, 55–8, 75, 81, 152–3, 164, 172
assimilation 32
auditory cortex 121–2
auditory learning style 41
authoritarian personality 108–9
autobiographical
    advertising 137–42
    memory 121–3
autonomic nervous system (ANS) 15

B
bar chart 198
Bartlett, Frederick 134–6
behaviour
    aggressive behaviour 9–13
    antisocial behaviour 6, 17–22, 93, 97–8, 106–7, 109
    collective behaviour 93, 95, 112
    criminal behaviour 3–5, 20–1
    crowd behaviour 93–6, 106, 109
    pro-social behaviour 21–2, 40, 93, 97–8, 100–1, 106–7
bias 18–9, 67, 73, 109, 138, 155, 176, 177–8, 200, 202–4
    age 18, 82, 140, 204
    confirmation 42
    cultural 31, 37, 47, 73, 82, 104, 109, 155
    experimenter 204
    gender 104, 109, 163, 204
    observer 188, 204
    questioning 204
Binet, Alfred 30
biological theory of schizophrenia 54, 68–73
brain
    activity 69
    auditory cortex 121–2
    brainstem 158–9
    cerebellum 122–4
    cerebral cortex 3, 15, 28, 131–2, 147, 158
    development 27
    frontal cortex 69, 71–2, 130–4
    frontal lobe 28, 122–3
    healthy 148
    hippocampus 54, 69, 108, 122–3, 127, 132
    imaging 121, 131–2
    occipital lobe 28, 72, 158
    prefrontal cortex 30, 92, 108
    structure 121–2
    temporal lobe 54, 69, 131

C
care in the community 59, 63
case study 130, 156–7, 181, 189
central nervous system (CNS) 15
cerebellum 122–4
cerebral cortex 3, 15, 28, 131–2, 147, 158
chart
    bar chart 198
    pie chart 198
    tally chart 198
childhood 27–30
clinical depression 54, 62, 73–86
clinical depression research study into Facebook 81–2
cognitive behavioural therapy (CBT) 85–7
cognitive development stage 32–5
    concrete operational stage 33–4, 36, 48
    formal operational stage 34
    pre-operational stage 32, 36, 48
    sensori-motor stage 32, 48
collective behaviour 93, 95, 112
compliance 94
computer game 9–12
concrete operational stage 33–4, 36, 48
condition 15
confabulation 121, 135
confederate 95, 99, 103–4
confidentiality 17, 133, 180
confirmation bias 42
conformity 92, 100–1, 105, 105–8, 115–6
    informational 95, 105
    normative 94
conservation 33
construct validity 82, 163, 181, 191, 202
content analysis 13
context cue 129
continuous reinforcement 7
control group 40, 44–7, 123, 125, 138–40
controlled observation 99, 187
Cooper & Mackie's (1986) study 3, 9–12, 22
correlation 18, 44, 81, 98, 108, 138, 170–71, 172, 181, 189–91, 196, 200
    negative 190
    positive 18, 190
    zero 190
correlational field study 44
counselling 85, 180
counterbalancing 11, 72, 175
co-variable 172, 189, 200
covert observation 187–8
criminal behaviour 3–5, 20–1
criminal psychology 3–26
criminal, gene 8
cross-sectional research 17, 36
crowd behaviour 93–6, 106, 109
cue 129, 141, 150, 202
    context cue 129
    state cue 129
culture 5
cultural bias 31, 37, 47, 73, 82, 104, 109, 155

D
data
    primary 193
    qualitative 131, 137, 163, 184, 189, 192–3
    quantitative 131, 137, 163, 184, 189, 192–3
    secondary 193
debate
    free will/determinism debate 78
    nature/nurture debate 8, 43
debriefing 104, 180

Index

decay 121, 124–5, 128, 141
decentration 34
deception 179
decimal 195
deindividuation 96, 100
delinquency 3, 17–8
delusion 64–5, 68–70, 130–4
demand characteristics 37, 61, 138–9, 175, 182, 202
dementia 130, 142
dependent variable 9, 36, 45, 71, 121, 138, 171–3, 181
depression 56, 62, 73–88
descriptive statistics 193–6
determinism 16, 54, 70, 78–9, 92, 101
deterrent 20
development 27–53
    brain development 28–30
    stage 27
developmental psychology 27
deviation from norms 5
difference 170
direct reinforcement 7
discovery learning 48
discrimination 54, 57, 62–4, 67, 75, 88, 92, 114–6
disengagement of individuals 54, 67
disinhibition 12
displacement 121, 124, 128
dispositional factor 92, 105, 108–9, 110–3
dispositional factors research study: Morrell (2011) 110–3
distortion 121, 130, 135–6
doing research 181–91
dopamine 15, 54, 68–9, 71–2, 84
    hypothesis 54, 68–9
    reward system 15
dopaminergic neuron 15
dreaming
    activation theory of dreaming 158–63
    Freudian Theory of Dreaming 152–7
    latent content 153–5, 157
    manifest content 153–5, 157
drug related offence 3
Dweck, Carol 27, 39

E

early socialisation 15
ecological validity 140, 182, 191, 202
egocentrism 33
electric shock experiment 99–101, 109
emotional stability 148
empathy 33, 108, 138
endogenous pacemaker 150–1
envy 54, 81–3
episodic memory 123
Equality Act (2010) 63
estimation 196
ethics 95, 99, 102, 107, 125–6, 128, 132–4, 179–82, 188–9
euthanasia 4
evolutionary psychology 76
exogenous zeitgeber 150
experience and expectations 135
experiment 181–2
    design 173–5
    electric shock experiment 99–101, 109
    field 182
    independent measures design 173–5
    laboratory experiment 182
    natural experiment 182
    repeated measures design 173–5
experimental group 46–7, 125, 138–40
experimenter bias 204
external reliability 201
extraneous variable 10, 43, 73, 104, 121, 136, 162, 172, 175, 188
extraversion 14–5, 17
Eysenck's Criminal Personality Theory 3, 6, 13–7, 22

F

Factor
    dispositional 92, 105, 108–109, 110–113
    situational 92, 94, 99–101, 108, 112–3
field experiment 182
fine 20
fixed mindset 27, 39–41, 44–7
foetal alcohol syndrome (FAS) 29
foetus 28
formal operational stage 34
fraction 195
free will 78, 92, 100–1
free will/determinism debate 78
frequency table 198
Freud, Sigmund 85, 152–8
Freudian Theory of Dreaming, Freud (1910) 156–7
frontal cortex 69, 71–2, 130–4
frontal lobe 28, 122–123

G

gender bias 104, 109, 163, 204
generalisation 37–8, 47, 57, 72–3, 92, 101, 109, 133, 154, 157, 176, 189, 202, 204
genetic inheritance 14
group
    control 40, 44–7, 123, 125, 138–40
    experimental 46–7, 125, 138–40
    norm 94–5, 115,
growth mindset 27, 39–41, 45–7, 49–50

H

healthy 148
Heaven's (1996) study 3, 17–8, 22
hippocampus 54, 69, 108, 122–3, 127, 132
histogram 199
holism 34–5
hypothesis 9, 36–7, 44–5, 71, 81–2, 102, 110, 137–8, 160–2, 170–1
    alternative 138, 170
    null 170
hypothetical thinking 34

I

identification 6
imaging 121, 131–2
imitation 6, 9
incremental theory 40
independent measures design 173–5
independent variable 9, 36, 45, 71, 104, 121, 125, 138, 171–3, 181
influence
    majority influence 92, 94–5, 114–5
    minority influence 114–5
information processing 121
informational conformity 95, 105
informed consent 45, 71, 85, 110, 179–80
in-group 96, 115
insomnia 152, 163–4
intelligence 30–1, 39–40, 44–7, 49
    innate 39, 49
internal reliability 17, 201
internalisation 7
International Classification of Diseases (ICD) 58, 64–5, 73–4
inter-rater 138, 161–2, 188, 201
intervention 44–6
interview 110–3, 156, 181, 183–4
    structured 183
    unstructured 16, 183
invariant 32
IQ 30, 49

K

kinaesthetic learning style 41
Kohlberg's (1968) theory of morality development 106–109

Index

L
laboratory experiment 182
latent content of dreaming 153–4, 157
learning styles 41
learning theories 20–2, 27, 39, 43, 49
LGBT 57–8
limbic system 30, 122, 147, 158
line graph 199
linguistic humour 34
locus of control 106
longitudinal
    research 17
    study 17, 44–5, 106, 131, 156
long-term memory 123–8, 131–3, 141

M
maintenance rehearsal 124–5
majority influence 92, 94–5, 114–5
manifest content of dreaming 153–5, 157
mean 194
measures of central tendency 193–4
measuring crime 5–6
median 194
melatonin 150–1, 163
memory 121–146
    autobiographical 121–3
    decay 121, 124–5, 128, 141
    displacement 121, 124, 128
    distortion 121, 130, 135–6
    episodic 123
    experience and expectations 135
    long-term 123–8, 131–3, 141
    Multi-store Model 124, 127, 130–4
    procedural 123–4
    reconstructive 134–40
    retrieval failure 121, 124, 129
    semantic 121–4, 130–4
    sensory store 124
    short-term 123–8, 131–3, 141
mental health 54–66, 68, 75, 83, 85–6, 92, 114–6
Mental Health Act (1959) 59
mental health continuum 55
mindset
    fixed 27, 39–41, 44–7
    growth 27, 39–41, 44–7, 49–50
minority influence 114–5
mode 194
morality 92, 94–6, 106–9
MRI scan 131–2
Multi-store Model 124, 127, 130–4

N
natural experiment 182
naturalistic observation 97, 187
nature/nurture debate 8, 43
negative correlation 190
nervous breakdown 56
nervous system 30, 147, 164
    autonomic nervous system (ANS) 15
    central nervous system (CNS) 15
    parasympathetic nervous system 164
    sympathetic nervous system 164
neuron 28–30, 68–9, 84–5, 136, 147
neuropsychology 15, 28, 69, 73, 84, 87, 108, 122, 142, 148, 150, 158
neuroticism 14–5
neurotransmitter 30, 68, 70, 80, 84–8
non-participant observation 187–8
normal distribution 196
normative conformity 94
null hypothesis 170

O
obedience 92–5, 98–105, 108–9
object permanence 32
observation 6, 11, 97, 99, 181, 187–9
    controlled observation 99, 187
    covert observation 187–8
    naturalistic observation 97, 187
    non-participant observation 187–8
    overt observation 187–8
    participant observation 187–8
observer bias 188, 204
observer effect 188, 202
obsessive compulsive disorder 56, 59
occipital lobe 28, 72, 158
of reconstructive memory 134–6
offence
    acquisitive 3
    anti-social 3
    drug related 3
    sexual 3
    violent 3
opportunity 102, 104, 176–8
out-group 96
overt observation 187–8

P
panic attack 56
parasympathetic nervous system 164
Parkinson's disease 30
participant observation 187–8
percentage 194
phobia 56
physical repair 148
Piaget, Jean 32
Piaget's (1936) Theory of Cognitive Development 32–5
Piaget's (1952) study into conservation of number 27, 36–8
pie chart 198
pineal gland 151
placebo 72–3
planning research 170–3
pons 151, 158
population validity 202
positive correlation 18, 81, 108, 190
positron emission tomography (PET) scan 88
post-traumatic stress disorder 56, 123, 130
praise 40
prefrontal cortex 30, 92, 108
pre-natal 27
pre-operational stage 33, 36, 48
Primary Care Trust (PCT) 76
primary data 193
prison 20
procedural memory 123–4
pro-social behaviour 3, 20–2, 40, 93, 97–8, 100, 106–7
psychoanalysis 156
psychological harm 133, 179
psychological problems 54–91
psychopath 108
psychotherapy 54, 85
psychoticism 14–5, 17–8
punishment 20

Q
qualitative data 131, 137, 163, 184, 189, 192–3
quantitative data 131, 137, 163, 184, 189, 192–3
questioning bias 204
questionnaire 9, 11–2, 17, 45–6, 82, 104, 108, 137–9, 181, 184–6, 201

R
random 9
    sample 176–8
range 194
rapid eye movement (REM) sleep 149, 158, 160–3
ratio 194
Rational Emotive Behavioural Therapy (REBT) 77
readiness 48
receptor 30, 68
reconstructive 134–40
reconstructive memory study, Braun *et al.* (2002) 137–40
reductionism 34
rehabilitation 21
reinforcement
    continuous 7
    direct 7
    vicarious 6

Index

rejection by society 54, 67
relaxation techniques 147, 163–4
reliability 31, 82, 138, 182, 200, 203
    external reliability 201
    internal reliability 17, 201
    inter-rater 138, 161–2, 188, 202
repeated measures design 173–5
representative 176
repression 153, 157
research methods 170–209
    analysing research 192–204
    cross-sectional research 17, 36
    doing 181–91
    longitudinal research 17
    planning research 170–3
restorative justice 21
reticular activating system (RAS) 15
retrieval failure 121–2, 124, 129
reversibility 33
right to withdraw 17, 45, 180
riot 95, 106, 110–3, 116
role model 6, 8–9

S

sample 176
sample
    opportunity 102, 104, 176–8
    random sample 176–8
    self-selected 176–8, 205
scatter diagram 200
schema 32, 49, 134–6
schizophrenia 54, 59–60, 62, 64–73, 83–8
schizophrenia research study, Daniel et al. (1991) 71–3
secondary data 193
self-efficacy 6
self-esteem 3, 17
self-fulfilling prophecy 62
self-report 6, 17–9, 58, 61, 81, 137, 160, 162, 183–4, 202
self-report survey 6
self-selected 176–8, 205
semantic memory 121–4, 130–4
sensori-motor stage 32, 48
sensory store 124
seriation 34
sexual offence 3
short-term memory 123–8, 131–3, 141
significant figure 195
Simon, Theodore 30
situational factor 92, 94, 99–101, 108, 112–3
situational factors research study: Bickman (1974) 102–5
skewed distribution 196

sleep and dreaming 147–69
sleep
    cycle 149
    hygiene 147, 163–4
    rapid eye movement (REM) sleep 149, 158, 160–3
social
    construct 4
    desirability 19, 202
    drift theory 54, 66–7, 88
    influence 92–120
    learning theory 3, 6–8, 12, 20–2
social rank theory of clinical depression 79
stage 27
standard form 195
state cue 129
stigma 59–64, 67, 92
stress 54
structure 121–2
structured interview 183
study
    activation theory of dreaming, Williams et al. (1992) 160–3
    clinical depression research study into Facebook 81–2
    Cooper & Mackie's (1986) study 3, 9–12, 22
    correlational field study 44
    dispositional factors research study: Morrell (2011) 110–3
    Freudian Theory of Dreaming, Freud (1910) 156–7
    Heaven's (1996) study 3, 17–8, 22
    longitudinal 17, 44–5, 106, 131, 156
    Piaget's (1952) study into conservation of number 27, 36–8, 48–9
    reconstructive memory study, Braun et al. (2002) 137–40
    schizophrenia research study - Daniel et al. (1991) 71–3
    situational factors research study: Bickman (1974) 102–5
    theories of intelligence 44–7
suprachiasmatic nucleus (SCN) 150–1, 163
sympathetic nervous system 164
synapse 30, 68
synaptic transmission 15

T

tally chart 198
target population 9, 176–8, 202
temporal lobe 54, 69, 131

Terman, Lewis 30
theories of intelligence 44–7
theory
    ABC model of clinical depression 76–9
    activation theory of dreaming, Hobson & McCarley (1977) 158–9
    biological theory of schizophrenia 54, 68–70, 73
    Eysenck's Criminal Personality Theory 3, 6, 13–6, 22
    incremental theory 40
    Kohlberg's (1968) theory of morality development 106–7, 109
    learning theories 20–2, 27, 39, 43, 49
    of intelligence 44–7
    of reconstructive memory 134–40
    Piaget's (1936) Theory of Cognitive Development 32–5
    social drift theory 54, 66–70, 88
    Social Learning Theory 3, 6–8, 12, 20–2
    social rank theory of clinical depression 79

U

unconscious mind 153–4, 157
universal 32
unstructured interview 16, 183

V

validity 19, 31, 188–9, 200, 203
    construct validity 82, 163, 181, 191, 202
    ecological validity 140, 182, 191, 202
    population validity 202
variable
    co-variable 172, 189, 200
    dependent variable 9, 36, 45, 71, 121, 138, 171–3, 181
    extraneous variable 10, 43, 73, 104, 121, 136, 162, 172–3, 175, 188
    independent variable 9, 36, 45, 71, 104, 121, 125, 138, 171–3, 181
vicarious reinforcement 6
violent offence 3
visual learning style 41

W

Wechsler Memory Scale 142
Willingham, Daniel 41–3
wish fulfilment 153–4
Wolfman 156–7

Z

zero correlation 190